Living Politics in South Africa's Urban Shacklands

Living Politics in South Africa's Urban Shacklands

KERRY RYAN CHANCE

The University of Chicago Press
Chicago and London

The University of Chicago Press, Chicago 60637
The University of Chicago Press, Ltd., London
© 2018 by The University of Chicago
Published 2018
Printed in the United States of America

27 26 25 24 23 22 21 20 19 18   1 2 3 4 5

ISBN-13: 978-0-226-51952-4 (cloth)
ISBN-13: 978-0-226-51966-1 (paper)
ISBN-13: 978-0-226-51983-8 (e-book)
DOI: 10.7208/chicago/9780226519838.001.0001

Library of Congress Cataloging-in-Publication Data

Names: Chance, Kerry Ryan, author.
Title: Living politics in South Africa's urban shacklands / Kerry Ryan Chance.
Description: Chicago ; London : The University of Chicago Press, 2018. | Includes
    bibliographical references and index.
Identifiers: LCCN 2017039629 | ISBN 9780226519524 (cloth : alk. paper) |
    ISBN 9780226519661 (pbk. : alk. paper) | ISBN 9780226519838 (e-book)
Subjects: LCSH: Urban poor—Political activity—South Africa. | Squatters—
    Political activity—South Africa. | Political activists—South Africa. | Abahlali
    BaseMjondolo (Organization) | Environmental degradation—Political aspects—
    South Africa. | Squatter settlements—South Africa. | Community organization—
    South Africa. | South Africa—Politics and government—1994–
Classification: LCC HV4162.A5 C43 2018 | DDC 322.40968—dc23
LC record available at https://lccn.loc.gov/2017039629

♾ This paper meets the requirements of ANSI/NISO Z39.48-1992
(Permanence of Paper).

Contents

Preface vii
Acknowledgments ix
List of Abbreviations xiii

Introduction: Elements of Living Politics 1

Fire / *Umlilo*

1 "Where There Is Fire, There Is Politics":
The Material Life of Governance 25

Water / *Amanzi*

2 Debts of Liberal State Transition: Liquid Belonging
and Consumer Citizenship 43

Air / *Umoya*

3 Coughing Out the City: Everyday
Healing in the Toxic Borderlands 63

Land / *Umhlaba*

4 Ashes to Ashes, Dust to Dust: How Territorial
Informality Builds Future Cities 85

Modular Elements

5 "The Anger of the Poor Can Go in Many Directions":
Rematerializing Identity and Difference 107

Conclusion: Liberal Governance and
the Urban Poor Revisited 133

Notes 147
References 165
Index 179

Preface

I recall driving past the building site for a gated community nestled between the mountains and the wealthy, largely white South African suburb of Somerset West. In the early 2000s, billboards, advertisements, and news reports lauded this and similar projects as the innovative answer to safe, luxury housing in Cape Town. I had visited the same site two years earlier, while assisting a local anthropologist, and got a glimpse of what lay beneath the clean suburban landscape. At the time, the site was a fifteen-year-old shack settlement. When we visited, the community was in the process of tearing down their homes. Families ripped out the nails that held together scrap metal roofs, shucked off the wood that formed interior walls, and threw what could be burned into a rising fire. The new owner of the land, after a protracted legal battle with the settlement's residents, had issued an ultimatum reminiscent of old apartheid days: clear the way for the gated community or be forcibly removed.

I spent time with an outspoken community leader, a woman who told me that, despite the well-meaning efforts of some state agents, development experts, and lawyers, outsiders could not understand what was happening to her community beyond the brute fact of relocation. Only by virtue of living there and knowing the people and their history could anyone begin to understand what they were undertaking. "She's a trustworthy neighbor," the woman said of the anthropologist, "She listens to our troubles when no one else will." Acting as a "trustworthy neighbor," indeed, as an anthropologist, showed me the possibility latent within this complicated form of listening. In my own research, I sought to train my ear, in a sense: my time in South Africa had already taught me that what we hear is shaped by our time and place in the world.

I began living in South Africa in June 2001, seven years after the fall of apartheid. It was still the honeymoon period of the new democracy. At that time, the euphoric optimism about either a revolutionary redistributive state or the "rainbow" nation—built on an ostensible reconciliation between white minority rulers and black liberation movements—had only started to wane. In the early 2000s, I spoke with workers who said unions were being rendered toothless by the power-sharing alliance with the ruling African National Congress (ANC). Yet they said they would vote for their ruling party until they died. Residents of council housing in race-based townships told me that their water was being disconnected amid aggressive cost-recovery experiments instituted under ideological pressure from the World Bank. Even so, they questioned the value of supporting comparatively weak opposition parties, doubting that their votes at the ballot box could serve as a protest against international institutions half a world away.

HIV-positive activists I knew viewed government inaction in the face of a mounting death toll as signaling a necessary return to civil disobedience. However, nearly all had faith that they could sway recalcitrant politicians and even multinational corporations to make antiretroviral medicine accessible to the poorest of the poor. Shack dwellers, who had spent their lives on a parcel of land in the city or who had moved from rural areas after the fall of apartheid, found themselves under threat of eviction and counted among the unemployed. Against the odds, they assured me that the promise of land redistribution and basic income would be fulfilled in their children's lifetimes, if not their own. Migrants and refugees who had been burned out of their homes and shops by neighbors told me that they were despondent about getting papers to stay in the country legally, but they continued to view South Africa as the continent's inclusive promised land.

From these multiple vantages in the early 2000s, optimism—revolutionary, liberal, or otherwise—was giving way to the imperfect processes that would consolidate South Africa as an actually existing democracy. In this book, I focus on what residents of shack settlements call "living politics" because it captures some of the complexities and contradictions of these processes. Living politics expresses how residents make their lives viable and secure and grapple with new global forces alongside the legacies of apartheid. Ultimately, living politics is about using everyday materials—fire, water, air, and land—to transform what it means to belong as a citizen. My aim in this book, if imperfectly accomplished, is to take advantage of what I feel anthropology, at its core, offers us—namely, an approach to understanding the lives and struggles of people who are commonly talked about but rarely listened to, on the African continent and elsewhere in the Global South. This book represents what residents in townships and shack settlements have taught me.

Acknowledgments

The research for this book was conducted in South Africa between 2005 and 2015. The project was funded by the Andrew W. Mellon Foundation, the Social Science Research Council, the Wenner-Gren Foundation, the Fulbright Foundation, the W. E. B. Du Bois Institute at Harvard University, the American Council of Learned Societies, the Marcus Garvey Memorial Foundation, and the American Philosophical Society. Along with receiving research support from Louisiana State University, I am grateful for the encouragement of my colleagues, in particular Joyce Marie Jackson, Micha Rahder, and Sunny Yang.

Thanks are due to colleagues at Harvard University, where I was fellow in the Department of Anthropology and at the Hutchins Center for African and African American Research. I owe thanks to Ajantha Subramanian and Vincent Brown, as well as Michael Herzfeld, for their mentorship and comments on manuscript chapters. The project benefited from conversations with Emmanuel K. Akyeampong, Robin Bernstein, Lawrence D. Bobo, Neil Brenner, Glenda Carpio, Steven Caton, Caroline Elkins, Arthur Kleinman, Achille Mbembe, Sally Falk Moore, Marcyliena Morgan, John M. Mugane, and William Julius Wilson. I am grateful to friends in Cambridge who provided critical insights and support: Aziza Ahmed, Hiba Bau-Akar, Naor H. Ben-Yehoyada, Anya Bernstein, Alex Blomendal, Matthew Desmond, Namita Dharia, Nicholas Harkness, Jason Jackson, Peniel Joseph, Anush Kapadia, Sohini Kar, Ju Yon Kim, Julie Kleinman, Doreen Lee, Keerthi Madapusi, Emily Madapusi Pera, Laurie McIntosh, George Mieu, Laurence Ralph, Rebecca Richmond-Cohen, Emily Riehl, Jeremy Schmidt, Brandon Terry, Anand Vaidya, and Dilan Yildirim.

I am especially grateful to Henry Louis Gates Jr., whose generous support made the writing of this book possible. At the Hutchins Center, special thanks to Krishna Lewis and Abby Wolf for their belief in the project. Chapter revisions benefited from discussions with colleagues at the W. E. B. Du Bois Institute, particularly Devyn Spence Benson, David Bindman, Floretta Boonzaier, Sara Bruya, Kathleen Neal Cleaver, Shahira Fahmy, Cheryl Finley, Philippe Girard, Vera Ingrid Grant, Sharon Harley, Gregg Hecimovich, Linda Heywood, Marial Iglesias Utset, Kellie Jones, Carrie Lambert-Beatty, Sarah Lewis, Wahbie Long, Xolela Mangcu, Kate Masur, Diane McWhorter, Sanyu A. Mojola, Stephen Nelson, Sarah Nuttall, Jonathan Rieder, Maria Tatar, John Thornton, and Charles Van Onselen.

In South Africa, I am thankful to the School of Development Studies at the University of KwaZulu-Natal (UKZN), where I was a visiting researcher, particularly to Vishnu Padayachee. Thanks to the Centre for Civil Society for hosting me, especially to Adam Habib and Patrick Bond. The project benefited from conversations with Keith Breckenridge, Catherine Burns, Mark Butler, Sarah Cooper-Knock, Tony Crookes, Jackie Dugard, Nigel Gibson, Jeff Guy, Paddy Harper, Gillian Hart, Marie Huchzermeyer, Mark Hunter, Martin Legassick, Monique Marks, Maria McCloy, Nashen Moodley, Thulani Ndlazi, Juliette Nicholson, Graham Philpott, Pravasan Pillay, Mary Rayner, Steven Robbins, Jared Sacks, Anna Selmeczi, David Szanton, Kate Tissington, Xolani Tsalong, and Stewart Wilson.

I was fortunate to have incredible support at the University of Chicago, especially from my advisors, Jean and John Comaroff. Their extraordinary generosity and mentorship made possible my scholarly trajectory. I am grateful to my committee members, Judith Farquhar and Susan Gal, who offered many valuable insights at the project's earliest stages. Thanks, in this regard, are also owed to Ralph Austen, Susan Gzesh, John Kelly, Joseph Masco, William Mazzarella, Emily Osborn, François Richard, and Danilyn Rutherford. Thanks to participants of the African Studies Workshop at Chicago, including Rob Blunt, Betsey Brada, Lauren Coyle, Zeb Dingley, Claudia Gastrow, Kelly Gillespie, Jeremy Jones, Kathleen McDougal, Kate McHarry, Michael Ralph, Mary Robertson, Theo Rose, Jay Schutte, Lashandra Sullivan, Joshua Walker, and Hylton White. I was fortunate to have an intellectual community at Chicago: thanks to Gopal Balakrishnan, Yarimar Bonilla, Filipe Calvao, Michael Cepek, Cassie Fennel, Rohit Goel, Elina Hartikainen, Larisa Jasarevic, Chelsey Kivland, Toussaint Losier, Maureen Marshall, Meredith McGuire, Marcos Mendoza, Marina Mikhaylova, Gregory Morton, Nerina Muzurovic, Lisa Simeone, Kaya Williams, and particularly Joao Goncalves. Thanks to Anne Ch'ien for all her support. Thanks to friends farther afield, particularly Ting Ting Cheng, Huffa Frobes-Cross, Dara Kell, Chris Nizza, and George Philip.

To those whose contributions are innumerable, I express my gratitude: Ashraf Cassim, Jerome Daniels, the late Bongo Dlamini, Mashumi Figland, Matilda Groepe, Gary Hartzenberg, Willy Heyn, Auntie Jane, Reverend Mavuso, Reverend Methetwa, Lindo Motha, Louisa Motha, Shamitha Naidoo, Mnikelo Ndabankulu, Zandile Nsibande, Zodwa Nsibande, Mama Nxumalo, Mazwi Nzimande, Mzonke Poni, Mncedise Twala, Philani Zhungu, and especially S'bu Zikode, Sindi Zikode, and their family. A very special thanks to friends without whom I could not have completed the project: Richard Ballard, Julian Brown, Sharad Chari, Vashna Jagarnath, Ismail Jazbhay, Naefa Khan, Clapperton Mavhunga, Mandisa Mbali, David Nsteng, Raj Patel, Richard Pithouse, and Niren Tolsi. Thanks to Mehmet Marangoz for all his support.

I am grateful for the editorial guidance of T. David Brent at the University of Chicago Press. Special thanks to Priya Nelson, whose editorial insights and expertise contributed to this project from the earliest stages. I thank Dylan Joseph Montanari and Christine Schwab at the press, along with Carol McGillivray and June Sawyers, for their essential work. I am grateful to the book's anonymous reviewers for their comments, which were extremely valuable. I am also grateful to the editors and reviewers of *Cultural Anthropology*, *Social Analysis*, and *Anthropological Quarterly*, where some of the ethnographic materials of chapters 1 and 4 appeared, and especially to Bjørn Enge Bertelsen, Dominic Boyer, Roy Richard Grinker, and Cymene Howe for their editorial advice. Many thanks are due to my family, who supported me throughout this process, especially my mother, Joan Chance; my sister, Erin Chance; and my grandmother Sally Chance; as well as Helen Craft, Sukha Jnana, and Suyin Karlsen. Above all, I thank Abahlali baseMjondolo and residents of Kennedy Road.

Abbreviations

ABM	Abahlali baseMjondolo
AEC	Anti-Eviction Campaign
ANC	African National Congress
BNG	Breaking New Ground
COPE	Congress of the People
DA	Democratic Alliance
EFF	Economic Freedom Fighters
GEAR	Growth, Employment, and Redistribution
IFP	Inkatha Freedom Party
KRDC	Kennedy Road Development Committee
LPM	Landless People's Movement
MK	Umkhonto we Sizwe
NGO	nongovernmental organization
PIE	Prevention of Illegal Evictions Act
PPA	Poor People's Alliance
RDP	Reconstruction and Development Plan
RN	Rural Network
SMI	Social Movements Indaba
TRC	Truth and Reconciliation Commission
UDF	United Democratic Front
UN	United Nations
UPM	Unemployed Peoples' Movement
WSSD	World Summit on Sustainable Development

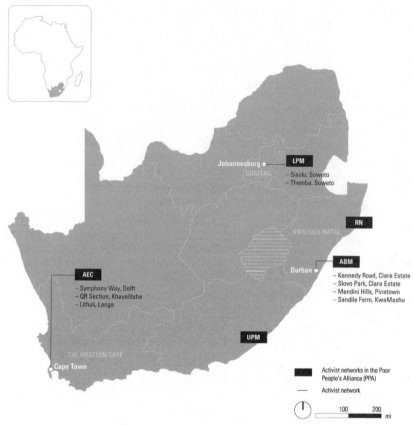

Mapping living politics in South Africa (Map by author with design by Joyce Lee)

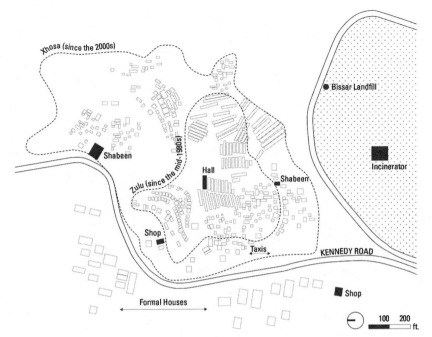

Kennedy Road shack settlement (Map by author with design by Joyce Lee)

Introduction: Elements of Living Politics

The neon-dazzled, art deco skyline slowly lights up in the distance, as the mild winter sun set on the unelectrified shacks. It was August 17, 2006. Hundreds gathered from shack settlements across the South African port city of Durban. The memorial service was held in the Kennedy Road settlement, home to about seven thousand African families who lived in makeshift shacks laboriously constructed from wood planks, plastic tarpaulin, and corrugated tin. Kennedy sprawled over a rolling hill in the postindustrial periphery of a historically "Indian" suburb called Clare Estate, stuck between a busy six-lane highway and the largest landfill on the African continent. This state-owned landfill asserted its presence with a polluting panoramic view and putrid-sweet chemical scent. The landfill was once the site of a World Bank energy project to extract methane gas emitted from the decomposing garbage. With only two outdoor communal standpipes and six functioning pit latrines, water and sanitation were a luxury this settlement could not afford.

The memorial service at Kennedy was for Zithulele Dhlomo, a seventy-year-old man who died in a sudden shack fire. Broken windows let chilly night air into the concrete block community hall. Mourners lit candles and sang reformulated liberation struggle songs, intermittently dancing and *toyi-toying*, a militarized stomping of feet. Dennis Brutus, a veteran activist who had served a sentence on Robben Island with Nelson Mandela, spoke to the circumstances of Dhlomo's death: "Tonight," he said, "we are talking about two kinds of service: a memorial service for the man who died, and service to the people for housing, water and electricity. The people were told that when we have freedom, services would be provided. But we know that tonight there are people shivering in the cold and darkness." He closed with "Amandla!"

to which the congregation replied, "Awetu!"—a popular anti-apartheid call-and-response meaning, "The power is ours."

"Baba" Dhlomo, as he was known, lived in Kennedy Road for twenty years. He was one of the longest-residing members of the community, which according to myth was founded in the mid-1980s when laborers occupied the edges of a white farmer's land.[1] Dhlomo shared a two-room shack with four other families and was in the back room when a candle, used for light after dark in unelectrified sections of the settlement, set on fire the plastic sheet walls. Unable to escape quickly enough, he burned to death. His children and grandchildren, whom he helped support by collecting scrap metal for resale, said that emergency services at the scene did not completely remove the body, despite pleas from family and neighbors. Dhlomo's lower arms and leg were later found, burned almost to the bone, in the ash and rubble. As residents told me, such treatment of the dead can be dangerous, even in the afterlife. Some say that those who die in shack fires cannot properly rest. Their spirits have been known to twist fitfully in the winds of the settlement years later. Even traditional healers, who commune with departed ancestors, found spirits intractable under such circumstances.

Offering a prayer at the memorial, a prominent Anglican bishop, Rubin Phillip, rose to the microphone. A confidant of slain liberation hero Steve Biko, Phillip had been placed under house arrest in the 1970s for his participation in the Black Consciousness movement. He spoke to the congregation about the composition of life, paraphrasing from the Gospel of John, an itinerant preacher who is said to have baptized Jesus Christ. "Life is about having water," Phillip exhorted the gathering, "Life is about having shelter. Life is about having food. It is about having medicine . . . so that children can grow up healthy. But when we look around us today [in South Africa and in Kennedy Road], we do not see this life." As he concluded, Phillip pledged his solidarity to Kennedy Road and said he would appeal to other religious leaders to do the same, calling on interconnected faith organizations that fought against apartheid.

Residents at "Baba" Dhlomo's memorial raised concerns about the criminalization of shack dwellers. Police and private security forces, they said, blamed the community for an "irresponsible" use of candles or cooking fires, as well as "illegal" energy connections. The crisscrossed wiring of these connections, albeit often unreliable and unevenly distributed, could be seen in any South African township or shack settlement. Commenting on criminalization, a resident from a nearby township attending the service said, "Better to lock us up in jail—in jail there is light, in jail there is water, in jail there is a toilet." Instead of basic infrastructure, which would prevent fires, she said

The Kennedy Road shack settlement, 2008 (Photo by Dara Kell and Christopher Nizza)

nongovernmental organizations (NGOs) came to "workshop the poor" on fire safety. In response to Dhlomo's death, activists committed to holding street protests across Durban to demand immediate electrification of the shacks.

I saw that the dissatisfaction of the people in Kennedy Road constantly told me about the slow pace of social and economic change among those who still struggle to make life viable and secure after apartheid. Kennedy Road residents led me to ask: What politics is possible for the world's most disenfranchised communities in emerging liberal democratic orders? How do communities enact sovereign claims, catalyze mobility across borders and boundaries, secure conditions for work and social reproduction, forge new engagements with the material world, or even imagine wholly other horizons for our world? Western democratic theory rests on the foundational principle that all citizens have an equal share in political life. In contemporary South Africa, the legacies of colonialism and racial segregation, along with new forms of economic inequality and environmental insecurity, test that very foundation. I began to approach politics as not merely defined by the laws, policies, or decisions of state-sanctioned agents, but by everyday practices and interactions among ordinary citizens.

Since the election of Nelson Mandela in 1994, the ruling ANC has endeavored to redress inequalities inherited from a colonial past while demobilizing the ungovernable street politics that characterized the late liberation struggle of the mid-1980s. The ruling party has cultivated participation in formal democratic institutions, such as voting, joining community policing forums, and local ward committees. A host of previously unavailable redistributive social grants have been created, including for child care givers, the elderly, and disabled.[2] Along with expanding basic infrastructure provision, the post-apartheid state has built nearly three million houses under a new South African Constitution, hailed as among the most progressive in the world.

Yet South Africa remains one of the world's most unequal societies. More than twenty years after the fall of apartheid, the unemployment rate is minimally estimated at 25 percent, millions live without formalized housing, and a top-ranking Gini coefficient reflects a yawning gap between rich and poor.[3] South Africa's shack-dwelling population roughly equals the populations of America's largest cities: 5.2 million, or Chicago and Boston combined.[4] Townships and shack settlements, while commemorated in liberation histories as heroic battlegrounds and shameful testaments to apartheid, have been recast in public discourse as "slums," earmarked for clearance or economic development. Those living in so-called slums—largely poor, unemployed black urbanites—have been moved, often en masse, from visible public spaces in the city: they have been dispossessed of land, informal markets, and the streets.

I moved beyond Kennedy Road to examine governance and political mobilization in the shacklands of Durban, as well as Cape Town and Johannesburg. Based upon ethnographic and historical research, I analyzed the criminalization in recent decades of popular forms of politics that were foundational to South Africa's celebrated democratic transition. Tracking interactions between state agents and residents of shack settlements between the mid-1980s and the present, I investigated rising urban unrest, which in the post-apartheid period has been characterized by street protests, labor strikes, and xenophobic pogroms. These protests have been sponsored by unemployed youths, anti-apartheid veterans, church leaders, and especially women and have focused on the means of making urban environments viable and secure. Residents, in the vernacular, refer to street protests as well as everyday practices of community building, such as occupying land, constructing shacks, and illicitly connecting to water and energy infrastructure, as living politics (*ipolitiki ephilayo* in isiZulu).

Living politics is premised upon a collective self-identification of "the poor" that cuts across historically "African," "Indian," and "Coloured" (or mixed-race) communities. As governance is increasingly managed by a globalized private sector, living politics borrows practices of the liberation struggle, as well as from the powers invested in new technologies and the recently desegregated courts. Protests by "the poor," as I demonstrate, have arisen not merely in reaction to the failure of the state and corporations to provide basic infrastructure, but also to the management of so-called slum populations by means of forced evictions and police violence. As the lines between

Women protest evictions at a new housing development site in Durban, 2008. (Photo by author)

"the criminal" and "the political" have become blurred in public discourse and through these interactions, shack settlements and the state yet again have been set against each other. The state, however, is inhabited by the party of the incomplete liberation and composed of diversifying governing institutions. This book shows how political spaces are redefined, state sovereignty is forcibly enacted, and new forms of citizenship and identity are congealed at the intersections of race, gender, and poverty.

Living Politics under Apartheid: Everyday Anticolonial Practices

The chapters of this book track the everyday interactions and practices of many residents but, in particular, Faku, a street hawker; Busisiwe, an aspiring teacher; Siboniso, a community activist; and Zinzi, a traditional healer. They are friends, political kin, and at times antagonists, whom I first met at Baba Dhlomo's funeral. My primary ethnographic research was based in the Kennedy Road settlement. From there, I followed residents' political networks outward to other shack settlements, townships, and new housing projects affiliated with Abahlali baseMjondolo, which emerged from street protests in 2005.

Abahlali baseMjondolo is an *isi*Zulu phrase meaning "residents of the shacks." Now a national movement, Abahlali claims about thirty-five thousand members to date.[5] It spans historically Indian and Coloured townships with large Hindu and Muslim constituencies. Along with maintaining its own website, listserv, Twitter, and Facebook accounts, Abahlali has regularly appeared in a spectrum of news outlets from *Al Jazeera* to the *New York Times* to the *Economist*. Abahlali also operates within cross regional and transnational networks of lawyers and grassroots activists, in part powered by digital media technologies, from Chicago to São Paulo.

I now turn to practices and interactions in Abahlali-affiliated settlements to describe how residents, on the margins of the city without formalized work or basic infrastructure, have come to inhabit political roles before and after the end of apartheid. Making life viable and secure in "slums"—in particular by constructing homes and accessing service supplies—has historically been a key contested site of governance in South Africa. Stories told by Abahlali members suggest how evictions from land, for instance, have been politicized over decades of struggle between residents and state agents. When I met Zinzi in 2006, she and her neighbors told me of events only five days prior to Baba Dhlomo's funeral that captured some of the historical dynamics of living politics in Durban's shack settlements.

On Youth Day 2006, a national holiday commemorating the 1976 Soweto uprising, Durban city officials and five car loads of private security arrived at the largely African shack settlement of Mendini Hills to identify and mark a spray-painted "X" on some 200 shacks for demolition by the Land Invasions Unit of the South African Police Service. I subsequently went to Mendini Hills to see these "Xs," which, in time, I would learn were common in settlements marked for imminent demolition. As the ANC-aligned city housing official overseeing the case explained, "We have adopted a zero-tolerance attitude to control the amount of informal settlements and . . . we are trying to eradicate such settlements."[6] The Durban city government, known as the eThekwini Municipality, resolved to "eliminate" all slums by the year 2014 in accordance with the United Nations (UN) Millennium Goals, a policy platform aimed at reducing poverty.

Zinzi, before becoming an Abahlali member and traditional healer, was born and raised in Mendini Hills. She helped lead a campaign against the demolitions in her community that, between boycotts, street protests, and emergency affidavits to the city courts, managed to successfully stave off the Land Invasions Unit tasked with carrying out the eviction. A year later, when the landowner and city renewed efforts to demolish the settlement, Zinzi said, "They act like it is still apartheid," recalling the 1960s, when security forces destroyed Mendini shacks, leaving her family "in the open bush like animals." The predominantly Indian residents of "tin-roofed" houses in Mendini, who also have been repeatedly threatened with eviction in recent years, work alongside Zinzi under an Abahlali banner.

Zinzi's comrade, Navi, and other families recall the 1980s, when Indian residents were forcibly removed under the 1950 Group Areas Act, after parcels of land near Mendini were rezoned for "whites only." Antieviction struggles in Mendini have been ongoing since at least the 1920s, beginning with riotous protests by an Indian residents' association. In 1923, the government passed the Native Urban Areas Act, which precipitated an early version of British colonial pass laws and other repressive forms of influx control, aimed at curbing the movement of Africans leaving the countryside for major cities like Durban. At the same time, the government, along with allied corporations, especially in the mining and textile industries, sought to maintain racial segregation and the availability of a cheap labor pool by tolerating, or even facilitating, the growth of shack settlements on urban peripheries or in small towns.

By the 1940s, with a heavy dose of colonial patronage, the government recognized townships that residents had increasingly formalized, like Cato Manor in Durban, by granting in situ infrastructure upgrades, building roads, and installing drainage and streetlights (Maarsdorp and Humphreys 1975). At other times and in other communities, including parts of Soweto and Cato Manor, residents were subjected to "slum clearance" and evictions. Some of Zinzi's relatives were sent to isolated, rural "Bantustans," allocated to African ethnic groups, such as the Zulu and the Xhosa. Whether formalized or not, so-called slums were not regarded by state agents as permanent communities, but as sites of squalor, spiritual and physical decay that existed only as a matter of temporary necessity (Beinart 2001)—a theme immortalized by the depiction of 1940s Sophiatown in Alan Paton's novel *Cry, the Beloved Country*.

Residents, however, sought to defend, often militantly, against state regulation as they did in Mendini, rebuilding their homes in defiance of evictions or "squatting" on new land. Early campaigns, like those spearheaded by the Commercial Industrial Workers Union and the religious front of Amafela—churches being key to these mobilizations—organized tenants in Durban and throughout the countryside. Near Johannesburg in 1944, James Mpanza led his Sofasonke (we die together in *isi*Zulu) movement of squatters to seize state-owned land, eventually managing to secure recognition and financial backing for the new settlement from a hostile municipality (Beinart 2001). Influenced by Mpanza, some shack dwellers staged a rent boycott after moving on to new land under the banner Asinamali ("We have no money").[7] Abahlali members cite Sofasonke and Asinamali as precursors of their own activist network.

With the election of the National Party (NP) in 1948, the government soon passed, and later rigorously enforced, legislation that struck out against life in townships and shack settlements. The notorious Group Areas Act led to the racial rezoning of Mendini Hills, while the 1950 Population Registration Act, and the 1951 Prevention of Illegal Squatting Act, reinforced segregation and the threat of forced eviction. Empowered by these acts and in an effort to ruralize black workers when they were not on the job, municipalities demolished whole communities, displacing hundreds of thousands of people. Among the communities targeted were those famed as vibrant intellectual, arts, and cultural centers, notably the predominantly African township called Sophiatown in Johannesburg, the largely Coloured District Six in Cape Town, and the racially mixed Cato Manor in Durban. Following one major forced removal, Cato Manor residents, at least seventy thousand people were scattered about racially segregated townships and shack settlements along the Durban periphery, including Arnett Drive, which today is home to an active Abahlali branch.[8] The removal in Cato Manor in the early 1950s, as elsewhere, was halted at least three times through riots and street protests led by organizations of women.

During these years, the apartheid regime continued to finance various government projects, borrowing some $200 million from the World Bank for infrastructural development, including electricity upgrades in townships.[9] By the mid-1980s, with many township streets rendered "ungovernable"—a strategy of decentralized civil disobedience—by the ANC and other anti-apartheid organizations like the UDF (United Democratic Front), the apartheid regime attempted unsuccessfully to recuperate dissent through new segregated governing bodies. Black local councils were formed and given marginal oversight in matters of housing rental agreements, and basic infrastructure payments (Greenberg 2004; Lumsden and Loftus 2003). However, the new councils only served to stir up further street protest and newly politicize housing as well as the supply and disconnection of water and electricity.

During the so-called honeymoon period that followed the fall of apartheid in 1994, the ANC swiftly acted to demobilize this rebellious popular politics. Six months after his election, President Nelson Mandela called for an immediate end to labor strikes, street protests, and consumer boycotts, explaining that their purpose—to destroy apartheid—had been achieved. These new demands for compliant "nonracial" citizenship coexisted with empowered vestiges of the old system—many police and bureaucrats occupied the same positions and, over the coming years, acted to suppress dissent much as they did under apartheid. As early as 1994, many residents continued to take to the streets, particularly when their homes were threatened or access to basic infrastructure denied. After the end of apartheid, however, street politics "reminiscent of the 1980s" would be considered a potential "danger" to the fragile rainbow nation and to the ANC.[10]

Practices and Protests of "the Poor" in Post-apartheid South Africa

Although living politics has been cultivated through retooled practices of previous generations, Abahlali-affiliated communities are responding to two inseparable sets of processes in the post-apartheid period. The first is South Africa's widely celebrated *political* liberalization, marked for instance by a de facto desegregation of social spaces and subjects, the opening of a clamped-down media sphere, and the adoption of new laws championing expansive social, economic, and political rights. The second is *economic* liberalization often associated with less desirable qualities of South Africa's state transition, marked for instance by the privatization, corporatization, and outsourcing of state functions and the reproduction of inequalities at the intersections of race and poverty.

In 2005, when Abahlali emerged on the political landscape, the South African Safety and Security Minister counted 881 "illegal" protests that year.[11] The national average has been estimated at five protests per day in the subsequent years.[12] Analyses from the mainstream news, academics, and state agents then identified protests in shack settlements as either a national assemblage of organizations and events termed "new social movements," or merely sporadic local dissent or "riots" lacking in political intelligibility. Abahlali has been described as both of these: as an activist network and a criminal organization bent upon stirring unrest. In spite of their criminalization, post-apartheid activists, after gaining prominence in the streets, have taken positions in state offices and nongovernmental organizations or played key roles in the leadership or formation of national political parties, such as the Economic Freedom Fighters (EFF). Here, I consider the competing claims of these activist networks, particularly with regard to criminality, looking first at the World Summit on Sustainable Development (WSSD), and then the so-called national service delivery protests.

To examine the term "new social movements," as it is used in South Africa, it is crucial to consider an event that is deeply associated with it, as well as the nexus of relationships it engenders between state agents and an emerging identity of a self-identified new urban "poor." A mass march against the

2002 WSSD in Johannesburg introduced new social movements by publicly seizing the platform of a world event. Marchers told me that the 1999 "Battle in Seattle" by antiglobalization activists was an inspiration. The anti-WSSD march was organized by a newly formed coalition, Social Movements Indaba (SMI), which assembled a range of post-apartheid organizations based in townships and shack settlements across the country. The march, which included activists in Durban, eventually took shape under the temporary banner of Social Movements United (SMU).[13]

First, the march publicly rearticulated the post-apartheid relationship between "the poor" and the ANC, now, as a ruling party. The protesters took on "the poor" as a self-fashioned political identity at the mass march and going forward. The anti-WSSD march moved from Alexandra, once the home of Nelson Mandela, a township with a famed history of struggle against the apartheid regime, its forced removals, labor extraction, and population influx control. Some activists who would later join the Poor People's Alliance and Abahlali participated in the march. From Alexandra, about twenty-five thousand protesters wound their way toward Sandon, the wealthiest suburb in Africa, an exclusive beacon for the rich in the post-apartheid period, which hosted the summit. Even at the height of revolutionary anti-apartheid fervor in the 1980s, the idea that tens of thousands of people would cross the boundary between "slum" and "suburb" was considered "unthinkable" (Bond 2004b, 25).

The ANC responded by attempting to straddle its origins as a mass movement and its present form as a political party, by at once taking to the streets and exercising the instruments of the state against SMU activists. They tried to reclaim "the poor" as their own constituents. Even before the summit, ANC-aligned city officials banned the anti-WSSD march for unspecified security reasons, arrested SMU organizers, and attempted to recuperate dissent by organizing their own legally sanctioned march to protest the summit, which it had nonetheless sponsored.[14] President Mbeki, who had delivered speeches at the summit and at the thinly attended ANC march, condemned the SMU a week later for "misrepresenting the poor."[15]

Second, the anti-WSSD march visually asserted—in news beamed out all over the world—an antagonism between an aggregate of organizations called "new social movements" and the global forces leading development. The march made it clear that these forces reached beyond South Africa's sovereign territories. Even before 1994, academics, policy makers, union leaders, and activists had spoken against liberal—as opposed to redistributive or radical—approaches to the economy, governance, and development (see Ballard, Habib, and Valodia 2006; Desai 2002). Experts within this framework typically posited "the poor" as a depoliticized category, an impoverished population passively awaiting governmental delivery. In the anti-WSSD march, such a position was articulated as an antagonism: an active and unruly "poor" versus state agents, affiliated corporations, NGOs, global institutions, and foreign investors.[16]

However, by early 2005, street protests in poor communities had become less centralized than the SMI, and more confrontational with security forces. These protests, which became known locally and internationally as "service delivery protests," have tended to be explained by experts as an economic reflex to scarce resources in "slums," an outgrowth of heightened and unreasonable expectations by a restless new citizenry, or inefficiency and corruption by the post-apartheid state. These explanations, along with often relying on worn-out colonial stereotypes of the African continent as a basket case, again, glossed over the political complexity of what residents themselves viewed as emerging in shack settlements.[17]

In the early months of 2005, thousands were arrested when protests over basic infrastructure erupted nationally in South African shack settlements from Durban to Cape Town to Johannesburg. ANC officials at the national and local levels suggested that a "dark force" was behind the protests, and by launching a National Intelligence Agency (NIA) investigation after Freedom Day 2005, deployed a measure usually reserved for serious threats to domestic security.[18] President Thabo Mbeki told Parliament that, though he did not believe the protests posed an "immediate danger," "they do reflect and seek to exploit class and nationality fault lines we inherited from our past, which if they ever took root, gaining genuine popular support, would pose a threat to the stability of democratic South Africa."[19]

In March 2005, the Kennedy Road shack settlement in Durban took to the streets when 750 residents—including Siboniso—blocked a six-lane highway with burning tires, clothes, and mattresses. They stopped traffic for hours. Prior to the march, the settlement had been in negotiation with state officials for over a decade, but the municipality had abandoned its plans to provide toilets and electricity to the shacks and threatened to evict residents to another parcel of land on the outskirts of the city. Fourteen Kennedy residents were arrested and many of the protesters were attacked and beaten by police, all of which was caught on videotape and played on the national news.

Three days later, on Human Rights Day, which in South Africa commemorates the Sharpeville massacre of 1960, over a thousand Abahlali supporters staged another march near the local police station, demanding that either the Kennedy fourteen be released, or that the whole community be arrested, because, "if they are criminal, we are criminal" (Pithouse 2006). The Durban mayor and other ANC officials concluded the protests had been "the work of agitators" bent on disrupting the local elections in 2006.[20] He and other national state agents ominously referred to the marchers as a shadowy criminal "third force."

References to a "dark" or "third force" in South African protests take on apartheid-era connotations. In the mid-1980s, the apartheid regime established its own secret police force, recruited spies in townships, and gathered "information" through torture and intimidation. As the Goldstone Commission publicly revealed in 1992 and later recounted in the TRC (Truth and Reconciliation Commission) hearings, the regime lent military support to Zulu ethnonationalist attacks on ANC supporters (Sparks 1995). The white and black apartheid agents involved in such campaigns became known in national public discourse as the "third force." The use of this term for post-apartheid protesters is, thus, pejorative and implies an organized effort to undermine the ANC and the democratic state.[21]

In the early 2000s, Abahlali and other movements increasingly entered the courts, not only defensively when activists were arrested, but proactively to challenge policy and legislation. Abahlali, for instance, vigorously protested "The Prevention and Elimination of Reemergence of Slums Act." Passed in KwaZulu-Natal in 2007, the Slums Act aimed to "eliminate . . . [and] prevent the re-emergence of slums" by the year 2014.[22] Abahlali and their legal team argued that the Slums Act, by compelling landowners to remove "slums," chipped away post-apartheid protections against arbitrary evictions. In particular, they argued that it violated the 1998 PIE Act, or the Prevention of Illegal Eviction from and Unlawful Occupation of Land Act, which effectively overturned apartheid-era legislation on influx control and squatting. The Slums Act eventually was successfully overturned after a challenge brought by Abahlali in South Africa's Constitutional Court, the highest court in the land.

Revealing of transformations in street politics after apartheid are mobilizations *against* relocation to new housing projects. At the time of the Slums Act case, these mobilizations were ongoing in every major South African city. State agents have been unable to explain why those demanding houses should refuse their delivery. As one perplexed housing official said about Mendini Hills in Durban: "When there are houses built for people from informal settlements, they do not want them and yet, when such removals occur, we as the council are seen as the harassers."[23]

Residents have explained, however, through press releases, affidavits to the courts, and memoranda from street marches that the new housing projects do not take into consideration what it means to actually *live* in existing settlements or in the new projects. Housing projects are built farther from the city than their existing communities, where transport costs are lower and proximity to jobs closer. Multiple families are prevented from living in a single residence, and they are not permitted to build onto their homes as families grow over time. State agents tend to allocate families of the same community to separate housing projects, especially when they are politically organized, residents note with suspicion. Many new housing projects are bonded or have income qualifications with incentives to save and to buy. These houses are fully equipped with flush toilets, water taps, and overhead lighting, but as residents point out, the electricity without payment is never turned on, and after the legally allotted amount of water per person is used (50 liters per day), the water is switched off. The Abahlali slogan, "Talk to us, not about us!" printed on T-shirts and banners, in part addresses state agents that are indeed talking about the poor, but as a population to be disciplined and regulated.

As residents explain further, forced evictions are often carried out with exceptional violence in excess of the law, which in turn become the subject of street marches and court cases. The 1998 PIE Act stipulates that residents slated for eviction have the right to appeal in court, must receive legal written notice at least thirty days in advance, and where residents cannot provide housing for themselves, the state must do so. As it happens, these "removals" are carried out typically by armed police or security forces, usually early in the morning, with no advanced or written notice. Moreover, existing houses, and sometimes the belongings within, are almost always destroyed on the spot, without recourse to any prior court review. The "Slums Act" in KwaZulu-Natal, which sought to expedite evictions, moreover did not guarantee the provision of new houses within the city, but only "transit camps" with sanitation and water located in undesirable areas on the urban periphery.

However, it soon became clear that activist networks like the SMI or Abahlali were not the only platforms to galvanize collective anger in historically race-based communities. In May 2008, xenophobic pogroms swept South African townships and shack settlements, including where I had been conducting research. Ethnic and national minorities deemed "foreign" were beaten, slashed, doused in petrol and set on fire—and untold thousands were displaced. President Thabo Mbeki eventually called in the army, causing dramatic shootouts in townships and shack settlements, again, called "reminiscent of the 1980s."

Those besieged and those leading the pogroms often were neighbors and all were overwhelmingly poor. Migrants from other regions and asylum-seeking refugees were certainly primary targets of the violence, but one-third of the people killed—twenty-one out of sixty-two—were South African citizens. Comedian Chris Rock, who was touring South Africa at the time, quipped, "It's not really black-on-black violence; its broke-on-broke violence." Those leading the pogroms subjected many South Africans to so-called elbow tests in which a potential victim is asked to supply the obscure Zulu word for elbow. People married to foreigners, those who speak a different language from their neighbors, anyone with complexions deemed "too dark" were targeted, whether or not they were "foreign." Rather than rooting out non-Zulus—for not all who administered the tests are themselves Zulu, or even *isi*Zulu speakers—the tests are about inscribing certain bodies with the taint of a racial or ethnic outsider.

Abahlali and many poor people's activist networks across the country rushed to protect foreign migrants, organizing community watch groups and antixenophobic street protests. "The poor," along with churches and aid organizations such as the Red Cross, have been at the forefront of the refugee-relief efforts in South Africa since 2005. Making life viable in townships and shack settlements always has required sharing resources such as energy, water, and land. Thus, Abahlali members posted online press statements asserting that living politics, premised upon sustaining communities, was the inverse of a "politics of death," which was defined by divisions among the poor on the basis of race, birthplace, or ethnicity.[24] They added discrimination on the basis of gender and sexuality to this list of divisions.

Ultimately, xenophobia goes beyond the hatred of foreigners, and beyond the scarcity of resources in settlements, but nothing about xenophobia in South Africa is, as a *Time* magazine headline claimed, "beyond racism." Rather, xenophobia is racism, wrought from the messy apartheid past and postcolonial present. The "elbow tests" used in the 2008 pogroms are instructive. The South African police used them for years. On the basis of such "tests," poor African migrants and refugees have been sent to the notorious Lindela repatriation center, a place of well-documented neglect and abuse, where suspected "aliens" await an uncertain fate. In Kennedy Road, residents spoke of Lindela with hushed and fearful tones.

"Elbow tests," say commentators in South Africa, recall colonial-era "pencil tests" that apartheid officials used to decide a person's race—and hence his ability to vote, to live, and to work in certain places—in essence, his or her citizenship—by sticking a pencil in his hair. In its simplest form, if it stuck, he was black; if it did not, he was white. Under apartheid, black South Africans were treated as foreigners, down to the notorious passbooks and curfews in the cities. The election of Nelson Mandela in 1994 meant that claims to citizenship based on race, birthplace, and ethnicity were forever

Nelson Mandela burning his passbook in 1952. (Photograph by Eli Weinberg, courtesy of the UWC-Robben Island Museum Mayibuye Archives.)

changed, but living politics captures how the struggle against a "politics of death" continues in historically race-based communities.

Living Politics beyond South Africa

The more I learned about living politics as an organic intellectual concept, the more I saw that it spoke to theoretical debates about liberal democracy that bridge anthropology, urban studies, and African studies. Anthropologists illustrate how democratic power has been differently shaped by existing cultural traditions and prior colonial regimes, affectively embodied through diverse rituals and representations, and reconfigured by civil strife and global neoliberalism (Ferguson 2006; Hansen 2008; Harvey 2005; Mbembe 2003; McDonald and Pape 2002; Marais 2011).[25] A growing number of scholars have attended to how the material world—from the installation of electricity to the extraction of fossil fuels to the toxification of groundwater—have become enfolded into biopower and other forms of late modern governance to constrain or open up democratic institutions (Mitchell 2009; Boyer 2014; Winther 2008; Murray 2009; Povinelli 2016).

Living politics illuminates how elemental forms of material life congeal political practices, interactions, and identities through time. In these ways, fire, water, air, and land are dynamic social relations that are intertwined with power. These elemental forms, in this case deployed by the urban poor, shape the demarcation of politics in liberal democratic transitions. By doing so, these forms cut across persistent dichotomies in social analysis between materiality and semiosis, the chemical and the historical, and the economic and the political. Scholarship on post-apartheid South Africa has established that "the political" in public discourse is often opposed to the antidemocratic or the criminal, expressed, for example, in racialized condemnations of violent protests and in fears of rising crime rates (Comaroff and Comaroff 2006; Morris 2006; Steinberg 2001; Gillespie 2008; Jensen 2008).

As part of my research in Abahlali-affiliated settlements, I considered how and what practices of the urban poor state agents name as criminal or antidemocratic, such as occupying public land or burning private property. Conversely, I interrogate how and what practices of state agents the poor consider illegitimate, such as banning street marches or disconnecting services for alleged nonpayment. I therefore theorize how the interactions of residents and state agents constitute contested demarcations of the political, most generally through a much-remarked relationship between crime and democratic state making (Siegel 1998; Kosek 2006). Fire, water, air, and land, as hermeneutics and technologies of state–citizen struggles, shape this relationship in the townships and shack settlements that continue to be hotbeds of criminalized popular unrest.

In addition to looking at interactions between residents and state agents, I examined how the material properties of fire, water, air, and land are used in everyday tactics of community building among the urban poor. An emerging literature on global slums documents their explosive urban growth around the world (Pieterse 2008; Simone 2014), as well as how residents survive on the edges of legality and state delivery without access to basic infrastructure (Appadurai 2006; Gupta 2012; Rao 2012; Roy 2011; Ross 2010; Huchzermeyer 2011). While an earlier wave of slum studies have cast these communities merely as "human dumping grounds" (Davis 2006), and therefore rarely as places of thriving politics, anthropologists have demonstrated how residents gain rights, resources, and recognition through appropriating state technologies (von Schnitzler 2013; Ong 1999; Langford et al. 2013), encroaching on urban space (Holston 2008; Bayat 2000), and refashioning themselves as biopolitical subjects of care (Chari 2010; Li 2007; Chatterjee 2004; Redfield 2012).[26]

With few exceptions, scholars have placed less emphasis on how residents render their material lives ungovernable to reconstitute their interactions with state agents. By transforming a burning match into a conflagration or by seizing an empty plot of land, the poor transform themselves and their urban environment. By using fire, land, or other elemental forms as a platform to redirect relations of power, they become legible to state agents, not as the governed but as the ungovernable. Even if fleeting or momentary, becoming ungovernable rarely leaves those involved wholly unchanged: a conflagration or land occupation could result in bodily injury or collective solidarity.[27]

Africanist scholarship, often critical of liberal democracy's theoretical antecedents, shows how elemental forms of material life have long been used, be it through war or witchcraft, to injure or terrify enemies, to regulate territories or social hierarchies, or to adjudicate punishment and disputes in the realms of customary or colonial law (Geschiere and Meyer 1999; Evans-Pritchard [1937] 1976). This work, focusing on the transformative properties of fire, water, air, and land, also has explored their roles in medicine and religion to heal the body and speak to ancestors, to protect local ecologies, and to make useful and necessary things, such as food, pottery, or coal (Comaroff 1985; Mavhunga 2013; Pooley 2012). To better understand how these productive and destructive—or even disastrous (Bank 2001; Kockelman 2016)—material properties shape democratic politics in South Africa's urban shacklands, I analyzed what residents of Abahlali-affiliated communities, in their own cosmological terms, call "living politics."

Members characterize living politics as eventful public dramas, such as street protests and court cases, as well as mundane domestic activities, including cooking with fire or carrying buckets of water. In this way, living politics transmutes the boundaries between the home and the streets to make the poor seen and heard in the city through means that residents ground in their own communities and contrast to expert, elite, or technical languages of formal state institutions. Living politics intersects with an emergent anthropological literature on the infrastructural imagination (Anand 2011; Appel 2012; Fennell 2011; Harvey and Knox 2012), but it emphasizes informally constructed domains, where residents make their material life and platform for politics by any means necessary.

For that reason, to examine living politics, I considered how the urban poor collectively mobilize and identify with each other. Studies of the past two decades have sought to capture the growing cross-regional and transnational nature of activist networks and to distinguish them from other forms of effervescent collective activity and assemblages (Nash 2005; Bertelsen, Tvedten, and Roque 2013; Heller 2001). Along with noting the use of elemental forms such as fire in riots or uprisings, they have high-lighted the role of spatial and organizational structures, the composition of crowds and multitudes, and the content of issue-driven action and public campaigns (Castells 1983; Paley 2001; Hardt 2010; Badiou 2012). Many theorists have argued that liberal democratic governance, which formally accompanied decolonization, has shifted popular movement politics away from the class-based struggles of the nineteenth and early twentieth centuries toward identity, whether ethnic, religious, or national (Benhabib 1996; Laclau and Mouffe [1985] 2001).

Well before the 2008 financial crisis prompted a reappraisal of this view, South African scholars observed that the primary self-identification of protesters in South Africa has shifted from "African" nationalism to loose activist networks of "the poor" (Desai 2002; Bond 2004a; Seekings and Natrass 2005). To consider how the poor came to inhabit this primary, but by no means singular or uncontested, collective identity at the intersections of race *and* class, one premised on shared and often criminalized material life, I consider the ways residents mobilize across historically African, Indian, and Coloured communities.[28] I show how the poor have melded old and new practices, for instance, by working within long-existing civic organizations and previously segregated state structures. By analyzing how residents of shack settlements make a platform for their material lives and politics, be it in the streets, the courts, or global media flows, we may better understand democracy as a lived concept in the tin-roofed houses of Mendini Hills, the *hokkies* of Delft, or the *imijondolo* of Kennedy Road.

Elements of Everyday Life in the Kennedy Road Settlement

My primary research—including ethnographic participant observation, interviews and life histories, and the analysis of relevant archival documents—was conducted in the Kennedy Road settlement. In the late 1980s, as pass laws were lifted, increasing numbers of people moved to Kennedy from the Eastern Cape, the largest among them from small towns and homesteads in Mpondoland. Many note with rural nostalgia an initial sense of urban alienation. But, typically, new residents moved, not into a world of strangers, but within kith and kin networks, building shacks upon plots close to those who would provide support, including connections to employment. As this suggests, Kennedy Road, like many shack settlements, is composed of people who have varied affective and material ties to urban and rural life.

Settlements, like Kennedy Road, are regarded by their residents as remarkably diverse also for the fact that they are composed of racial and ethnic groups, which historically were forced to live separately from each other. These are among the reasons that theorists have seen the influx of people into urban "slums," globally, as containing the conditions of possibility for new social and political formations. It is also for these reasons that, at times, residents today descriptively map the settlement in terms of these "old" and "new" sections, as well as sections that can be identified by their linguistic and ethnic character. The "oldest" section, where the oldest members of the community live is said to be composed of *isi*Zulu speakers, whereas the other sections, constructed in the 1990s, are largely identified as *ama*Bhaca, *ama*Mpondo, and *ama*Xhosa peoples. The newest sections, built after apartheid around the periphery of the settlement, are marked for their continual growth and for housing the youngest members of the community, also predominantly *isi*Xhosa-speaking.

Between 2005 and 2008, when Abahlali was at its peak of mobilization in the community, this imagined map of ethnic diversity was cited by residents as evidence for Kennedy Road embodying the spirit of the nonethnic nationalism of the liberation struggle and of a unified "poor." After 2008, in the years that followed so-called xenophobic attacks in much of the country, residents referred to this map as evidence of political fractures within the community, wherein ethnicity aligned with opposing political party affiliations. In spite of the conflicting ways in which this map was mobilized across time and across groupings, there was little dispute among residents about its basic territorial contours.

There have been disputes in the settlement, with employers and with the local councillor, over the just distribution of jobs at the site, as well as over the benefit (or lack thereof) to residents of the World Bank–led methane project. Although coveted, these jobs can prove dangerous—during the course of my research, several workers sustained serious injuries from the explosive underground gas. Other residents work for security companies, in factories, in restaurants, shops, or as domestic laborers. Like in most settlements, the vast majority of those living in Kennedy Road are unemployed. Those with jobs, typically, work on a casual or temporary basis and rely on pensions and other state grants to survive.

The Kennedy settlement has been an ANC stronghold since 1994. During early Abahlali protests, residents often wore ANC paraphernalia alongside signature red Abahlali T-shirts bearing the slogan "No Land, No House, No Vote." In Kennedy Road, most residents attend nearby Christian churches; indeed, some rallies are inflected with religious ceremony such as a mock funeral for their local councillor. Outside the Durban-metro, I also conducted site visits to affiliates in rural KwaZulu-Natal, as well as to settlements in the cities of Cape Town and Johannesburg. The research, as formulated, was deeply cross regional, in an effort to understand interactions with state agents in their particularities, an eviction in the Mendini Hills settlement for example, and what could be identified as systematic across Abahlali-affiliated communities: that, in every major metro, forced evictions are carried out by police and private security outside the bounds of proscribed post-apartheid legal procedures. These included settlements that were not ANC aligned.

In these sites, then, daily participant observation included attending events such as street marches, mass gatherings, court hearings, and regular Abahlali meetings. Kennedy Road Hall, a locus of community activity, served as an area health clinic, day care center, and Abahlali headquarters, and often was a critical node in such events. At the Hall, I observed administrative operations, informal discussions among residents, and interactions with state and political party officials. As I have suggested, these activities typically were interlinked with routine episodes of violence, in Kennedy and other communities. This is violence that bears the mark of the state either in its absence— when fire consumes an unserviced settlement—or in its presence—when city security shoots live ammunition at residents during a road blockade.

Also from these sites, I followed close contacts—elected Abahlali leaders and ordinary residents, men and women from various backgrounds— through their day-to-day activities: from gathering water to connecting electricity, from selling goods in an informal convenience store (known as a *spaza* or tuck shop) to working as a security guard, from attending church services to visiting bureaucratic state offices. These were activities not necessarily toward organizational solidarity or an articulated living politics, but that defined a milieu of the ordinary in shack settlements, meaningful in and constitutive of mobilization. A local councillor's office, for instance, is intelligible as a target of a street march, not only because it is, materially, a local manifestation of the state, but also as a space of contested day-to-day exercises of bureaucratic state power, such as in the issuing of forms required for shack dwellers to apply for state grants, ID books, or bank accounts.

I conducted semistructured, group and individual interviews with residents, focused on particular events, notably during a relocation to transit camps, before and after the national presidential elections, as well as following police assault. I anticipated conducting formal, recorded interviews with experts and state officials, requests that, for various reasons, were either deferred or declined. Some officials expressed concern that sharing information was not permitted, or could place their livelihoods at risk. In lieu of formal interviews, experts and officials spoke with me, often openly, off the record. I also observed day-to-day, on-the-ground interactions with officials, who at multiple levels—local, city, and provincial—were involved in projects at Kennedy Road or affiliated communities, or who were present during events such as shack demolitions, or court hearings.

Last, I read and produced an archive of texts, each tied to on-site discourse and events. These included local or national news, English and *isi*Zulu, as well as press statements issued by state agents or Abahlali, with usually competing narratives. I also read relevant policy, Breaking New Ground (BNG) for example, which has since 2004 newly guided national housing projects. Legislation and court documents were also key, in particular the "Elimination and Prevention of Reemergence of Slums Act," which challenged in 2009 by Abahlali in South Africa's highest judicial body, the Constitutional Court.

When my research began, with preliminary research in 2006, Abahlali was centralized around shack settlements in the city of Durban. It had yet to become a provincial and national activist network recognized as a force on the South African political landscape. Branches have been launched throughout the province of KwaZulu-Natal and in the Western Cape provinces, from rural homesteads to formal housing. Although visits to all of these sites was impossible, those who attended regular meetings at Kennedy Road from new affiliated communities brought with them articulations of practices and interactions with state agents in areas outside Durban, which contributed to further cross regional nuance of this book. In 2008, Abahlali launched the Poor People's Alliance (PPA) with other South African social movements, including the Anti-Eviction Campaign (AEC) in Cape Town, the Landless People's Movement (LPM) in Johannesburg, the Rural Network (RN) in KwaZulu-Natal, and later the Unemployed Peoples' Movement (UPM) in the Eastern Cape.

Chapter Outline

Each chapter of this book is structured by an element of living politics: fire, water, air, and land. These elements entail a specific set of practices among the poor, such as responding to a shack fire, illicitly connecting water, managing air pollution, and occupying land. Each element also entails a set of interactions with state agents, for instance, workshops on fire safety, police raids to disconnect service supplies, summits on climate change, or legal battles over evictions. While elaborating how the poor collectively self-identify through these everyday practices and interactions, the chapters are organized with attention to certain historical shifts in the liberal democratic transition: (1) ngovernable civil disobedience of the mid-1980s; (2) the forging of a new social contract in the 1990s; (3) the late honeymoon period of the 2000s; and (4) a fragmentation of sovereignty and the return of ethnic politics in the 2010s. These historical shifts reflect transformations in the possibilities of governance and political mobilization in urban townships and shack settlements.

The first chapter draws from empirical material on the uses of fire in settlements to consider how poor residents and state agents understand "the political" and "the criminal," categories that have transformed under liberal democratization. The second chapter tracks how the supply and disconnection of water in townships shifts from a race-based system to a logic of globalized liberal contract in the mid-1980s, which spelled out new terms for so-called nonracial citizenship. In the third chapter, focusing on air pollution, I examine how ritual gatherings stage public confrontations with state agents, which designate movement leadership, effervescent collective identification, and an emergent politics. The fourth chapter analyzes forced evictions of shack dwellers to transit camps—the latest technology of "slum elimination" rapidly reshaping the urban periphery—to chart how the management of "slum populations" spatially reproduces historically race-based inequalities. Whereas each of these chapters suggests how the poor might be constituted through shared everyday practices and interactions in communities, the final chapter combines elements to show how this identity breaks apart in countermobilizations over territorial sovereignty, which explosively differentiate certain residents as ethnic and national others.

Preceding each chapter is a digital "dispatch," an excerpted online press statement written collectively by Abahlali members. These statements, which focus on the elements of living politics, were featured on the activist network's website, circulated via text messages, shared, and reposted on social media. They offer a glimpse into how residents articulate politics in their own words, and how they use the elements of fire, water, air, and land as technologies to connect with members and affiliates in ever-broader circuits in South Africa and across the globe. These statements also follow Abahlali's emergence in 2005 to its violent routing from Kennedy Road in 2009.

Fire / Umlilo

Dispatch

A State of Emergency: Statement after the Fire Summit
Submitted by Abahlali on Wed, 2008-10-08 06:41
OCTOBER 8, 2008

The day before the shack fire summit we held a mass prayer to mourn all those who have died in the fires. . . . Our struggles start from the fact that we are all human beings. . . . If the rich were being burnt like this in their suburbs it would be taken as a crisis for the whole country. But because it is the poor that are suffering this crisis is taken as if there is no crisis, as if it is just normal for poor people to burn. . . . Our lives matter as much as anyone else's life. Our communities matter as much as anyone else's community. Therefore these fires are a crisis for the whole country. They are a state of emergency.

"Where There Is Fire, There Is Politics":
The Material Life of Governance

Faku and I stood surrounded by billowing smoke. In the Durban shack settlement of Slovo Park, flames flickered between piles of debris, which the day
before had been wood plank and plastic tarpaulin walls. The conflagration
began early in the morning. Within hours, before the arrival of fire trucks
or ambulances, the two thousand households that made up the settlement
as we knew it had burned to the ground. On a hillcrest in Slovo, gathered in
a mass meeting, were members of Abahlali. Slovo was a founding settlement
of Abahlali, which emerged from a burning road blockade during protests in
2005. In part, the meeting was to mourn. Five people had been found dead
that day in the remains, including Faku's neighbor. "Where there is fire, there
is politics," Faku said to me. This fire, like others before, had been covered by
the local press and radio, some journalists having been notified by Abahlali
via cell phone text message and online press release. The Red Cross soon set
up a makeshift soup kitchen, and the city government provided emergency
shelter in the form of a large, brightly striped communal tent. Residents,
meanwhile, took up tools for several days of hard labor, digging foundations
and hammering nails to construct new shacks. By midday, local officials in
luxury vehicles rode down the winding dirt road of the settlement, leaving
piles of blankets and stacks of canned food. A Slovo resident, with a megaphone, shouted that those seeking the goods first had to display African National Congress (ANC) membership cards. A riot nearly erupted.

Fire is a familiar sign of life in the sprawling shacklands that populate
the margins of Durban's city center. Behind securitized suburban landscapes,
glossy shopping plazas, and beachfront tourist attractions, residents like Faku
routinely use fire as a source of light and heat at home, and as a weapon of

protest on the streets. By tracking everyday interactions with state agents between the mid-1980s and the present, this chapter analyzes how residents of
shack settlements leverage the material properties of fire to secure claims to
energy infrastructure, and more broadly to political inclusion and economic
redistribution. As I illustrate, residents are deploying the distinct destructive
and productive capacities of fire through practices, borrowed from liberation
movements, which have been criminalized during South Africa's democratic
transition. By approaching fire as intertwined with power, I illustrate how the
urban poor, those living on the margins of the city, come to inhabit political
roles that transform—and are transformed by—material life.

Fires in settlements occur because of household accidents or deliber-
ate political acts. Official statistics suggest that shack fires happen ten times
per day throughout the country, with one death resulting every other day. A
shack fire is estimated at once per day in the city of Durban alone (Birkinshaw
2008, 1). During my own research, I recorded at least one shack fire and street
protest every month in Abahlali-affiliated communities. Street protests are
estimated at about five per day nationwide.[1] These fires, as I found, are regular fodder for local tabloids, national television, and social media, ensuring
that news of flames spreads quickly through South African media spheres.

The aftermath of the Slovo Park fire in 2008, in which an estimated two thousand homes were destroyed.
(Photo by author)

Abahlali baseMjondolo website, asking "Why Are the Poor Left to Burn?" (accessed March 18, 2008)

To analyze the intertwining of fire and living politics in urban South Africa, the first section of this chapter illustrates how liberation movements and apartheid state agents made use of fire during the ungovernable years of the mid-1980s, searing it into the life histories of the next generation of activists in townships and shack settlements. The second section, focusing on burning barricades, suggests how Abahlali members are adopting and redeploying practices of liberation activists, which have been recast in the post-apartheid period as the work of "electricity bandits" and other shadowy "criminal elements."[2] The last section, returning to shack conflagrations, suggests how forms of endangerment attributed to a lack of electricity and the promise of infrastructure have become a platform for innovative forms of political mobilization in poor communities.

Living Memories of Fire: Insurgency in 1980s KwaZulu-Natal

Prior to the election of Nelson Mandela in 1994, fire was linked to the atrocities of apartheid, counterrevolutionary activities, and the very possibility of liberation. During the 1952 Defiance Campaign, a young Mandela and other activists torched their passbooks, the notorious identity documents that regulated and restricted the mobility of African people under apartheid. The campaign, which swelled membership across ethnic and racial lines by the tens of thousands, would mark the ANC's birth as a mass movement. By transforming a tangible symbol of apartheid into ash, Mandela showed up the illegitimacy of the race-based state's power to divide and rule, while issuing a performative claim on inclusive "nonracial" citizenship within a new democratic polity. The ANC had been inspired by Mohandas Gandhi's 1909 nonviolence campaign in KwaZulu-Natal, when South African Indians likewise broke the law to burn their passes—which prohibited crossing into unauthorized zones—in defiance of British colonialism, suggestive again of fire's potential power to destroy and redraw lines of difference.

A quotation by Winnie Mandela, at times cited in present-day protests, captures the spirit of these turbulent times and helped make her its controversial icon—then and now. In 1986, she said, "Together, hand in hand, with our boxes of matches . . . we shall liberate this country."[3] Her words suggest how the properties of fire constituted its threat to state security and its importance to urban insurgency. Unlike guns and other weapons that required a supply chain and orders from above, fire was always within the grasp of ordinary men and women, made from ordinary, on-hand materials found inside the home. The primary tools of its ignition, matches, are not only affordable and accessible to all, and in this sense highly democratized, but they are also highly mobile, easily transported from place to place; they can be secreted, if necessary, hidden away in one's palm, pocket, or kitchen cupboard. Once set, flame spreads rapidly and consumes what it touches, making its illuminant effects highly visible, but leaving the agents who have lit the match often invisible, mysterious, or unknown.

Abahlali members often point to the Defiance Campaign as a fiery precursor to post-apartheid civil disobedience. Yet residents of contemporary shack settlements—in life histories, in texts produced by them, and media representations—identify their mobilizations involving fire with one historical moment in particular: the insurgency of the mid-1980s. Persuaded that the time had come "to submit or fight,"[4] the ANC established Umkhonto we Sizwe, the MK or "Spear of the Nation," in 1961, following the Sharpeville Massacre, in which sixty-nine people were gunned down during a mass gathering against pass laws. The MK's guerilla military cells, by way of matches and petrol bombs, set on fire government buildings and blew up electricity pylons.

By the mid-1980s, with many of the earlier generation of fighters such as Mandela in prison, the ANC famously called for the townships to be rendered "ungovernable," thereby expanding and popularizing the role of militant activities beyond the rigid hierarchies of the MK. Oliver Tambo, then president of the ANC, referred to the militant operations of the party as "the terrible but cleansing fires of revolutionary war."[5] Fire during this period served not only as a popular political metaphor but also as a choice weapon for youths coming of age during the struggle; they notably set about blocking roadways with fiery barricades and burning the homes of despised local councillors. The term "ungovernable" generally implied intervening in interactions with state agents by breaking the law, and destroying—through unrest, disruption, or violence—material manifestations of the prevailing order.

Yet as the South African Truth and Reconciliation Commission (TRC) re-

Recruitment poster for Umkhonto we Sizwe (MK), the ANC's military wing, with a bombed electricity pylon in the background. (http://riseandfallofapartheid.tumblr.com/post/75897895825/poster-for-umkhonto-we-sizwe-armed-wing-of-the, accessed July 23, 2015)

vealed in gruesome detail, apartheid state agents harnessed some of the same properties of fire during the mid-1980s for their most shadowy operations. Security forces were known to burn the bodies of the disappeared, which along with preventing proper burial, destroyed evidentiary traces of the identities of both victim and perpetrator.[6] Inkatha fighters, Zulu nationalists known as "the third force," were armed by the old regime to target their neighbors during the liberation struggle and made a practice of burning rural homesteads, a memory that lives on for many in Durban shacklands. Burning homesteads dually served as retribution for supporting ANC operatives and as a sovereign claim on disputed territories.

All sides—the apartheid state, Inkatha, and the ANC—deployed so-called necklacing, setting on fire a rubber tire around the neck of a suspected *impimpi* (spy, colluder in *isi*Zulu and *isi*Xhosa), who would slowly burn to death. Necklacing as punishment for political disloyalty was a practice viewed by some in the ANC as evidence that populist violence had run amok. One of the earliest recorded cases of necklacing was brought to light by the TRC, which documented the burning of a young girl, Maki Skosana, in July 1985, accused of being an informant. Dramatically, while attending the funeral for one of the young comrades she had supposedly had a hand in killing, she was set on fire. Necklacing, along with the torching of shops and homes, would reemerge after apartheid in the wake of "xenophobic attacks" targeting ethnic and national minorities, as well as in acts of vigilante justice aimed at suspected witches and criminals (Comaroff and Comaroff 2001; Hickel 2014)—including at sites where I conducted research.[7] In Kennedy Road, fire was used during ethnicized armed attacks by ANC supporters, which were aimed at movement members in 2009 (Chance 2010).

As the above historical outline suggests, during the mid-1980s, while apartheid state agents cultivated fire to fuel the counterinsurgency, residents cultivated it as a guerilla weapon. These interactions are relevant not simply because practices of the mid-1980s continue to be enacted in present-day shack settlements but also because fire conjures powerful living memories of organized warfare. Many residents of Abahlali-affiliated settlements were involved in various capacities with liberation movements, including the ANC, whether through military operations, churches, or trade unions. Others, especially young people, characterize their political activities and involvement with what they even now call "the struggle" (*umzabalazo*) as beginning with the fall of apartheid and battles emerging over adequate housing, work, and access to infrastructure in the newly desegregated cities. All residents I spoke with who lived through apartheid were subject to, and witnessed enactments of, state violence, frequently mediated by fire: forced removals, political killings, and military occupation. The racialization, and indeed ethnicization, of social spaces and subjects implied by this violence, again, highlights fire's ability to draw lines of difference.

Life histories of Abahlali members and other residents I spoke with clarify how fires, past and present, punctuate life in settlements. Siboniso and I sat in colorful plastic chairs at the movement's then national headquarters in the Kennedy Road settlement to speak about his memories of fire. With the din of children playing in the day care center next door, we talked about Bellcourt, where he grew up. Bellcourt is a small town amid the rolling green hills of northern KwaZulu-Natal, a land of livestock and white commercial farming. Siboniso moved to Durban in 1998 to find work and study law at the local university. When he first arrived in Kennedy, the shack conflagrations brought back memories of his rural hometown. He would awaken at night screaming, uncertain why or from what nightmare, but certain it had to do with the fires. While staying with relatives in a nearby township, he landed a job as a gas station attendant filling tanks. When his employer learned of his membership in Abahlali—not long after his arrest and torture in police custody linked him to the formation of the movement—Siboniso lost his job, allegedly under pressure from the mayor. After two years of study, no longer able to afford his tuition bills, he was ejected from the university.

Although popular national histories draw the battle lines of apartheid-era civil war between the old regime and the new dispensation led by the ANC, there remain at the regional level other powerfully felt fields of conflict and other actors that tell of fire. In the mid-1980s and the early 1990s, Bellcourt was a hotspot for battles between the Zulu-nationalist movement Inkatha and the supposedly nonethnic nationalist forces of the ANC.[8] The area of Bellcourt in which Siboniso's family lived was an Inkatha stronghold. Siboniso, like others in the province, characterizes his hometown as divided, homestead by homestead, into two camps of opposing party affiliation. "Party politics," he said, "was one being an enemy to the other," with fire being of deadly importance to this distinction: "[As a child] I did not understand party politics, other than as an opportunity to learn to shoot well. If you are IFP, then the ANC would kill you; if you are ANC, then the IFP would kill you—your house would be burned down or you would be shot to death."

Siboniso and other residents I have spoken with liken the process of acquiring organizational status in an activist movement to gang initiation, a violent and masculine rite of passage. But where guns took aim at men, fire took aim especially at women and children. The deployment of fire targeted the home, the site of the domestic sphere, of social and biological reproduction. Against this stark picture of civil war, Siboniso joined the Boy Scouts, whose activities—not perceived as a threat to Inkatha territorial sovereignty—proved a permissible refuge. Often drawing parallels between the Boy Scouts and Abahlali, Siboniso suggests that the organization contributed to a prominent formulation of his movement's politics, a living politics (*ipolitiki ephilayo*) or a "home politics" outside nationalist party structures.

Busisiwe, another Kennedy resident, grew up in an ANC stronghold called Nortown, a hundred kilometers from Bellcourt. We first talked at length about fire while visiting her relatives in a township adjacent to a dusty, abandoned main street, which in earlier days had drawn vacationers to nearby hot springs. Along with her mother and two siblings, Busisiwe moved to Durban and the Kennedy settlement in 2003 in search of decent schools and upward mobility in the city. In contrast to the concrete block house her family had built in Nortown, their shack in Kennedy was a one-room affair with the basics—a few pieces of furniture, a paraffin lamp, and wallpaper made of a mixture of juice and milk cartons. Busisiwe particularly loved the wallpaper for the childhood memories it evoked. In Nortown, her family had lived along a contested road, where Inkatha and ANC operatives targeted each other with arson and petrol bombs. "Every time these two were fighting. They would just come and camp by the corner of our house. One would shoot up the road, the other would shoot down the road." After one long day of fighting on the road, Busisiwe's family received news that her uncle had been killed. As a known ANC loyalist, he had apparently been the target of a "plot."

What emerges in Siboniso's and Busisiwe's narratives in two distinct party strongholds is the mediating force of fire in the spatiopolitical configurations of rural towns in late apartheid-era KwaZulu-Natal. Alleged arson, a fire with a suspected yet obscured agent, hinged on "operations" aimed at designating a suspected *impimpi*. "If your house is set with fire," said Siboniso, "then that would mean it would have been planned. There would have been a conspiracy. There would be a lot of people knowing that you were a suspect, so you would not retaliate." Intervention in the public designation of an *impimpi* could risk perceived affiliation with the suspect. Under apartheid, amid the banning of activists and organizations and police crackdowns on public gatherings, funerals took on a strong political valence as potential sites of mobilization.

But funerals also were sites where kith, kin, and organizational loyalties could be identified by opposing factions. "I had family members and friends whom we couldn't even bury," said Siboniso, echoing a sentiment shared by many who lived through these years. "If your family member or friend in the area was a suspected ANC operative or sympathizer, you could not be buried under the ground of an IFP stronghold." Many would be too fearful to attend the funeral. As Siboniso and Busisiwe suggest, territories were regulated by violence tied to talk of shadowy secret colluders, their plots, and their alignments with one or another enemy party.

Street Protests and Shack Conflagrations: Politicizing Energy and Endangerment after Apartheid

If the mid-1980s marked the popularization of fire in street politics against apartheid, the turn of the millennium marked its unanticipated return in street politics against neoliberal policy reforms and ongoing inequalities in poor African, Indian, and Coloured communities. Activists deployed fire, as they did in the mid-1980s. They capitalized on fire's highly mobile and affordable qualities to render visible spaces ordinarily hidden from view in the city, while disrupting urban activities by blocking roadways, and therefore the circulation of traffic, goods, and people. Residents of townships and shack settlements torched sites tied materially and symbolically to the state (*uhulumeni* in *isi*Zulu),[9] including old targets such as local councillors' homes, but also new sites of technoinstitutional management, such as the offices of nongovernmental organizations. Police and private security forces have officially condemned these acts as "criminal" and "counterrevolutionary" (Agence France Presse 2005), meeting them with arrests and violence (Alexander et al. 2012; Chance 2015a). Protesters, at times, have been referred to as *izimpimpi* (spies, colluders).

The deployment of fire by activists in South Africa in the post-apartheid period has thus become a distinguishing criterion between civil and uncivil society, the former associated with nongovernmental organizations (NGOs) aligned with state or international institutions, and the latter associated with movements of the poor or populist community-based mobilizations.[10] A public dispute over fire, for instance, erupted between Abahlali and a leading NGO for those living with HIV. Though they at times work together and share members, the NGO, echoing official discourse, posited burning barricades as criminal acts. Abahlali in Cape Town responded that fire formed part of daily life in the communities that are the locus of living politics: "We are not a professional organisation with millions of rands of donor funding that can operate in the middle class world. We are a movement of, for and by the poor. We therefore have to struggle where we are and with what we have. If that means burning tyres on Lansdowne Road then that is how we will struggle."[11] The press statement emphasizes the enduring power of fire to galvanize collective anger into concrete political action when other means of civic action remain unavailable.[12]

The identification as the poor also reaches into the spiritual realm. Fire, Abahlali members told me, is associated with forms of spiritual consciousness arising from conditions of—and threats to—life in shacks. Siboniso used the motif of "invisible fire" to describe popular anger "that burns within us, inside every poor person." Resonating with both Black Consciousness and Christian theology (Gibson 2011), Siboniso suggests that "invisible fire" signifies that "our humanity is not rated the same as a middle-class person." Fire is used in significant rites and rituals across faiths that comprise the activist network. Residents use fire in age-set initiation, in traditional medicine, and in Hindu and Muslim communities, during significant religious holidays. In some settlements, communal outdoor fire pits, whether burning or not, is likewise a site where residents gather, for Abahlali meetings or for casual socializing.

Often less visible to middle-class publics, but pivotal to making living politics, are political mobilizations within settlements. In Abahlali-affiliated settlements, shack fires are the subject of summits and gatherings attended by thousands. Routine practices have emerged to respond to the aftermath of fire, including collective rebuilding, organized distributions through aid organizations, and making a registry of families requiring the replacement of school uniforms, ID books, and other items often lost to flame. Abahlali members characterize fire, and the activities that surround it, as an existential condition of living in shacks. Flame leaves inscriptions on the homes, belongings, and bodies of the poor, identification in contemporary South Africa rendered through intersections of race and class (Ballard, Habib, and Valodia 2006; Seekings and Natrass 2005; Hart 2014). An Abahlali leader named Mnikelo makes this point saying, "When a white man lights a candle, it is supposed that he is being romantic. When a black man lights a candle, it is supposed that he is poor." The stereotyped race/class identity of the poor, as Mnikelo suggests, is inscribed in fire. For Abahlali members, the use of candles and the routine quality of fires in infrastructurally bereft settlements distinguish the poor from the middle or upper class, categories that are themselves racially marked.

The opposition posited by Mnikelo, moreover, points to post-apartheid reconfigurations between race and class, for the ranks of the white political and economic elite have not so much been displaced by the collapse of colonial orders as joined by a small, but growing black elite. By self-identifying as the poor, Abahlali members emphasize a racialized status tied to ongoing experiences of lived material conditions in shack settlements, while recognizing the persistence of racism across class lines. An allegory, frequently heard at Abahlali meetings and in day-to-day talk, captures how these race/class reconfigurations map onto urban dwellings and, more broadly, onto spatial arrangements of the city: imagine yourself accidentally falling asleep with the light on. If you live in a shack and your light is a candle, it could mean the destruction of life and limb, community and property. In the wealthy suburbs, it is of little consequence other than perhaps a higher household electricity bill. An estimated three times as many deaths occur in shack settlements than in formal dwellings (Birkinshaw 2008, 1). Inasmuch as fire has everyday productive capacities—in the making of food, light, and politics—inside homes of the poor—unlike in those of the rich or the middle class—its destructive capacities are injurious, even deadly.

Although burning barricades have been criminalized with reference to

"counterrevolutionary" activities in the post-apartheid period, shack conflagrations have been criminalized with reference to another sort of power:
"electricity banditry." Residents I spoke with mobilize numerous, overlapping, and at times conflicting explanations for shack fires, including witchcraft, winter winds, drunkenness, and lovers' quarrels. The most commonly
cited source is tipped over candles. However, residents in Kennedy Road and
Slovo Park most broadly attribute fire to a lack of electricity. When one is
without the services needed for a viable urban life, their absence tends to be
understood as bearing the inherited legacies of "the state."

In recent years, shack fires have been a cause for alarm among state agents,
at various levels and offices, in the city of Durban. At times, city officials propose that shack fires are a natural phenomenon, brought on by dry weather
and exacerbated by the geographic terrain of settlements. Yet in press statements and off-the-record interviews, the most readily mobilized explanation
for shack fires by Durban officials is so-called illegal connections (Ngcongco
2011), wherein residents connect themselves to the energy infrastructure, at
times under the banner of poor people's movements. Activists call it Operation Khanyisa ("Let There Be Light"), a slogan since appropriated by state
agents for programs aimed at stamping out illicit energy. Within settlements,
those who do the technical work of connections are often called "guerilla
electricians" or "people's electricians." The result, crisscrossed wiring, can
be seen throughout South African townships and shack settlements, which
officials regard as "electricity theft" (Mchunu 2008), a criminal seizure of
power by the poor from the legitimate monopoly held by the state and its
often multinational corporate partners.

If shack fires and protests are posited as symptoms of criminal agency,
the force of technical and legal interventions by the state is framed as their
cure. When another fire tore through a settlement near Slovo Park, Durban's
mayor called for a citywide investigation, warning that if "illegal electricity connections" were involved, "criminals"—those caught connecting and
those using the electricity—would "soon be brought to book" (Khuzwayo
2011). As Abahlali responded in an online press statement, "When self organized [electricity] connections are done safely they protect us from fires. But
when we connect ourselves in a safe and carefully disciplined manner we are
called criminals."[13]

The measures to control illicit connections in the city of Durban include
a heady mixture of armed raids and surveillance, both of which establish
settlements as de facto zones of criminality. At Slovo Park, police disconnect shacks almost every night, only to find electricity cables repaired the
next morning. The removal of illicit connections would be enacted, said one

municipal statement, by deploying "contractor teams" to regularly patrol "identified areas." In practice, these contractors and armed security forces are outsourced private labor. Police often also accompany or participate in the work of these teams. In addition to reconfiguring electrical cabling and installing "anticlimb devices" to electrical poles, the municipality promises the use of "forensic investigation" including surveillance cameras and photographs (Mdlalose 2009).

The municipality frames electrical service theft not as an act against the corporate interests of Eskom, the parastatal that supplies South Africa with its power, operating with private and multinational partners. Rather, Eskom and the municipality emphasize that this supposed theft makes for a quantifiable incursion on the private property of consumers. As one television advertising campaign put it: "Electricity theft is not a victimless crime. The victim is YOU." The advertisement plays on racialized and class-based post-apartheid fears of crime. Residents of shack settlements illicitly connecting to the electricity grid have been blamed for the increasing frequency of rolling blackouts, a measure taken by Eskom to conserve energy to prevent a total loss of power. At times, the municipality, in newspapers and press statements, boasts a record of successful arrests of shadowy "electricity thieves" (Mchunu 2008). In January 2011, the city reported that twenty-five people had been arrested for alleged electricity connections near Siyanda, an area home to many Abahlali supporters (Ngcongco 2011). The endpoint of these investigations, ultimately, is to ensure the electricity disconnection of unauthorized households, but also submitting "electricity bandits"—those connecting and those connected—to the might of the law through the courts and the prisons.

The municipality further calls for residents "to follow the right steps" by applying for an electricity connection and providing phone numbers to the Metro Customer Services Centre (Ngcongco 2011). The call charges a technocratic state with the recuperative possibility of curing fires by connecting potential customers, if not to the energy grid, at least to the realm of law and order. It is, however, a fictive connection—although steps may be in place to apply to be connected to the energy grid, the provision of electricity in shack settlements, including Slovo Park, was suspended in 2001. The 2001 policy states: "In the past (1990s) electrification was rolled out to all and sundry. Because of the lack of funding and the huge costs required to relocate services when these settlements are upgraded or developed, electrification of the informal settlements has been discontinued" (Birkinshaw 2008, 4). Since then, with the implementation of "slum clearance" initiatives, shack settlements were recast as temporary dwellings and earmarked for removal.

Liberal state discourses on fire elide the politicization of racialized en-

Eskom's campaign against electricity theft, invoking anti-apartheid slogans and icons. (https://web
.archive.org/web/20140830111651/http://www.operationkhanyisa.co.za/index.php/resource/entry/report
-posters, accessed July 23, 2015)

dangerment among residents in Abahlali-affiliated settlements. In Durban's
shacklands, scars on bodies tell stories, often about fire. There are three common injuries associated with fire: the first is to livelihoods, the second is to
the burning of the body, and the third is death. In 2008, in the same month
Slovo Park was swept away by flames, Abahlali convened a Shack Fire Summit
in the Kennedy Road community hall, the locus of activities in the settlement
and national headquarters of the activist network. There, with a candle lit in
vigil on the floor, Busisiwe spoke about a time when her family's one-room
shack in Kennedy had been set on fire. It happened when she arrived from
school and began cooking supper. While chatting with her mother, Busisiwe
moved back and forth to stir and stare at the pot. Suddenly, she said, "smoke
was coming out and it was smelling nasty. I said to mom, 'What is wrong with
this stove?'" The stove was brand new: an NGO had been selling new ethanol
gel stoves hailed as "safer than paraffin" in Kennedy Road. Busisiwe's family

purchased one, knowing the hazards of paraffin—an expensive substance, a hassle to acquire, and easily combustible. Aside from its foul smell, the clear liquid was sometimes accidentally ingested by young children, resulting in death. Ethanol gel, a renewable resource often made from sugarcane, is regarded as a "green," ecofriendly alternative.

While Busisiwe wondered what might be wrong with the new stove, she again stared at the pot. Then, "POOF!" The stove exploded:

> The flames caught my clothes. My clothes: that is how I got burned. It just burst into flames. I only saw the flames and nothing else, and I ran away. I just ran outside.
>
> I wanted to get rid of the fire, and so I was rolling down on the sand. My neighbors, seeing me run out of my shack with the flames, ran to remove the stove, so that the fire would not catch the other homes. I rolled outside, and then [my mother and neighbors] poured me with water.

Once back inside, Busisiwe sat down on the bed, when suddenly she began "feeling the heat." She saw that the only objects burned were the duvet cover and the milk-and-juice carton wallpaper. Her mother called the ambulance, but after more than an hour, it had not arrived. Eventually, she was given a lift to Addington, a public hospital that serves as the main access point to medical care for poor residents in the city, where she underwent two skin grafts. They did not take: the fire left her with permanent scars across much of her arms, legs, and torso. Busisiwe's mother told me that thereafter the younger children would awaken at night shouting: "There's a fire! There's a fire! There's a fire!" I asked Busisiwe if she too had nightmares. She says, "No, I just take things I see into my eyes—not into my head." But it did reorient her future. After spending months in recovery, she was prevented from taking a scholarship that would have allowed her to go to a private school. She says, "It wasn't only me that burned down; all my plans were burned down in that fire." Through the body, the injuries sustained by fire extend indefinitely into the future to shape life and politics inside the home and on the streets.

Emblematic of the complex entanglements of energy and endangerment are the measures taken within settlements to prevent fires. In 2009, I went with Kennedy residents—including Busisiwe, Siboniso, and Faku—to a mass meeting to prepare the memorial of sixteen-year-old Sakhephi Zenda. With the illicit electricity supply cut by private security earlier in the day, the nighttime meeting was conducted in complete darkness, save for a single electric lamp. Suddenly, a police helicopter appeared shining bright spotlights on the residents gathered below. Flying low in the sky, the helicopter swung back and forth like some deus ex machina, recalling the theme of criminalization at the Shack Fire Summit.

The newspapers at the time had announced that KwaMashu had been named a "murder capital" of the world,[14] according to international crime counters for the statistical prevalence of gun- and gang-related deaths. However, Zenda had not been killed by a stray bullet, but by electrocution from a badly made electricity connection. Perhaps, said his neighbors, Zenda had attempted, unskillfully, to repair the broken live wire to ward off shack fires. Or, as most thought, he stepped on it, absentmindedly, his head full of school the next day or of his grandmother's recent passing, while he walked home to his family's modest shack. While Zenda's body was transported for burial at his family's rural farm outside Durban, Abahlali issued a statement online and via cell phone text message, criticizing the municipality's policy suspending energy installation in Durban shacks: "Electricity could have saved Sakhephi's life just as it could have saved . . . Baba Dhlomo's life. . . . We will do what ever it takes to make sure that each person counts [in this city and this system]. If that means going to court we will go to court. If that means going to the streets we will go the streets. . . . If that means resisting disconnections we will do that."[15] Although it is difficult to know what influence residents had in the halls of power in the city, after nearly a decade, the electricity policy in Durban was overturned.

Conclusion: Agents of Fire under Democratization

I conclude by suggesting that there is a double edge to the promise of infrastructure. Electricity protects against shack fires and connects people to a world that increasingly relies on energy to access information and participate in politics. As Mnikelo put it, "We do not need electricity, but electricity is needed for our lives." Yet licit or illicit infrastructure also can enable unwelcome state interventions, such as policing settlements as criminal zones. By promising "life"—or the health and integrity of the body and community—infrastructure becomes a staging ground for injuries that map onto longstanding configurations of urban space at the intersections of race and class. That is not an argument against the installation of electricity, but for better understanding its dynamics of power.

When prepaid electricity boxes began to be installed in Kennedy Road shacks, it exacerbated tensions between community members by redrawing lines of difference: between those who could pay for electricity and those who could not; between those who had a job and those who were unemployed;

between those who could access state patronage and those who could not. At times, these lines were perceived as marking age, ethnic, or national difference as well. As Kennedy residents found, even with electricity installed, connections are likely to break, be disconnected, or become interrupted over time, particularly if prepaid electricity meters cannot be fed with a steady supply of cash. Electricity raids to switch off households have frequently led to violent clashes.

In other words, there is no endpoint to the installation of infrastructure. Endangerment to the body and community do not depend only on whether residents are connected to energy but rather more broadly on the place still accorded to racialized bodies in distributions of political and economic power. The promise of liberation—or what liberation movements fought for—is to fundamentally transform these distributions, which cannot be achieved by infrastructural interventions alone. For Abahlali members, fire spells a line between rich and poor, white and black, Global North and Global South, which maps onto urban public space.[16] That does not suggest that nothing has changed since 1994 in South African townships and shack settlements, but rather that, from the vantage point of the shacks, it is clear who burns and dies in fires, and who does not. It is here, between life and death, that fire draws its ultimate line of difference.

I move from deadly fire to life-giving water in the next chapter. I also follow Abahlali's political networks from Durban to Cape Town shack settlements. The everyday practices and interactions that flow from water, as I demonstrate, offer different insights than fire about the material conditions and outcomes of a living politics of "the poor." What can be learned about the political roles actualized in protest if the properties of water, now, are taken as an optic of analysis?

Water / Amanzi

Dispatch

Pemary Ridge Settlement Disconnected from Water
Submitted by Abahlali on Fri, 2006-11-03 01:52
NOVEMBER 3, 2005

Yesterday Pemary Ridge . . . had their water disconnected. This is yet another act of direct aggression towards shack dwellers from [city government] that could cost lives. Imagine raising a child without water throughout the whole day in the Durban summer. . . . Imagine if AIDS, as it does, produces diarrhea and you simply can't wash all day. . . . When the local Councillor . . . was challenged today he said that the water had to be turned off because people were 'abusing it' as consumption had gone up. . . . It was pointed out to [him] that water consumption had gone up because the settlement had in fact grown from 50 families to over 200 families in this time. He was unrepentant. . . . [Government officials] don't realise that it is the utter inhumanity of their own policies that produces resistance.

Debts of Liberal State Transition: Liquid Belonging and Consumer Citizenship

QR was thirsty. Hundreds of residents of the QR shack settlement gathered for a march to downtown Cape Town, a city crescented around the Atlantic Ocean. M'du, who soon would be elected Abahlali's provincial chairperson, led the congregation of young and elderly women. Their starting point was District Six, the site of an infamous apartheid-era forced removal. District Six was chosen, residents explained, to dramatize QR's own place in a genealogy of urban displacement. QR is located on sandy, low-lying land in township formalized under apartheid. South Africa's energy company Eskom now owns the land. Each year, QR is consumed by massive floods, which are brought by cold winter rains. Those shacks not swept away are filled with water that residents bail out of their homes with plastic washing buckets. As QR grew in size and density since the 1990s, the floods have wreaked greater havoc.

This chapter analyzes water (*amanzi* in *isi*Xhosa and *isi*Zulu) as a vital, if perilous, force in political belonging. Water connects sovereign territories to each other; the body's cells to the means of life; domestic spaces to institutions and commodity flows. It carries and surfaces state–citizen relations. Until the fall of apartheid and colonial orders in 1994, South African citizenship—a claim of inclusion, recognition, and redistribution in the polity—was formally an explicit racial status, which excluded African people. Whereas the previous chapter focused on fire's power to draw lines of racial and ethnic difference, this chapter examines how water acts as a conduit between activist networks and state agents to renegotiate historically race-based citizenship.

The QR marchers' route into the city, from the dusty abandoned lots of District Six, is paved with manicured municipal gardens and white colonial-style buildings. Up above, built into the jagged sides of flat-topped Table

Mountain, sit homes gleaming with blue swimming pools. The "table cloth," condensed moisture that forms a misty cloud above the mountain, can be seen from the street. Facilitated by *toyi-toying* and anti-apartheid anthems, QR residents arrived swiftly at the steps of the Provincial Parliament, a coral-colored building with impressive colonnades that houses the Western Cape province's executive. Police and journalists already had arrived.

The congregation, at first, stood quietly holding handwritten cardboard signs, which read in English: "We are tired of the Mayor's empty promises," and "This city is only accountable to the rich." Although the slogans were aimed at the then mayor and opposition party figurehead Helen Zille, the women were sidestepping the city government to address a higher provincial authority, which at the time was the ANC. The congregation demanded that a member of the ANC's provincial cabinet appear in person to receive a memorandum. Submitting a memorandum is a ritual feature of post-apartheid street protests. It involves a representative of a state or corporate office publicly signing a list of collective demands.

QR's memorandum, though copies were lost in the aftermath of the flood, focused—as their meetings and marches did at the time—upon water's compound properties. The memorandum spoke to the ecological disaster that was their rain-engulfed community. It addressed a lack of infrastructure, in particular that no resident in QR had access to functioning toilets. It spoke to extreme water scarcity: "An estimated 620 people shared eight outdoor communal water taps." Like many post-apartheid activist networks, QR residents posited water as a natural resource held in common, rather than as a commodity to be bought and sold. In these multiple forms, the ebbs and flows of water—whether arriving in QR as too much or too little—make life in shack settlements viable or unlivable. Water is what politically united QR.

Memorandum in hand, M'du noticed that the waiting crowd was growing impatient. The provincial official did not appear, but eventually sent his spokesperson. The women met him shouting, "Down with pit toilets! Down! Forward flush toilets! Forward!" Still, the memorandum signing did not play out peaceably as expected. With M'du at the megaphone, police moved to forcibly break up the march, to which the women responded, "Down with apartheid police! Down!" The scuffle was featured on the national news, and in Cape Town's most widely read newspapers. Abahlali and affiliate movements posted the story to their websites and sent text messages to members.[1] Not captured were the tense interactions with police prior to the march. For unspecified "security reasons," police denied QR's permit request to march on local government offices—a historical flashpoint over water infrastructure.

When the women returned to QR section, they continued to march and

A memorandum signing between Abahlali members and state agents, 2011. (Photo by author)

burned tires in a road blockade. There had been blockades over flooding before, but this one marked escalation from the theatrics at Parliament. As I explored in the previous chapter, fire issues an implicit threat to power. The memorandum ritual, by contrast, is an open-ended negotiation. The ritual mirrors a contract signing, where residents and state agents play the part of mutual partners in a process of transforming existing infrastructure. Between these two distinct kinds of mobilizations, one consultative and the other confrontational, QR did get a response. The following day, Mayor Helen Zille called M'du's cell phone, and told residents to cease all "violent protests." She assured him that an acceptable solution, possibly including relocation, would be reached in QR. Meetings would commence.

I tracked water, and the forms of belonging it engendered, in Abahlali-affiliated communities. Water is an element of living politics because it sustains life, but also obliges residents to interact with state states, be it by paying a household water bill to a local government council, or drinking from an outdoor communal water tap managed by state agents. Official statistics suggest that 43.3 percent of the national population has piped water inside their homes, 28.6 percent have access to water in their yards, 2.7 percent have use of a neighbor's water tap, and—like nearly all the residents I know—14.9 percent rely wholly on outdoor communal taps. Approximately 10.5 percent have no access to piped water at all (Rademeyer 2013; Statistics South Africa 2013). The new South African Constitution guarantees 25 liters of free water per day. This right has been a matter of several high-profile court battles, including those brought by Abahlali. However, there are no adequate systems to regulate or protect it, especially in settlements without necessary infrastructure. A lack of indoor plumbing typically means households rely on women's labor to carry water, at times long distances, for cooking, bathing, and other domestic activities. It also is typical—for water often commingles with waste—that toilets in such homes are composed of a hole in the ground ("pit toilets"), a bucket ("the bucket system"), or a plastic bag, jokingly known as "fly toilets," for you swing it above your head and let it land where it may.

Although these statistics sound dire, they are actually thought to be optimistic by water researchers in South Africa (Rademeyer 2013). Access to piped water means that you have access to a pipe, not necessarily that drinkable water flows through it, or that the pipe works all the time. When water dwindled in Abahlali communities, residents supplemented by borrowing, accessing illicit connections, or gathering from natural sources such as springs or rivers. A lack of water ripens the ground for shack fires. Of increasing concern among policy makers is the sustainability of South Africa's overall water supplies. These have been depleting for reasons attributed to climate-change-related rain shortfall, water-guzzling industries—mines, oil refineries, and commercial agriculture—as well as the steady degradation of existing dams and other infrastructure upon which the flow of water depends. Water falls from the sky and makes up most of our bodies and the planet's surface; it is relatively plentiful in South Africa, yet it remains most dear in poor communities.

To grasp how water acts as a political conductor, I focus on how activists used it in the mid-1980s to mobilize consumer boycotts, a collective refusal to engage in commodity exchange with the apartheid state. During this period, apartheid state agents responded by framing household water disconnections in townships as the neutral termination of a liberal contract; rather than what it principally was: a counterinsurgency operation in the final moments before state transition. Activist networks' efforts to consolidate their members during the transition binds water to national citizenship (*ummi* in *isi*Xhosa), which itself is constantly being remade in relation to other often contrary conceptions of political belonging.[2] Among them is a long-standing fluidity of residence in townships and shack settlements (*umhlali* in *isi*Xhosa and *isi*Zulu), where Abahlali derives its name.

Water is essential to demobilizing township street politics, not primarily by producing racialized criminal agents as fire does, but by according a new status and mode of political belonging as "nonracial" consumers. This liberal social contract, struck between an infrastructure-supplying state and a consumer citizenry, is conditioned upon being willing and able to engage in exchange with the state: to trade cash for water. In this way, water disconnection serves to discipline as well as cultivate desires for civic inclusion, and therefore stores the debts of colonial citizenship. The binding of citizenship to consumption, moreover, serves to discipline not only paying customers in townships, but also those who cannot pay in shack settlements.

Waterfronts: Liquid Geographies of Belonging

A week before M'du marched with the women to Provincial Parliament, Cape Town mayor Helen Zille visited the flooded QR settlement. She was photographed stepping through the pools of fetid water that residents called the Waterfront. Like many of South Africa's present-day politicians, Zille positions herself as a former activist. Along with participating in anti-apartheid protests by white progressives in the mid-1980s, she was arrested for violating segregationist "Group Areas" laws. Visits by politicians like this one in QR serve to reaffirm these "struggle" credentials and rally townships, which became major voting blocs with the conferral of post-apartheid citizenship.

Zille visited the section of QR known as the Waterfront. To any Cape Townian, calling flooded shacks the Waterfront is understood as a jab at wealth disparity in the city—and a reminder of the liquid geographies of South Africa's colonial past. "The V&A Waterfront" is an exclusive high-end shopping mall in central Cape Town, boasting such global brands as Gucci, Prada, and Louis Vuitton. It is named after the British Queen Victoria and her son Alfred. The rocky shoreline that the mall overlooks was constructed by the Dutch East India Company, as a refreshment stop for ships en route between African and Asian colonies. It also is where ferries depart for guided tours of Robben Island, the leper-colony-cum-insane-asylum-cum-prison that held Nelson Mandela and other activists. At the Waterfront, as the mall is better known, water serves as a majestic backdrop to luxury consumption, a channel for indentured labor and colonial trade, and the treacherous natural mote of a notorious prison. By shifting the proper name of this complex intersection of the city to the disaster zone that is QR in the wintertime, residents surface unexpected, and ironic, connections between these otherwise spatially and temporally disparate sites.[3]

Residents in Abahlali settlements characterize the presence (or absence) of water infrastructure, from bridges to wastewater systems, as the imprint of colonial governance.[4] The British colonial state in South Africa (von Schnitzler 2013), as it did in other colonies (Larkin 2008), actively laid water pipes to demarcate their colonial territories under indirect rule, a system that maximized power by localizing authority. The pipes meant more than opening up

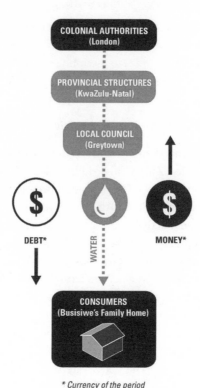

COLONIAL AUTHORITIES
(London)

PROVINCIAL STRUCTURES
(KwaZulu-Natal)

LOCAL COUNCIL
(Greytown)

$

DEBT*

WATER

$

MONEY*

CONSUMERS
(Busisiwe's Family Home)

* Currency of the period

Flows of water governance in 1901. (Chart by author with graphic design by Joyce Lee)

or closing down flows of water through dams, reservoirs, or filter systems. It was an entry into, and the maintenance of relations between, sovereign authority in London, local government, and white water consumers, for the pipes were laid where there were British citizens. It was a citizenship status like apartheid, which excluded African, Indian, and Coloured households. One 1901 Act of Parliament identifies the indebted, asymmetric but reciprocal terms of these relations with reference to Nortown, where Busisiwe grew up and where her rural family now resides. The act enables the local government "to borrow a sum not exceeding Twelve Thousand Pounds for the purpose of supplying . . . water; to construct the necessary works; to levy a water rate; to prevent the pollution of water; and generally to exercise all powers necessary for the purpose aforesaid" (Colony of Natal 1901, 38).

The colonial act further declares that if payment is not received from consumers via local government, interest will mount. Eventually, consumers may have their land appropriated, or serve time in prison—"not exceeding one month"—in lieu of the payment of debt (Colony of Natal 1901, 41). The act, echoing liberal contract theory, characterizes water as a special kind of property: "If the taking, impounding, diversion, appropriation or convey-ance of water . . . shall deprive any person of any water, or right of water, which he may at the time . . . possess, or be entitled to possess, and shall thereby cause damage to such person or his property, such person shall be entitled to recompense or compensation."[5] By granting British citizens the ability to sue for damages, water is posited as at once a consumable public good that connects nodes of South African rule, as well as a valuable form of private property, a commodity whose circulation is unseemly to disconnect.

Like the two "Waterfronts," the 1901 Act suggests that the intertwining of water and race-based political belonging runs deep in South Africa, but, moreover, that at particular moments this history comes bubbling up to shape lives in present-day townships and shack settlements. In the apartheid era, with the passing of the Separate Amenities Act of 1953, water would be-come further segregated: beaches, bathrooms, swimming pools, and water fountains would be racially designated "black" and "white," noncitizen and citizen. As Abahlali members and archival sources suggest, the mid-1980s also is one of these moments, when state transition put the very substance of citizenship dramatically into flux, and, with it, the status of water consump-tion in race-based communities.

Transitional States: From Exiled Militants to Citizen Consumers

During the volatile unrest of the mid-1980s explored in the previous chapter, scores of anti-apartheid militants were exiled or became political prisoners. As Abahlali members who were detained attest, few substances were as im-portant in carceral life as water. Through the act of drinking and food prepa-ration, water sustains biological existence. Through acts of cleaning, it keeps away illness and pests. Through rites of medicinal or religious purification, it shields against defilement, or even the depths of madness.[6]

Winnie Mandela meditates on water's properties in her journal smug-gled out of prison, where she spent 451 days in solitary confinement. She writes:

> My daily routine in all three cells was the same. . . . After cleaning the cell, I washed my mouth, face, and hands in the sanitary buckets with the drink-ing water poured into the mug. There are no lavatories . . . so I had to use the same bucket for everything. I trained my stomach to work once a day, in the morning, just after washing my mouth, face, and hands, because this "pon" [a bucket used as a toilet] is changed once a day, in the morning only. (Madikizela-Mandela 2013, 14)

By leaving prisoners thirsty, dehydrated, or unwashed—or by forcing them to bathe under inspection—her captors used water as an instrument of sovereign power. As many of apartheid's prisoners describe, water was used to achieve control or humiliation, to inflict and deposit wounds invisible to the naked eye. The long-term effects of dehydration can bring on nightmares, or manifest in chronic conditions at the organic level. Prisoner accounts of this period, likewise speak to water—especially because of its necessity for survival—as central to psychic warfare.

As Nelson Mandela writes from the perspective of Robben Island, between the Atlantic Ocean and its uses inside the prison walls, water is among the warder's most profound tools in making the familiar hostile and strange. The Truth and Reconciliation Commission (TRC) revealed that security forces in the mid-1980s used water in interrogations to water board for confessions by covering a prisoner's mouth with a wet bag to simulate drowning. Winnie Mandela recalls prison wardens putting her meager daily allotment of water in "filthy" containers. She notes that her "Dixie" (a metal plate used for meals) was placed atop "the pon" (Madikizela-Mandela 2013, 15). Using water in torture, withholding or giving contaminated water and food, centers on the individual prisoner and her biological processes, but targets a larger political body, to break each down and weaken its life force.

Winnie Mandela, like other prisoners, nevertheless used what little water she had to tend to her body and organize her time around a routine, both otherwise so much subject to the prison. Water could be used in fleeting acts of subversion, or self-possession, or as a reminder of everyday practices of home. Prisoners also collectively organized around water in prison. These acts of discipline and protest suggest how imprisonment was implicated in what was happening on the streets outside, and, in turn, how carceral life extended from the prison into urban townships. Water transmuted prison walls, literally through systems of pipes, but also through logics of infrastructural disconnection.

When Winnie Mandela returned to her township home in 1987 after exile and imprisonment, she found battles over water all around her. One hundred forty-two people would be killed in the Vaal uprising.[7] Although known primarily as a popular anti-apartheid revolt, it began when the local apartheid agents raised the cost of state-supplied water in townships, and increased the rent in state-owned housing. Tariff increases, and corresponding water disconnections, were endemic in the mid-1980s. Household disconnections targeted the homes of prominent anti-apartheid leaders and politically mobilized communities.

Arresting the flow of water targeted activists, whereas refusing to pay for water sought to compromise apartheid state agents and institutions. The 1980s rent and services boycotts, as they became known, would last for over five years. Residents in fifty-six townships—which contain settlements now affiliated with Abahlali—refused to pay for infrastructure owned or supplied by the apartheid state. More than half of the 2.5 million residents of Soweto (Southwest Township), where Winnie resided, withheld payment for water, rent, and electricity.[8] The boycotts were organized, the ANC announced, "to protest housing policies, the state of emergency, the presence of troops in townships and other aspects of government policy toward the vote-less black majority."[9] Umkhonto we Sizwe, the ANC's military wing, meanwhile targeted nodes of transportation and infrastructure, such as bridges and water mains.[10]

Abahlali members recall and even participated in the boycotts. Monique, a former anti-apartheid union organizer in Cape Town, observed that refusing to pay for water dovetailed with other consumer campaigns. The Boycott Movement was founded in 1959 at a meeting of South African exiles in London. Locally in South Africa, activists—and, particularly, women responsible for stocking the household larder—were asked to boycott neighborhood shops, and to go without essential products, such as flour or eggs.[11] Boycotts endeavored to regain control over practices of consumption in townships, which from the sale of morally charged products such as liquor to the establishment of black-owned businesses such as *spaza* shops (informal convenience stores) were historically restricted under apartheid.

The boycotts had a profound political and economic impact. Activists aimed at, and succeeded in, bankrupting segregated local councils under whose purview the billing, collection, and keeping record of water payments fell.[12] By some estimates, the cost to local councils exceeded $100 million in Soweto alone.[13] The combined effect of nonpayment across the country, activists correctly calculated, would put pressure on the national government already increasingly isolated on the world market by sanctions and trade embargos. What emerged from the boycotts were forms of political belonging, premised not upon national citizenship, but cross regional participation as empowered consumers grounded in one's community or civic organization (*umhlali* in isiZulu and isiXhosa).

Winnie Mandela in 1987 publicly announced her participation in the water boycotts.[14] Soon thereafter, heavily armed police arrived at her home in Soweto. Witnesses describe the spectacle as culminating in an exchange of gunfire. A police spokesman, alluding to the ANC's militarization, told reporters that he could "neither confirm nor deny" that a police officer was shot. Winnie denied shooting at security forces.[15] She told the press that the water disconnection was pure political intimidation. Although released from prison, state agents still had power over her water supply.

Winnie suggested that water was being used to turn her home—then also an activist base in Soweto—into a place where apartheid state agents could display their power to a national public. Whereas petrol bombings and arson happened as covert operations under the shroud of nightfall, water could be disconnected in the bright light of day, through official channels, and with the press recording the proceedings. The all-white Soweto council made recourse, *not* to counterinsurgency or upholding racial segregation— increasingly unpopular political grounds—but rather to a "nonracial" liberal contract. They denied that Winnie's water disconnection had anything to do with her political activities or her race, and rather claimed it was her failure to pay her bills on time.

This liberal contract was further articulated at the national level as "Operation Switch Off." The operation, launched in 1990, targeted townships participating in the rent and services boycotts.[16] As Planning and Provincial Affairs Minister Hernus Kriel—the man whose hand was on the nation's water taps—put it: "Suppliers of [water] have no choice but to discontinue their services to certain communities, especially those with a poor record of payment. . . . The government simply does not have the funds to continue to provide bridging finance, and the onus to pay for these services rests with the consumers themselves."[17] In Kriel's formulation, those long regarded as "militants," "criminals," and "terrorists" would acquire a new status: "consumers." Here, consumer status is infused with the logics of water as a "nonracial" commodity. The status shifts the responsibility for water disconnection from the apartheid state—which had the sovereign power to connect or disconnect its supplies—to individual households.

Liberation movements, at times, promoted township residents not merely as citizens-in-waiting, but frustrated consumers. As one ANC organizer told the international press, "We want to make it very clear that . . . [township] residents are prepared to pay rent and services charges, if their demands are met. We don't want to use services free of charge."[18] In 1990, as Nelson Mandela was released from prison, prominent activists "painstakingly hammered out" a deal with provincial and local apartheid state agents.[19] The deal, known as "The Soweto Accord," erased some boycott-related debts. Yet it also established payment plans for water in Soweto and other townships, which would extend beyond the apartheid era.

Water as a "nonracial" commodity remained controversial among black and white South Africans. In the 1990s, liberation activists and apartheid agents, while consolidating leadership around a negotiated democratic transition, were hemorrhaging control over water at local levels. As desegregation followed the repeal of the 1953 Separate Amenities Act, water disconnections struck dozens of townships and shack settlements. White local councils retaliated against negotiations with the ANC. Not only did these so-called rogue councils deprive black residents of water, they refused to integrate swimming pools, water fountains, and other public amenities. They viewed, and desperately clung to, water rights as a racial entitlement.

At the same time, ordinary township residents understandably balked at paying for life's basic necessities—especially to local councils seeking to retain apartheid.[20] Some within liberation movements—notably, Winnie Mandela—vocally opposed concessions made by the ANC to the apartheid government and international institutions. Water, again, was at stake in these concessions. As early as 1990, liberation activists were negotiating future repayment plans with the World Bank for debts accumulated under apartheid. These were national debts. The apartheid state borrowed some two million dollars from the World Bank for infrastructure development projects, including for toilet installation in townships.[21]

The contradictions surfacing over "nonracial" citizenship may be captured by water battles in Wesselton, a township outside of Johannesburg. Wesselton supplied disenfranchised black workers to the water-guzzling Ermelo coal mine.[22] In 1990, on the cusp of state transition, the white local council disconnected the township's water.[23] About fifty thousand people were affected.[24] Provincial apartheid authorities—falling into line with the national government—responded by circumventing the white local council. Water supply trucks were sent from South Africa's capitol, Pretoria. But rumor abounded that the water was poisoned. Residents refused to drink it, and instead gathered from wells in historically Indian and Coloured communities miles away.

Gas station owner Mohammed Tilly told a reporter that he saw apartheid security forces puncturing residents' filled water containers, a failed attempt to force them to use the supplies from Pretoria.[25] When police interrogated Tilly for allowing residents to use the gas station's water taps, he said, "You can't refuse water. It is a gift from God."[26] Tilly's comment problematizes the notion that township residents were willing customers in waiting for fair charges on government services. Rather than positing water as a commodity, Tilly emphasizes it as a sacred substance of gift exchange between neighbors.

His formulation, echoed by Wesselton residents, stands in striking contrast to exchange with apartheid state agents on the basis of liberal contract or racial patronage.

The water disconnection in Wesselton points to growing anxieties in South Africa's private sector over the status of water and belonging at the mines. Amid conflicts between township residents and the white local council, mining activities at Ermelo were disrupted. The mine's management reportedly donated $50,000 to cover overdue water payments and reconnect Wesselton households.[27] Ermelo opted to provide free water in exchange for resumed productivity. In exchange for water, however, the mine demanded compliant labor.

It has become a truism in South Africa to date the commodification of water with neoliberal reforms between the late 1990s and mid-2000s. That water commodification crystallizes under apartheid, and echoes the 1901 understandings of water as a special kind of property tied to political belonging, suggests overlooked continuities between colonial and postcolonial periods. Faku pointed out to me that the late Lucky Dube, South Africa's most famous reggae musician, grew up near Ermelo mine. Dube is popular in Abahlali settlements. In 1999, Dube released an album titled *The Way It Is*, reflecting on apartheid's brutal legacies. The chorus of the track titled "Till You Lose It All" repeats: "You don't know what you've got / Till you lose it all again / You never miss your water / Till your well runs dry."[28] The lyrics powerfully suggest that water carries debts of previous generations. Dube warns listeners that "the wolf"—of deadly thirst—"is always standing at the door."[29]

"The Freedom to Pay for What We Use": Citizenship after Apartheid

Even after the fall of apartheid in 1994, residents of townships and shack settlements continued to boycott water payments. However, now, it would be recast as a failure of civic duty. During a speech in 1995 at the township of Marconi Beam, newly elected President Nelson Mandela launched the nationwide "Masakhane Campaign." Marconi Beam, named after the colonial telegraph facilities built there, is about thirty-five kilometers northwest of QR section. *Masakhane* means "stand together" in *isi*Xhosa and "let us build each other" in *isi*Zulu. To the residents and journalists gathered that day in February, Mandela characterized the campaign as a new exchange between a state responsible for supplying basic infrastructure and a citizenry responsible for paying for what they consume. Mandela announced that water pipes, sewerage, and electricity cabling would be installed in twelve hundred

Marconi Beam homes, but required, in turn, that residents play an active role in developing a post-apartheid "culture of payment":

> What is happening here [in Marconi Beam] . . . is a partnership of a community determined to take responsibility for its own upliftment; and a government which has assumed the responsibility of planning for the most efficient use of the country's resources in order to address the legacy of the past. The Masakhane campaign will build partnership, so that we can build one another. . . .
>
> From Soweto to Mitchell's Plain, from Chatsworth to Khayelitsha, democracy brings to neighbourhoods and communities the power to make sure that the changes working through our country will reach them. The Masakhane campaign will help communities turn government programmes into the projects they need.
>
> With freedom comes responsibility, the responsibility of participation.
>
> Each brick that is used to build a wall, every drop of water from a tap, is the result of many people's work and uses our country's resources. Government is putting massive investment into programmes for housing and services. We all have the responsibility to pay for what we use, or else the investment will dry up and the projects come to an end. We must ensure that we can, as a nation, provide for the millions still without the basic needs.
>
> The laying of this brick symbolises the building of our nation, by all of us, working together in partnership to bring a better life for all South Africans.
>
> Let us all build together and let us build each other.
>
> Masakhane![30]

The campaign resonates with the Reconstruction and Development Plan (RDP), the ANC's election platform in 1994, which set out redistributive national policies. Mandela later told Parliament that Masakhane was an effort to put an end to the 1985 boycotts, for the "nonpayment of services had been aimed at fighting apartheid, [which] was no longer necessary."[31] Masakhane was popularized through various media, notably including theatrical performances in townships of plays written to encourage water payments. In these iterations, the campaign reflects a post-apartheid conception of citizenship, which hinges not merely on an ability to vote, but upon consumption in historically African, Indian, and Coloured communities.

In his speech, Mandela identifies water—"every drop . . . from a [household] tap"—at one level as a commodity, something that congeals human labor and natural resources, which can be bought and sold. Along with its economic value, however, water is phrased as materializing state–citizen relations. Political authority, flowing from state agents and institutions, is

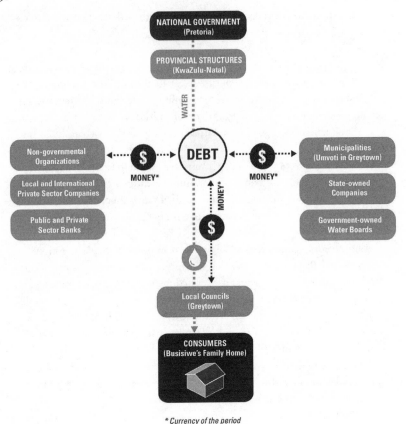

Currency of the period

Flows of water governance in 2009. (Chart by author with graphic design by Joyce Lee)

enacted through the supply of water to households, particularly in communities deliberately underserviced by colonial and apartheid governments. In turn, citizen belonging is enacted through conventional electoral participation, as well as rituals of reciprocating consumption with the payment of a monthly bill.

The unintended consequences of Masakhane would become evident in Phola township outside of Johannesburg, when some twenty thousand people were disconnected from water and electricity. The community reportedly owed nearly $1 million in debt to the local council. The council itself owed an estimated $2 million to Eskom, South Africa's soon to be multinational parastatal energy company. Then head of the Phola council, Edwin Sibiya, blamed the disconnections on apartheid-era debt, "President Nelson Mandela and [the last apartheid head of state] F. W. de Klerk's agreement that some of the arrears would not be written off was a blow to us."[32] He continued, "People do not want to pay for their services and most cannot afford to pay."[33]

Following the disconnections, residents of Phola intensified their services boycotts and threatened to burn down the local council's offices, in part, to destroy the record of their debt. As Phola resident Solomon Mahlangu—who shared a name with an icon of the liberation struggle—said, "If they want us to start paying, then they must scratch our arrears and let us start from the beginning."[34] Councillor Sibiya suggested, however, that nothing could be done, "Even if they burn our offices, the fact remains that at the end of the day they will still owe their arrears."[35]

Phola residents' debt was accumulated under the ANC, but also under the apartheid regime. Where payment agreements had not been reached in townships, debt even lingered from the rent and services boycotts of 1985. Mahlangu and Sibiya explain that the demands of a "payment culture" always are more than "paying for what we use"; residents also were expected to pay for what they used according to apartheid records. In this case, Phola residents are bound as citizens to pay their bills—often without the money to do so—and are responsible for paying off debt to a regime that no longer exists.[36] Although the history books have been rewritten, apartheid-era debts would continue to be taken as binding material facts.

Moreover, state agents and corporations in Phola and other townships treated every water debt as if it were the same. It is no matter whether a payment is overdue because the household cannot afford to pay, has taken a political decision to refuse payment, has leftover debt from the 1985 boycotts, or any number of other reasons for how and why debt is accrued. Far from being seen as political or even circumstantial, nonpayment is regarded as a breach of contract between consumer and supplier, as well as a personal and communal abnegation of civic duty. In effect, the short history of an overdue bill is denied any consequence, as is a longer history of struggle that called on residents to protest by boycott. As the escalating situation in Phola suggests, these contradictions inadvertently repoliticized nonpayment and water disconnection in QR and other settlements.

Activist networks emerged across the country, demanding cancelation of South Africa's international debt and communities' localized debt. Repoliticizing nonpayment coincided with experiments with water privatization, which yet again reconfigured consumer citizenship. In 1999, the same year that Lucky Dube's album warned of the wells running dry, the South African government awarded a thirty-year contract to a British multinational corporation called Biwater. The Congress of South African Trade Unions

(COSATU) and the Pan-Africanist Congress (PAC), in an uncharacteristic show of solidarity, teamed up with civic groups in a mass boycott of water payments to Biwater. Along with water delivery problems, residents said Biwater raised rates by some 400 percent.[37] Households that refused or were unable to pay were switched off.

Household debts and disconnection in South Africa had circled back to London, the former colonial metropole. Although water remained a negotiation with state agents, redistributive demands now were to be directed to a corporation half a world away. With echoes of Hernus Kriel, the head of Biwater Graham Corrod in London blamed rate increases and dire water shortages on black consumers. He pointed to nonpayment, "wastage and indiscriminate use of water" in urban townships.[38] Amid the controversy, then president Thabo Mbeki—Mandela's successor known to be astute and aloof—told the local council "under no circumstances must Biwater be allowed to collapse."[39] A special police unit was called to monitor the situation. A legal firm was hired to track down water defaulters and threatened to sue residents with outstanding arrears. Local state agents suggested that the boycotters be treated as criminals: "[they are] just individuals who are misbehaving; the police are dealing with them."[40]

Yet Biwater created a public health catastrophe: cholera was reported in the townships it serviced. By some measures, post-apartheid experiments in privatization resulted in hundreds of deaths in African, Indian, and Coloured communities. Following the collapse of Biwater, the Water Services Act of 1999 prevented the South African government from outsourcing water to the private sector. However, the act has been diluted over the years. The question of privatization remains one of management, rather than simply the shifting hands of ownership. Public–private partnerships include complex networks of subcontractors, consultancy firms, security forces, and an array of other private actors and global institutions. These networks participate actively in South Africa's water provision (Bond 2004a; Greenberg 2004; Huchzermeyer 2004; McDonald and Pape 2002). Public–private partnerships have consequences for political mobilization, for activists are protesting not only state power, but multinational corporate and nongovernmental power as well.

Conclusion: Historical Accounting, or Renegotiating the Social Contract

This chapter has examined how water (*amanzi* in *isi*Xhosa and *isi*Zulu) materializes citizenship as a negotiated exchange with state agents. The refusal to exchange cash for water galvanized political protest and belonging in townships and shack settlements during the mid-1980s. However, by the nineties, liberation movements and apartheid state agents reintroduced liberal logics of contract to govern water provision that drew from the wells of British colonial rule. Residents of townships and shack settlements, taking on a new status as consumer citizens, were granted the civic responsibility to pay or be disconnected. "Nonracial" citizenship, then, demanded a separation between payment and protest, which also meant the depoliticization (and criminalization) of certain political subjects like the Biwater boycotters, certain forms of protest such as debt accumulation, as well as certain histories of unequal distributions of water infrastructure.

Returning then to QR section in Cape Town, M'du's efforts to address the state "in person" take on a new light. As M'du and the women wait on the Parliament steps for a cabinet member who never appears, the memorandum ritual nevertheless serves as a collective and performative refusal of the realpolitik of water governance. Living politics responds to global and local flows of power that have sought to reduce life and belonging to commodity consumption. As this suggests, residents' claims to water, in such instances as QR's protest, push against national "nonracial" citizenship, and the privatization of water. In the post-apartheid period, residents of townships and shack settlements are mobilizing forms of community (*umhlali* in *isi*Xhosa

"Down with Water Cut-Offs": Abahlali affiliates gather at the Cape Town High Court. (Photo by author)

and *isi*Zulu) against the terms of so-called nonracial citizenship. Against the autonomy of the present implied by a culture of payment, they are demanding water infrastructure, but moreover an accounting of their community's deep histories and liquid geographies. Their demands, most broadly, are to renegotiate conditional access to the democratic state grid, which enacts a disconnection from the past.

The next chapter looks more closely at these contrary forms of political belonging (*umhlali* in *isi*Xhosa) by moving from water to air, and particularly residents' struggles to breathe freely in urban areas. These mobilizations, in contrast to the burning barricades of Kennedy Road or the memorandum rituals of QR, do not necessarily seek to garner the attention of state agents. Rather, they seep into the body to realign the soul in urban poor communities. Traversing the water back to Durban's port in the mid-2000s, shack settlement residents after the fall of apartheid were contending with ongoing infrastructural disconnection, as well as environmental pollution. This time, they draw from spiritual practices—some with precolonial referents—that inform contemporary belonging.

Air / Umoya

Dispatch

iPolitiki ePhilayo: The Abahlali baseMjondolo Manifesto
for a Politics of the Poor
Submitted by Abahlali on Sat, 2008-12-27 05:16
DECEMBER 27, 2008

- We are all created in the image of God therefore everyone is important.
  God does not want us to suffer. . . .
- We rebel because we are oppressed. We are oppressed because we are
  excluded and exploited. We are excluded and exploited because the war
  waged on our ancestors forced them into tiny pieces of land only big
  enough to raise workers for the factories and the mines and the farms and
  kitchens. Our parents' wages were not enough to escape poverty. We came
  to the cities searching for a way out. . . .
- Our rebellion is also justified by the fact that we and our parents and our
  ancestors struggled for justice in this country.

Coughing Out the City: Everyday Healing in the Toxic Borderlands

The air (*umoya* in *isi*Zulu) in shack settlements, as residents told me, is not empty, but full of all sorts of enigmatic particulates: sounds, scents, ancestral spirits, and digital signals. On a windy Saturday morning in 2009, Busisiwe, Faku, and I walked down the narrow pathway tightly surrounded by shacks that led to Kennedy Road's Community Hall in Durban. We joined about fifty other members representing branch areas, most wearing Abahlali's signature red T-shirts. Everyone was sharing gossip before the weekly Saturday mass gathering. Although many of us had become inured to certain putrid smells in the settlement—sewage seeping into muddy rivulets, the Bissar landfill with its gas-emitting incinerator, and sickly sweet perfumed sprinklers—it always struck the noses of members traveling from other areas in the city, as it did Zinzi, a movement leader and *sangoma* (traditional healer) from Mendini Hills.

Like the interior of any body or home, each shack settlement has its own ever-changing composition of air. Balances, or imbalances in this composition—sweet or sour relations with ancestors, the clamor of taxis jostling for customers, or the powerful aroma of a *shisa nyama* (an informal barbeque stall)—can inspire comfort and familiarity, or the sense of contagion and congestion. This potentially polluting composition can affect the most intimate and sensitive regions from the lungs to the soul (*umoya* in *isi*Zulu). Gatherings, like the one being assembled by Abahlali at the Community Hall, is where the autonomous accumulation of these particulates could be shifted to a settlement-wide body, and therefore redistributed, reordered, and productively managed. Gatherings were where the business of the activist network was done, where protests and court cases were planned, but as organic intellectual and ritual spaces, also where airborne particulates could be used to heal and protect against pollution at once chemical, spiritual, and technological.

From the Kennedy Road Community Hall, Abahlali members have a unique vantage on the well-known geography of the city's air. On the highest hilltop ridges is the Berea, where orange-roofed mansions house Durban's oldest wealth. Until racial integration began in the historically white suburb, residents told me that the Berea was distinct for its fresh, clean air: at a remove from the polluted industrial periphery and busy Indian Ocean port. From the Hall, Abahlali members also could glimpse Durban's downtown through a faint haze of smog, which wafts upward from the trafficked streets and northward from South Durban's petroleum refinery hub, where the Engen refinery vaporizes crude oil to manufacture gasoline and lubricants. Sulfur dioxide (SO_2), Durban's most prevalent chemical pollutant, has a devilish vinegar smell and, if inhaled for long periods, can result in prematurely divined death. According to official reports, SO_2 concentrates in the poorest African, Indian, and Coloured communities in Durban.

The previous chapter showed how water acts as a conduit for so-called nonracial citizenship, and therefore how residents interact with state agents. This chapter illustrates how air comes to structure being-together in shack settlements, and therefore how residents identify with each other. I focus particularly upon a tension between breathing and being unable to breathe, a state that residents describe as characteristic of living in poor urban communities. A key practice in mediating these states is what residents of South African shack settlements call "coughing out" (*ukubhodla* in *isi*Zulu). Coughing out is when you clear your lungs of pollution to breathe—whether to sing, pray, or speak—in ritual space. Coughing out at mass gatherings produces networks, which—like air—are found everywhere, and yet nowhere in particular. These networks, in spite of their seemingly fleeting and ephemeral properties, give substance to collective solidarity between residents.[1]

To track such an ungraspable substance as air in Kennedy and other Abahlali-affiliated settlements, I examine how the tangible practice of coughing out transmutes what are presumed to be the worldly domains of political-ecological life and the metaphysical realms of spiritual ancestors. I consider how this practice produces collectivities inside shack settlements, which, in turn, via digital technologies reach outward to globalized networks. Then I return to violent forces of pollution that suffocate, or inhibit breathing, while having the generative effect of designating movement leadership and consecrating symbolic kinship (Chance 2015b). These practices, I argue, reflect upon postliberation South Africa, which promised a decolonized state—or to free bodies and souls from the stranglehold of apartheid.

"Coughing out" at a mass meeting in front of an electricity pylon, soon broken up by police, 2008. (Photo by author)

Coughing Out: Liberating Lungs, Liberating Lives

In 1950, thousands flocked to a Johannesburg township called Kliptown to witness delegates sign the Freedom Charter. The document spelled out the principles of the multiracial coalition that became Nelson Mandela's ANC. The Congress Alliance—which Abahlali members frequently invoke as symbolic ancestors—included delegates from the African, Indian, and Coloured Congress. Accompanied by jubilant song and prayer, the charter was read in its entirety. When police broke up the gathering on the second day, Nelson Mandela disguised himself as a milkman to elude arrest. Those later charged with treason alongside Mandela, which resulted in his twenty-five-year imprisonment, were key delegates of this Congress Alliance gathering in Kliptown.

From 1950 onward, legislation such as the Riotous Assemblies Act, the Suppression of Communism Act, and the Unlawful Organization Act criminalized gatherings in African, Indian, and Coloured communities. Traditional authorities in segregated rural "Bantustans" also outlawed unauthorized meetings. Abahlali members, such as Zinzi, Siboniso, and Faku, recall that gatherings were held in the dead of night and in secret locations, so as not to be seen except by those in attendance. Gatherings were prime targets of surveillance and infiltration by *izimpimpi* (apartheid spies, or colluders). Anti-apartheid activities were hidden in other more visible ways, for instance, within networks perceived as apolitical by state agents, notably musical performers, soccer teams, and spiritual groups.

Abahlali's mass gatherings were initially structured in relation to liberation movements, such as the Congress Alliance.[2] Among the most frequently attended gatherings are Saturday "Branch Area Meetings" (iBranch Area Meeting in *isi*Zulu). Depending upon the size of the branch and the degree of its mobilization, these local settlement-wide meetings might draw between fifty or several thousand people. Along with active ordinary members, such as Faku, Busisiwe, and Siboniso, Branch Area meetings are coordinated and attended by elected representatives—known as "Branch Area Committees" (or "iCommittee"). Members of these committees, such as Zinzi from Mendini Hills, are expected to attend biweekly cross regional meetings of usually thirty to fifty people, simply referred to as "Movement Meetings" (or iMovement Meeting).

Intended to bring branch matters into cross regional discussion, Movement Meetings are described as thoroughly public, open to all members, ordinary residents and to those outside the activist network. Their duration ranges from four to eight hours. Members of the annually elected "Executive Committee"—the president, vice president, public relations officer, secretary, treasurer, and coordinator—also attend. Members might hold multiple positions, as Zinzi did in certain years, occupying a local position as well as a presence in the "Executive" national leadership. Last, there are "Poor People's Alliance Meetings," wherein other affiliates outside of Durban and across the country gather, such as the Anti-Eviction Campaign from Cape Town. These meetings, which last several days, are attended by a rotating group of elected Abahlali representatives, and bring "Branch" and "Movement" matters into national coordination.

In addition to gatherings that imply a structure across geographic areas, there are meetings called by particular activist structures within Abahlali. "The Executive," the highest-level positions in the activist network but not necessarily always the most powerful, and other elected bodies, such as the Women's League and the Youth League have their own meetings. There also are "Task Team" meetings by members elected to work on a particular short-term project with a narrowly defined mandate, such as formulating a response to a piece of climate change legislation, or making administrative arrangements for a street protest.

Although some meetings may be geographically or structurally defined, there also are Abahlali meetings that respond, in real-time, to unfolding crises or events. An "Emergency Meeting," which may be called by anyone and could include anywhere between five and several thousand people, can happen at any time of day or night. In these meetings, accounts of the crisis—such as a police raid, a forced eviction, or a sudden death—are shared with the assembled group, and usually a plan of action is formulated. In addition to those that are oriented toward crises, there are meetings that are oriented toward producing large-scale events. A mass event might be hosted, for instance, to respond to a shack fire that happened the previous night, or a Shack Fire Summit might be organized months in advance. Funerals might be considered gatherings as well, depending upon the circumstances of the person's death, whether he or she was an active member or died for reasons interpreted as political by members at the branch or movement levels.

Along with these event-oriented meetings, there are gatherings whose explicit purpose is social reproduction, or what is sometimes called "movement building." Under the banner of "University of Abahlali baseMjondolo," members might discuss a topical issue or movement concept, such as air pollution or living politics. "Branch launch" meetings take place when Abahlali members meet with a group in preparation for the election of a new local committee structure. As this suggests, there are many elections held by Abahlali, some which are more formalized than others. The most formal of all is the "Annual General Meeting" that elects "the Executive Committee," wherein hundreds of people—who are themselves elected as representatives of Branch Areas—vote in a secret ballot.

All of these gatherings, with few exceptions, take place within shack settlements and townships. Meetings outside of poor communities are less frequent and usually aimed at negotiating or building support with state agents or professional affiliates. Members might have meetings with police, local and city officials, and political party representatives. There are gatherings with civil society affiliates, such as church leaders, nongovernmental organizations, or funding agencies. There also are "technical" meetings with lawyers, housing experts, architects, and journalists. Last, an Abahlali member might be elected to meet international affiliates outside the country to places such as Turkey, India, Brazil, Haiti, and the United States, to name a few.

With the exception of funerals or meetings with officials and professionals, which have their own rituals and codified forms, Abahlali meetings have a few common and expected features. Generally, people sit with their branch-area comrades, by generational affiliation, with kith or kin. If there are few attendees, everyone might sit in a circle, but if there are many, the assembly will face leaders, who sit at a front table. Any meeting table is adorned with a South African national flag and Abahlali paraphernalia, such as banners, photographs, and awards. The opening of meetings is signaled with the singing of the national anthem, "Nkosi Sikelel' iAfrika" (God Bless Africa), with fists raised or placed on the chest. The lyrics of the national anthem combine Christian religious and African spiritual traditions. The original version of the anthem, sung under apartheid and at some present-day ANC events, asks the Holy Spirit or the ancestral winds (both *umoya* in *isi*Zulu) to come to the congregation and unify a liberated African continent. The last few stanzas emphasize *umoya*:

Nkosi Sikelel' iAfrika	God Bless us Africa
Maluphakanyisw'uphondo Iwayo	May her glory be lifted high
Yizwa Imithandazo Yethu	Hear our petitions
Nkosi Sikelela, thina lusapo iwayo	God Bless us, Us Your children
Woza Moya	Come Spirit
Woza Moya Woza	Come Spirit Come
Woza Moya	Come Spirit
Woza Moya Woza	Come Spirit Come
Woza Moya Oyingewele	Come Spirit Holy
Nkosi Sikelela	God bless us

A prayer typically follows the anthem. At the time of my research, an elderly woman from a long-standing branch area delivered the prayer. She is an African Zionist said to have spiritual powers. At times, she is overcome with emotion, weeps, grasps for breath, or falls to the ground. Her occasional speaking in tongues, I was told, meant that spirits had overtaken her. Reformulated liberation struggle songs are peppered throughout meetings to enliven people, whether between agenda items when the crowd becomes quiet, or when something is said that the assembly finds particularly moving.

Following song and prayer, a member of the "Executive Committee" will call for the agenda to be set. Ostensibly, anyone can add anything to the agenda, but new members rarely do. An agenda tends to have three primary components: (1) reports on upcoming events such as a street march, media briefing, or court case; (2) reports on movement-wide matters, such as a new housing policy or a branch launch; and (3) "Area Reports," the longest in duration, that concern any goings-on in communities represented in the meeting. As they begin, gatherings often end with singing, and a great deal of informal talk afterward—an hour of postmeeting lingering is not atypical, unless on the rare occasion that food is served, in which case several hours would be expected.

There are many reasons that this ideal-typical meeting composition may not happen in practice: agenda items might be interrupted, meetings could be postponed, or disagreements might emerge among members. Notably also, meetings have been the target of violence or disruption by groups who perceive the activist network as a threat, particularly during Branch Launch meetings when new members and leaders are initiated.

A significant practice structuring collective solidarity at these gatherings is known as coughing out (*ukubhodla* in *isi*Zulu). The practice of *ukubhodla*, like coughing itself, principally is to relieve discomfort by dislodging and expelling polluting particulates. Traversing the body's interior and exterior, it involves inhaling air and then exhaling it with a force that can be felt and heard by others. The Zulu term *ukubhodla* implies making a noise, and can also mean to roar or to bellow.

Busisiwe and other Abahlali members told me it means, quite literally, "coming out of silence," which implies a change from one state to another accomplished by sound. This turn of phrase—"coming out of silence"—puts into perspective apartheid-era bannings and a suppression of mass gatherings, when politicized singing, praying, or speaking could get you arrested, or even killed. It resonates with the Truth and Reconciliation Commission's (TRC) political theological mandate to unearth past violence through public confessional narration (Ross 2003). But this phrase, at the same time, invokes emerging post-apartheid corporeal and environmental conditions. "Breaking the silence" is a slogan used to promote testing for HIV and tuberculosis. It is a slogan used in South Durban environmental activist newsletters.

Coughing out, like some other cathartic activities, is intimately associated with pain, but also sensuous relief, pleasure, or joy.[3] *Ukubhodla*, for instance, is entwined with popular musical styles associated with the liberation struggle. A style of South African township jazz, known as *mbanganga*, has Zulu migrant laborer roots. Its most famous icon is Mahlathini, "The Lion of Soweto," so-called for the gravelly, roaring cadence of his distinctive voice. He toured and appeared with international celebrities, such as singer-songwriter and civil rights activist Stevie Wonder. Kin to the "Lion of Soweto" are homegrown heroes Ladysmith Black Mambazo, who via American folk singer Paul Simon's album *Graceland* helped internationally popularize the a cappella choir music called *isicathamiya*.

These styles still may be heard wafting through the air in shack settlements. Kennedy Road has its own award-winning *isicathamiya* choir, the Dlamini King Brothers, who perform at gatherings across the city and the province.[4] Residents formed the choir in 1999, and, when Abahlali emerged, they began composing anthems for the movement. They competed with and recorded their tracks, winning several trophies, which are placed at the front

of the room at every Abahlali mass meeting. The Dlamini King Brothers'
most well-known track—circulated with a music video online (see https://
vimeo.com/7657178)—is titled "Abahlali baseMjondolo." Translated from
*isi*Zulu, its lyrics emphasize an embodied spiritual discomfort and the force
of coughing out:

> Abahlali baseMjondolo you experience pain
> You experience pain and misery and being looked down upon
> Because you live in the shacks.
> But we say, now is the time to be with us.
> And make ourselves heard about the issues that concern us
> And the future of our children.
> We say there shouldn't be anything that is done for us, without us
> To make peoples' lives better in this land
> The government should work hand and hand with the shack dwellers
> And the shack dwellers should work hand in hand with the government

The lyrics move from a second person "you"—objectified, isolated, and
outside—to a third person "we" an active, agentival, and speech-filled col-
lectivity. Unified participation is emphasized lyrically, in the layered staccato
baritone singing as well as in the polished accompanying dance. The dance
is performed with soft-stepping movements in circular—or semicircular—
mobile unison with only the designated choir leader breaking form for di-
dactic emphasis. Although the performance is about vocalizing politics to be
"heard," in this case by state agents, the dance is almost entirely silent: a signature Dlamini King Brothers move is to firmly grasp the air with two fists, a
visualization of working hand-in-hand on state infrastructural projects, such
as the installation of electricity or the provision of water.

Isicathamiya is a musical style cultivated by migrant miners, or men taking on the role of migrant miners, such that air is analyzed by way of sociality
in these coal, platinum, and gold-rich underworlds (see also Coplan 1987).
For Abahlali members in Durban, while temporary construction and security
jobs are the most common type of economic migrancy, the mines of Johannesburg loom in songs and stories of the past. The soft stepping, I was told,
was to not wake the mine bosses, or the authorities while politicized coun-
terpublics were in formation. Performatively, the style connects a laboring
underground with living in the suffocating hostels and shacks of Johannesburg, often faraway from what is considered home. The music, although a
meditation on the present, reaches spatially and temporally back to imagined
ancestral grounds, and to extended kin networks. Although the Dlamini

King Brothers are a multiethnic group—some members self-identifying as *ama*Pondo—Zulu "tradition" is often invoked as the *Ur* ethnic personification of masculinity, which is the flipside reflection of the hardened gender performance demanded by the coalface (Breckenridge 1998; Moodie 1994). *Isicathamiya* groups typically are all men, but when a woman takes on the form by singing, she is considered toughened, savvy, and androgynous.

To sing *isicathamiya* is to breathe the air of the familiar and the nostalgic in relation to the toxic dust that permeates your lungs inside the mineshafts, or the smoky coal fires outside the hostels and shacks at nightfall. The mines become an affectively felt metaphor for the daily suffocations of poverty. Rather than positioning performers as victims or supplicants, singing is an assertion of empowered masculinity.[5] These musical styles have built-in modes of respect (*hlonipa* in *isi*Zulu), particularly for the skill and status of the performer, how he breathes and measures air being one important index. Amid widespread unemployment in Abahlali areas, where paying *lobola* (a marriage rite involving payment to a would-be wife's family) increasingly seems a luxury of the few (White 2004), respectability is embodied by the performer but also transferred to listening publics. The performances posit the liberatory possibility of mobility against labor migrancy (or labor scarcity), the latter a fracturing of masculinity and constricting the possibility of family.

Making Things Public among the Living and the Dead

The musical roots of coughing out reveal how the practice among Abahlali members is tied to ancestral kin, such that the regulation of purity and danger is in embodied yet dispersed spiritual networks (Douglas 1966; Ashforth 2005). Not every resident I spoke with wholly espouses a so-called ancestor cult, and some actively reject it as a colonial construct, a capitalist mystification, or a challenge to Christian doctrine. Others speak openly about ancestors, but actively taboo public discussion in the movement of related forces such as witchcraft, positing these as reactionary superstitions that uphold social hierarchies (Evans-Pritchard [1937] 1976; Geschiere 2013). However, any Mhlali will know of their ancestors—or the fact that others have them—and nearly everyone I know has respectful, or sometimes secreted, interactions with them. Some say they have lost their ancestors because migrant labor or land dispossession meant they were severed from meaningful burial places. Others say their ancestors' spirits may be rendered mobile by carrying earth from their gravesites to other public spaces.

Among the most primary difference between you and your ancestors is that you breathe, and your ancestors do not. They are not exactly dead in the determined biomedical sense, but in a stage of the continued life process that you eventually also will enter (Comaroff 1985). As one resident told me, they are like networks produced via social media. Ancestors are virtual networks that compress time and space, but have pragmatic effects upon your life in the here and now. Your ancestors, depending on them and how well you maintain your relations with them—as when they were breathing—can contribute to your good fortune, or misfortune. They can help bring you windfalls of profit or the wild winds of love, but also illnesses and calamities. Neglecting to maintain your relations with your ancestors can leave you vulnerable to witchcraft—a charged substance in the air arising from the jealousies of your neighbors.

Coughing out also touches upon the curative knowledge practices of *izangoma* (traditional healers), who can help readjust ancestral harmony and ward off the polluting hazards of witchcraft. They can also treat ailments common to residents of poor African, Indian, and Coloured communities. Residents often complain about the damp air, which seeps up from the mud floors or through the mildewed wood plank walls, as well as the winds that cut through the cracks of informally constructed tin roofs, all which exacerbates other illnesses. So common are chest infections that mass meetings in the Kennedy Road Community Hall often were a cacophonous symphony of shifting bronchial phlegm. Residents in Abahlali-affiliated settlements tended to see doctors for such ailments, if they could afford it, but also *izangoma*.

In treatment, *izangoma* may make the sound of roaring lions or other animals (*ukubhodla kwengonyama* in *isi*Zulu), a manner of speaking in tongues that evidences and makes public audible communication with ancestors. Roaring, like coughing out, can be therapeutic, or violent and unpleasant, especially for the *sangoma*. A Kennedy resident drew my attention to a story in the local newspaper about a *sangoma*, who at 13 years old, was too young to control spiritual visitations and roared (*ukubhodla*) disruptively at school. A *sangoma* may "breathe in" the ancestors in order to access them, and then "breathe them out" into divinatory totem objects. In this case, her coughing out was too powerful so as to become a polluting sound instead of a lifeline to the past.

One *sangoma* whom Faku and I visited breathed upon and whispered to a smooth and shapely, palm-sized gourd. It was chirping at the time, as if a small bird were inside of it. Faku had lost his cell phone during an Abahlali meeting and wanted to consult the *sangoma*, who was known as one of the best—and evidently, the richest—in Durban. Lines of people waited from the early morning outside his massive township compound. The *sangoma* told us that the gourd was a direct line to the ancestors. Faku explained that his own cell phone had been lost at a mass gathering with members who were close and trusted comrades, but also from potentially polluting areas outside the city. He wanted to know who was seeking him harm by appropriating his technology, especially as he was up to date with kin and ancestral demands. In fact, he had spilled some goat's blood for me, as I was afflicted with frequent chest infections.

The *sangoma* told him that his cross regional and global networks—raising a finger to point in my direction—were inspiring local jealousies, but that it was not any serious risk to health or property. He said the phone would be returned in three days. In the meantime, Faku was to arm himself with *muthi* (traditional herbs). The *sangoma*'s dark, dank office was full of it: countless little jars filled with carefully arranged and unlabeled medicines. Again, breathing is of consequence. Those seeking healing or protection from a *sangoma* might be given *muthi* to inhale its vapors, or inhale smoke from the burning of the herbs. The powers of healing relied upon what you, and the *sangoma* breathed in and breathed out. Suffocation—for instance, from *muthi* smoke—might be a temporary state of healing, but the aim in seeing a *sangoma* is to achieve and sustain the ability to breathe.

Undergoing rites of initiation to become a *sangoma* also can be temporarily suffocating. Zinzi became a *sangoma* after joining Abahlali. She said the activist network helped her find her "voice." Zinzi grew up in the Mendini Hills settlement next to shuttered colonial textile factories and a dumping site for industrial waste. According to rumor, it was near where the iconic *isicathamiya* leader of Ladysmith Black Mambazo spent his childhood. *Izangoma* do not choose their line of work, but are called by ancestral spirits, who often appear in dreams. Before her calling, she worked at a cafeteria in the factories and—like her mother—as a domestic laborer. Zinzi's most continually defining memories are of the Black Jacks. These were apartheid police in black uniforms, who along with checking passbooks, would spill over the hill to repeatedly demolish her family's shack. State agents sought to remove her from a tract of land from which she and her mixed race—Indian and African—neighbors resolutely refused to move since the 1920s.

Zinzi's most significant dream, which confirmed her calling as a *sangoma*, happened in 1998. She said her late mother and other spirits, though she never saw them, "spoke into her ears." The sound afflicted her. At the time of the dream, she said, "I was SICK! Sick, sick, sick, sick, sick, oh God!" In the dream, her ancestors led her to a "Mandela" house, the government houses built after the fall of apartheid. Her ancestors said, "Go in there. There is a key for you. It's your house." She said, "I opened the door to that house, and went from the kitchen to the bedroom to the sitting room. All the furniture [inside] was oak. Even the toilet [was made of] oak." Some of the factories near where Zinzi grew up made expensively detailed wood furniture, found inside many white suburban homes, like those she used to clean.

In the dream, her ancestors handed her two large envelopes, the paper-work for the house, and told Zinzi to go to the bank. She marched straight to the bank, and two white ladies opened the envelopes and read the paperwork inside. Then they wrote numbers on the paperwork and said, "This money is for you, for your whole life until you die." The money would "pay for the house." The dream emphasizes the role of ancestral power in her path to be-come a *sangoma* in her polluting illness and a postliberation dream deferred. "I wish that dream [at least about the house] had come true. Oh God!" she said. Zinzi remains under threat of eviction in the settlement, where she grew up. Still, she said her calling was "proof that God was good."

Air Pollution as Pentecostal Problematique

As Zinzi's comment indicates, the practice of coughing out does not have any singular or stable spiritual referent. In fact, multiple open-ended spirit worlds might be at stake simultaneously. The Zulu word for air and wind (*umoya*) is the spiritual breath that leaves you when you die. It is also the word that missionaries used for the soul. Along with the ancestral realm, coughing out is associated with contrasting Christian theological traditions, which have their own notions of pollution (Comaroff 1985; Chari 2004; Pype 2012). Notably, among Abahlali members, these are Anglicanism and African Zionism.[6]

The Anglican Church, while seen as an institution of the liberation strug-gle, is also viewed as complicit with colonization and the post-apartheid po-litical establishment, central as it was to missionization and decolonization. Anglican constituents in Abahlali are associated with Black Consciousness churches. Its leaders are former anti-apartheid activists, who broke away from Nelson Mandela's ANC to follow such figures as Steve Biko.[7] They ar-gued their mission was to liberate not only South Africa as a nation, but also the depths of consciousness from suffocations of white rule (Fanon 1965; Biko [1969] 2002; Gibson 2011).

Across either of these religious traditions, but particularly among Afri-can Zionists like Zinzi, some members believe in the rapture (Marshall 2009; Meyer 2013). Others, in the manner of Pascal's wager, view the rapture as possible future worth considering. With echoes of environmental apocalypse predicted in the worst-case scenarios of climate change science (Hardt 2010), the rapture involves joining the dead when the world expires from an excess of pollutants. For Pentecostal churches, these may be imbalances with the spiritual ancestors, toxic industrial gases, or sexualized sin. In biblical sources most used by Abahlali members, the rapture is described as the living and the dead "caught up together . . . in the clouds, to meet the Lord in the air." The rapture, as a moment of damnation for the polluted and redemption for the pure, is a spiritual struggle over earthly contaminants.

Features of coughing out overlap with Pentecostal practices that refer to breathing or not breathing, which include Christian confessional, channeling the Holy Spirit (*umoya*), or bearing witness by speaking in tongues. These are modes of purgation, and therefore knowledge of the divine sovereign, that mediate spiritual powers in preparation for a contagious, and all-consuming future effervescence. Some residents suggested to me that dynamics of sin and confessional, in turn map onto technological concerns. Facebook, Instagram, and Twitter posts, which produce digitally networked publics, simultaneously reveal what is socially acceptable, and violations of social norms. Members of Abahlali, at times, turn to these virtual forums to praise God, admit sin, or pray for salvation in the end times.

In some shack settlements, especially areas that demobilized from Abahlali, self-identified youth churches would crop up, run by usually unemployed men and women in their twenties or thirties. In Slovo Park, for instance, young members of Abahlali, such as Faku, established their own church in a large corrugated-tin shack, constructed specifically for that purpose. They listened to and circulated American Christian pop music, and Evangelical sermons. These churches, they explained, were outside the control of the older members of the community, who wielded the most power in both the formalized Anglican and African Zionist churches. Although they did not necessarily abandon their respect for ancestors or *izangoma*, these practitioners rejected the notion of traditional authority associated with gerontocratic power in the rural areas extended to cities like Durban.

Their youthful appropriation of Pentecostal traditions was viewed as urban and Afro-cosmopolitan (Mbembe and Nuttall 2008), a distinctive outgrowth of a post-Mandela South Africa. Their technological access, and savvy— finding global sources of spirituality online, for instance—reaffirmed this urbane and mobile identity, for many rural areas were still bereft of digital connections. These influences, however, were viewed as politically polluting in some corners of Abahlali, particularly among the elder leadership.

Suffocations of the City

These youth churches suggest how many residents feel "betwixt and be-tween" urban and rural, as geographically and generationally imagined zones (Turner 1967; Beinart and Bundy 1997; Van Onselen 2001). This liminal state, reflected in the cross generational intersections of *isicathamiya* music and tra-ditional medicine, is exacerbated by what members described as not feeling fully admitted to the center of the city, living in polluted, economically and politically disenfranchised peripheries like Kennedy Road or Mendini Hills.

Although some Abahlali members such as Zinzi grew up in Durban, many were raised in rural areas, or segregated former "Bantustans." These residents, particularly, dreamed of the city as a place to "breathe freely," re-leased from the hold of elders and ethnicized expectations of identity forma-tion. When Faku first came to the city of Durban, he thought that people who lived in the shacks must be deeply destitute, or certifiably insane. He never imagined living in a shack himself. Residents found that traversing boundaries between urban and rural, instead of liberating brought on their own polluting suffocations: congested traffic on industrial highways, noxious gases spewing out of Bissar Road's incinerator, or hearing every word said on television in the closely built shacks next door.

Emblematic of the spatialized tension between breathing and suffocation is a failed mass gathering in Red City, in a rural area north of Durban. In this instance, the expected effervescent ritual elements of the mass gatherings dis-sipated. I spoke with residents via cell phone as it unfolded. A delegation of ten Abahlali leaders, including Busisiwe, Siboniso, and his four-year-old son, traveled to Red City for a Branch Launch in August 2009.

Soon after the first songs of the launch were sung, a speeding car, without warning, drove through the congregation. People leaped from its path, scat-tering and screaming. The driver, jumping from the car, shouted in *isi*Zulu, "Who organized this meeting? These are my people! This is my territory!" before manhandling a Red City resident. Two more cars full of armed men suddenly appeared. The men were thought to be associated with the local council and a taxi boss. Their cars blocked the single exit point out of the settlement, preventing the Durban delegation from leaving. They effectively were being held hostage.

The men then loudly debated whether to kill the delegation or beat them bloody. The men assaulted one Abahlali member, a local DJ from a commu-nity radio station, who was present to act as the MC for the gathering. After Busisiwe in secret managed to call the police, the armed men ordered the

Durban delegation to go, warning, "Never return, or you will be killed." The delegation left Red City, while two unmarked cars followed closely behind. The delegation directly went to the police station to lay a complaint. Two members of the Red City Abahlali branch, identified by armed men as the co-ordinators of the gathering, were forced to flee to a place of hiding elsewhere in the province. While the Durban delegation waited in a local restaurant to take the two coordinators to safety, the local councillor slowly pulled into the parking lot. He was waiting, and watching. He and the armed men were not the kind of spectators that this gathering was meant to produce.

Here, rather than collective solidarity being achieved through coughing out in ritual completion, it is built through the sharing of violence among those in attendance. The failed launch became shared further online, and by those who coughed out at the next Abahlali meeting in Durban. Members collectively composed an online press statement, which emphasizes how even failed gatherings facilitate "coming out of silence." Gatherings, the statement suggests, are a process of transforming the particulates in the air, historically and in relation to post-apartheid conditions:

> [We] have not seen a situation like this since the [19]80s, not in the 15 years since democracy.
>
> Apartheid was a time when people lived in fear of the authorities. . . .
>
> Apartheid was a time when people were assassinated. Today . . . [t]hey must not face politically motivated murder, threats of murder, or violence.
>
> The people of [Red City] are living in fear, and are in fear to talk. The [gathering] was an attempt to come out of the silence they have lived for a very long time. People need to come out of this silence. In a democratic society, it is unacceptable that people cannot have political gatherings, talk and associate with each other. . . .
>
> We . . . ask government officials . . . to honour the proposed invitation for a consultative meeting with Abahlali, so that we can expose all evil activities that hinder development in our communities. The situation in [Red City] looks calm, but is very volatile.
>
> Abahlali stand firm that this is a democratic country . . . and that everyone has a right to associate and hold meetings.
>
> All people, whether they live in a shack or a house, have a right to freely speak and express themselves.[8]

This process of coming out of silence, equated with the post-apartheid period, is a practice that calls for and enables public collective speech. Coughing out, then, rather than being simply liberatory also carries the burden of past and the risk of present-day violence.

Air Pollution as Corporeal Violence

Although, thus far, I have focused upon highly visible instantiations of the practice of coughing out by focusing on the production of publics at mass gatherings, there are sacral figures and spaces that are politically consecrated but *not* publicized. These figures and spaces are as revealing as what becomes the subject of Abahlali meetings or online press statements. Among the many instances of arrest and torture that I documented during my research with Abahlali and other poor people's movements before and after the 1980s, the story of Sisipho stands out.[9] An arrest often is a rite of passage into leadership, but many just want to put their lives back together again. Those who refuse an elected mantle are treated with reverence and respect within Abahlali, whether or not they remain active. These narratives highlight how unreported cases of police violence contribute to Abahlali's idiom of "coughing out."

The first time I talked at length with Sisipho was in a tranquil, grassy park in the middle of the city. Her boyfriend, Bulelani, had been arrested on trumped up criminal charges. He was acquitted but languished in prison for eleven months. Sisipho and Bulelani first met in 1998, while living in adjacent, rural hometowns. He said his town "ended at the river, where her town began," which he meant both in the literal, geographic sense and in an unconcealed expression of his love for her. After meeting by chance through Sisipho's sister and dating for four years, they decided to move to the city of Durban together, where the odds of getting a job, however limited, were better than in the rural areas. He went first, and landed a series of "temporary jobs" in construction. He stayed in a shack settlement where the couple both had kith and kin. She eventually followed, but they were not yet married, so they dutifully kept separate residences next door to each other. Like many unemployed women, Sisipho opened up a *spaza* shop in the settlement to make ends meet. Her shack had two rooms then, one for dwelling, and one for selling goods like matches, sweets, crisps (potato chips), and her specialty, *koeksisters* (a South African donut). By virtue of their work and networks, they were known as up-and-comers in the settlement, those who very well could "make it," if not as middle class, at least with a security that shack life did not typically afford.

As Sisipho and I sat talking in the park, she suddenly began trembling, grasping for air, and burst into tears. Not only was her boyfriend awaiting trial, her shop had been looted and destroyed as part of an apparent ethnically based xenophobic attack, which targeted Abahlali members and those from outside the province. While local and international media coverage of xenophobic pogroms in 2008 focused upon violence targeting foreigners, in areas such as Kennedy Road, these tensions manifest in heightened violence between ethnic groups (Chance 2010). However, it was not only the destruction of her shop that made Sisipho tremble. A year later, I found out that she also had been tortured. It all began at the prison, while visiting Bulelani. Police phoned her to say that they wanted to talk with her and were waiting outside the gate. Seeing no alternative, she met them outside. They put her in a car and took her to the police station near her home. She spoke to a provincial crime intelligence officer, known to the community, who told me he had cut his teeth as a policeman during the bloodiest years of the liberation struggle. They brought her into a room otherwise empty aside from a bench "tightly up against the wall." According to her, the crime intelligence officer told the other two police officers to "bring the plastic things," for which she did not know the name. They are best described, she said, as a 50 kg sack, not "the plastic [bags] used for shopping, but a strong one that when you bring it up [over your face and mouth], you breathe in a small space."

The crime intelligence officer left, and two remaining police officers handcuffed her with her hands behind her back. She said, "Then, they put the plastic." They began repeatedly suffocating her with "the plastic," covering her head. She said she kept moving so one police officer held her down, while the other punched her and continued "putting the plastic." They demanded that she bring them evidence against her boyfriend, specifically clothes with bloodstains or a gun. Although many of the local police officers are recognizable to the community, she had never seen them before and suspected that they were not from the area. She said she thought, "I was going to die on that day because when I breathed, it kept on cutting and cutting and cutting and cutting."

After they finished with her, they put her alone in a cell with blankets. She said she was kept at the police station a total of seven hours. She remained in the cell until the police returned. Without saying anything, they opened the door, and she walked out into the fresh air. She kept walking all the way to the settlement, where she lived, only to find the supplies in her shop had been looted along with some furniture in her home, and both had been chopped up with axes and bush knives. Fearful of what would happen to her if she stayed, she moved with her family to another settlement out of the area. By virtue of the police beating, her ears were blocked and bloody. She could not immediately see a doctor, but later went to a local clinic and a public hospital. The doctor told her that her ear should be back to normal, but she said more than a year later, she still felt the injury, for "if someone was speaking in a soft voice, I couldn't hear that person."

Bulelani found out what happened to Sisipho when friends next visited him in prison. He said that hearing the news was "a blow to the heart." "First, you are arrested for a case you don't know [anything about], then you hear someone who is close to your heart has faced such a problem. Then, it was like the sun set during the day." He said he did not expect to see her again because, after he had been beaten in custody, he feared the police were capable of worse. Bulelani had never seen the inside of a prison before he was arrested. He said during the first three weeks, he could not eat, not because of a boycott, but a complete loss of appetite. Even when visitors like Sisipho would bring him food, Bulelani said he could hardly eat it. He said the jail was suffocating. "Being in jail," he said, in multiple ways, "was like being a tied up pig. You cannot go here, you cannot go there, and your body will automatically be un-hygienic." He said that the water inside the prison will not help you without soap, and if you do not have soap, you will get lice and fleas. "When the policeman opens the door for you, even if you are running quick and doing what you are told, he will kick you." He said you have "no other option but to eat that thing," by which he meant absorb that suffocating humiliation.

Sisipho and Bulelani saw each other immediately when he was released from prison. They were "very, very, very excited" to see each other. However, now five years later, they still struggle to find a footing to reestablish their lives. Both of their homes were destroyed, Bulelani lost his job while awaiting trial, Sisipho lost her shop. They had to stay with family and still owe money that they borrowed from neighbors. They still hope to be able to marry one day, though. For Abahlali members, that which can be readily felt—seen, heard, smelled, tasted, touched—is not necessarily the same between spaces in the city, such as the prison, the shack settlement, or the middle-class suburb. It is here, in places like Kennedy Road, that potential participants of political activities are created, through gatherings, but also through the quiet stories that residents tell each other.

Conclusion: Ecologies of Postcolonial Pollution— All That's Solid Does Not Melt into Air

In long segregated cities like Durban, the air that you breathe depends upon your own and your ancestor's historical location. Through practices of living politics, residents use the air as an instrument to counterbalance hazardous accumulations of corporeal and environmental pollution. Rather than privileging expert epistemologies, nonhuman agency, or far-flung networks of elites (Latour 2013), postcolonial approaches resonate with, and yet productively complicate, understandings of climate change science.[10] The management of pollution among residents in shack settlements may offer unconsidered innovations. These bridge climate science and precolonial practices, both which respond to emergent knowledge about the material world (see also Mavhunga 2013). These innovations include novel modes of calculating atmospheric risk, notably by deploying digital community-based mobilizations in monitoring and accumulating knowledge about climate change. Ancestral rites—policed by the earliest colonial authorities—posited air as a potential health risk long before biomedical inquests into climate pollution gathered storm. Likewise, juxtaposing Pentecostal end times with environmental apocalypse suggests how climate activists trade on common and familiar spiritual tropes to establish the urgency of environmental crisis. Abahlali's approach to pollution calls for a role reversal between so-called global experts and local innovators in the production of knowledge about ecological purity and danger.

International scientists and climate experts have become increasingly interested in Durban's air since the collapse of apartheid. Protection from air pollutants is reflected in post-apartheid policy and legislation, which guarantees the right to "a clean environment." The city of Durban played host to the United Nations global climate change meetings called COP 17 (the 17th Conference of the Parties). It is where state signatories of the 1992 Kyoto Protocol meet to discuss the world's air. The Kyoto Protocol, a treaty that commits states to reducing the emission of greenhouse gases, acknowledges

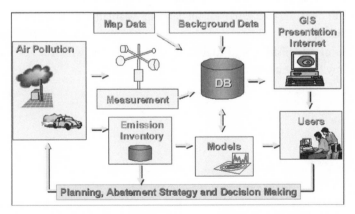

Flow chart from Durban's 2015 air quality plan. "Users," or interpreters of climate data, are featured as white global experts. (eThekwini Municipality 2007)

global warming as induced by human activities. Yet it does not specify how or what activities might be racially distributed.

Among South African scientists and activists, there is consensus that industries—even those long gone, such as the colonial textile factories in Durban—have come to shape our bodies, as they have the composition of the air. Abahlali members living in the effluent waste of factories and landfills like Bissar Road have observed that airborne particulates can affect life processes in the short and long term. Chronic respiratory illnesses, widespread in shack settlements, can make you lose sleep, workdays, or even intimacy. The links between coughing—by way of tuberculosis—and HIV can carry the stigma of infection. Activists in the South Durban Community Environmental Alliance (SDCEA) recognized that air contaminated by oil refineries was causing asthma and even cancerous growths. Some residents, combining practices of the liberation struggle with climate science mobilized court cases against the refineries by gathering daily samples of air pollutants.

In spite of this consensus, ten thousand activists—including Siboniso, Faku, Zinzi, and Busisiwe—joined spirited street protests against COP 17. As Abahlali discussed in their own climate gatherings, they protested because members perceived that the UN meetings were not enough concerned about how pollution is lived and breathed in poor communities, or about knowledge that residents had accumulated about their own environmental vulnerability. The public spectacle of COP 17 revealed that the role of air in South African governance and political mobilization has galvanized around pollution, but through human activities that cannot be explained by the expert tools of climate science alone. Breathing, as the most taken-for-granted of all human activities, remains a highly differentiated practice.

As the next chapter explores, the land in Abahlali-affiliated shack settlements has spiritual value as well, but it is moreover viewed by residents as a means of establishing and maintaining community, which offers earthly autonomy from state agents.

Land / Umhlaba

Dispatch

City-wide Summit on Land, Housing and Dignity
Submitted by Abahlali on Fri, 2014-05-23 03:08
MAY 23, 2014

We are clear that there will be no landlord or messiah that will deliver land or have all answers pertaining to land but ourselves. We are clear that it is sinister to be landless and homeless in a country that has produced multi-millionaires in this sector. We are clear that it is unreasonable to buy land that already belongs to you. We are clear that state land is our own land. We have been very clear that the social value of land must come before its commercial value. We are clear that land occupations are a form of land reform carried out from below. We are clear that without land and without decent housing our dignity is compromised. We are clear that without dignity our citizenry and humanity is at risk. We are clear that if we continue to pretend as if politicians will one day come up with a one size fits all solution we will be self-deceiving. And yes, we are clear that one day our children and our next generation will put blame on us if this question of land is not resolved now.

Ashes to Ashes, Dust to Dust: How Territorial Informality Builds Future Cities

In the mid-1940s, James Mpanza, leader of the South African shack dwellers' movement Sofasonke (we die together in *isi*Zulu), captured how his constituents accrete and erode power over land. Abahlali traces its roots through Mpanza. "The Government," he said, "was like a man who has a cornfield which is invaded by birds. He chases the birds from one part of the field and they alight in another part of the field . . . we squatters are the birds" (Stadler 1973, 93). Occupying land (*umhlaba* in *isi*Zulu) in urban shack settlements is to establish power over territory. If backed by force or the possible use of force—which, for residents, often means occupying in numbers— this power may hold into an unforeseen future. Forced eviction, conversely, is to reset interactions of power in shack settlements, and, if successful, to establish a new governing order. In the forty-year-old settlement of Kennedy Road, systems of informal tenure mean that Siboniso and other residents "own" or "rent" their homes and the land beneath them. However, as a matter of law, the land belongs to the government. It can be seized, if state agents dare—and more than once, they have tried in Kennedy Road. Territorial sovereignty, as residents understand it, may be temporary and informal like ever-shifting grains of sand. But that does not make claims to it any less powerful. Land is central to living politics because residents use it to enact sovereignty and sustain their homes.

The previous chapter focused upon coughing out that produces, sometimes fleeting and sometimes lasting, political collectivities through differentiated practices of breathing. If air (*umoya*) is the most basic element that brings the urban poor together, perhaps the most complex and fractious is land and territorial sovereignty. At least, it is in South Africa. Land is complex because it remains so unevenly distributed along explicitly racial lines.

A land occupation marked with an Abahlali baseMjondolo banner demanding land (*umhlaba*) and housing (*izindlu*). Abahlali's logo has been turned into soccer balls in protest of evictions happening during the 2010 Soccer World Cup. (Photo by author)

Following the 1913 Land Act, only about 13 percent of the soil was in African hands. Whites still own a disproportionate amount of the best agricultural land. It is also complex because land comprises so many other elements: precious liquids, volatile gases, as well as a multitude of earthly organisms and mineral compounds, which give life to and decompose organic matter. Each stone of rural soil, grain of shoreline sand, or chip of urban pavement in a shack settlement, then, contains an archeology of spirits past, their dwelling places, and their everyday practices—as well as their forced displacement. The land, for residents I spoke with, is not an ontological essence to which they are bound, but a historical sedimentation with concrete effects upon the future. In this chapter, I show how residents use the land in all its complexity to construct, gain access to, and transform post-apartheid housing. To do so, I return to Abahlali's affiliates in Cape Town, for their struggles in the streets and the courts would inform community mobilizations in Durban and Johannesburg.

The Space-Time of Land Occupation

I met Monique two weeks after the eviction. At dawn, a team of heavily armed police and private security moved into Delft, a sandy sun-blighted township on the outskirts of the South African city of Cape Town. Delft is the site of a national flagship project in urban land and housing, called the N2 Gateway. With armored vehicles and sniffer dogs in tow, the eviction team removed about sixteen hundred residents from unfinished houses they had occupied two months earlier at the alleged authorization of their local councillor. Many families had moved from wood and corrugated tin shacks located in the backyards of nearby homeowners, in historically Coloured and African townships. The concrete block structures the residents occupied were known as BNG houses after a popular 2004 national policy called Breaking New Ground. The policy aimed at making the delivery of state infrastructure more efficient by expanding the role of the private sector in housing programs.

The eviction, broadcast on national nightly news, was violent. Siboniso and Busisiwe saw it on television from their shacks in Kennedy Road. Without warning, police fired rubber bullets at crowds gathered in the streets, shooting residents and trampling them as they ran for cover. At least twenty injured people were rushed to the hospital. With nowhere else to go, Monique and about a thousand others remained on the pavement. The municipal government, together with the Democratic Alliance (DA), the largest opposition party to the ruling ANC, responded by providing about five hundred of the evicted families with large communal tents; some of a dark-green military make, others brightly striped or white with frilly awnings. Latecomers were given "black sails," or plastic sheeting, which they used to build tiny, makeshift shacks behind the tents, unseen from the surrounding highways. The camp, referred to by residents as "Section 1," was eventually encircled with barbed wire and supplied with water taps and portable toilets.

Monique and approximately five hundred other residents, however, refused to work with the DA or sign the forms required to acquire space in Section 1. Under the banner of the Anti-Eviction Campaign (AEC), then a leading poor people's movement, they instead constructed shacks out of a motley assortment of collected materials at the scene of their eviction. They founded the settlement of Symphony Way, named after the highway that ran through the center of it and was henceforth blockaded in a protest and land occupation that would last for more than two years. In time, their collective grievances would center upon not only their eviction but also "transit camps," which occupants referred to as *amathini* (tin cans in *isi*Zulu), *blikkies* (little tins in Afrikaans), or government shacks.[1]

Transit camps are government emergency shelters located in controlled sites. The camps house those displaced by routine environmental disasters in shack settlements, such as floods or fires. However, the majority of camp occupants are those displaced by processes of urban development, such as the construction of roadways, bridges, and housing projects like the N2 Gateway. Transit camps typically take the form of tent villages like Section 1, or settlements built from corrugated tin and other "temporary" materials. Tens of thousands reside in transit camps, and many more shack dwellers are slated for relocation. Their occupants have no security of tenure on the land or inside the tin structures. Transit camps are rapidly reshaping the urban periphery of Cape Town and other cities across the country.[2] The largest camp in South Africa is located in Delft.[3]

State proponents of transit camps posit them as a temporary stopgap toward the delivery of permanent and secure "formalized" housing. The camps, some told me, are an investment in an urban future that is spatially desegregated and democratically governed. For residents refusing relocation, like those on Symphony Way, living conditions in the camps are inadequate, even if temporary and even by the standards of "informal" dwelling. They posit the camps as reproducing segregation, where space-time is defined by waiting for future inclusion in the city. Living in camps is qualitatively different from living in shacks, for state agents do not recognize residents' territorial claims in these liminal zones.

I focus on instances where power over land is fragmented with no sovereign at its center and, like much of urban life for shack dwellers, is already foreclosed as informal and temporary. Delft, to wit, briefly had a prince. Known as Prince Xhanti, he was the first project manager of the N2 Gateway. A successful businessman from an esteemed Eastern Cape royal family, he ran the private company called Thubelisha, which was outsourced to manage the site in Delft. However, this prince's power was sustained through a complex web of public–private partnerships. This fragmented and liminal terrain of sovereignty, structured by a colonial past and emergent present, gave way to the resurgence of forced evictions from prime urban land to peripheral transit camps. These evictions intensified as South Africa prepared to host the 2010 Soccer World Cup. The management of so-called slum populations, which aimed at curbing urban informality by filling a gap in housing stock, wound up spatially reproducing historical race-based inequalities and peri-urban precarity.

At the same time, forced evictions have given rise to cross regional networks among the urban poor, such as Abahlali and the AEC, as well as affiliated teams of lawyers. Residents, by cultivating the land inside these networks, endeavor to convert their dwelling places into tangible urban futures for themselves and their children. I focus on the informal spatial practices, which include building shacks and occupying land, as well as mobilizing street-based activities, such as gatherings at the courts. I draw from participant observation in transit camps across all three major South African cities. Notably, along with Symphony Way in Cape Town, these include Richmond Farm in Durban and Protea South in Johannesburg. Activist networks across these three transit

Symphony Way shacks. The sign in Afrikaans reads, "We are ass full [*gat vol*] of empty promises." (Photo by author)

camps launched landmark legal battles over post-apartheid land and hous-ing policy in the South African courts. This newly afforded legal status—not only as citizens, but as respondents in a court case—did not gain residents permanent or formalized housing, but turned around the space-time of wait-ing onto state agents by delaying forced eviction to the camps.

Ordering Informal Territorial Sovereignty

Transit camps, as sites that order or eliminate informal dwelling, might be seen as securing ever-more efficient control over "slum" populations.[4] In theory, the camps localize poor families (one to a home) and their location within the city (on the periphery). The spatial layout is aimed at control-ling bodies, making individuals and their behaviors more visible and policing more effective. In addition to disciplinary measures aimed at bodies, there are regulatory mechanisms that apply to the population. These encourage opting into state housing databases, rules on hygiene that seek to optimize public health in the city, and bans on building that constrict the growth of poor families and therefore control sexuality (Foucault 2003, 251). Though centered on managing the health and welfare of the population, transit camps were designed above all to remove the poor from crowded shack settlements, long regarded as disorderly and criminal.

In practice, my time spent in Delft suggests that the camps instead have developed conditions for protracted insecurity, which affects socioeconomic stability and the likelihood of unrest among the urban poor (see also Huchzermeyer 2011). What is not accounted for in this control model is how land and housing are transformed by the informal spatial practices of the poor, whether by their refusal to be removed, seizing access to homes by illicit occupation, or by using carceral spaces like the camps as platforms for collective mobilization. As spatial practices, they have an ambiguous, or even outright criminalized, relationship to the laws and institutions that govern urban areas, but nonetheless are so commonly enacted as to have taken on the status of an infrastructural norm.

Recent studies of infrastructure, some following the work of urban philosopher Henri Lefebvre, have breathed new life into how theories of space and informality might be rethought and recombined in post–Cold War, postcolonial African cities. Indeed, activists too, including Abahlali and the AEC, have made use of Lefebvre's famous phrase, "a right to the city," in their placards and press releases, emphasizing that space is not a preexisting or empty container, but rather is lived, made, and remade.[5] Where governments and corporations have failed to provide available and affordable land and housing, the urban poor have constructed their own dwellings, complex rental schemes, property agreements, and communal lives. Those without formalized housing, inasmuch as they might desire and await government delivery, do not do so passively, but rather their activities constitute an autonomous capacity for generating not only economic growth, as scholars of the informal economy have argued (Hart 1973), but also specific infrastructures for their lives in the city (see Simone 2004b; Chalfin 2013; Chu 2014). Transit camps, which look and feel very much like shacks—or worse, tents, as at Section 1—suggest how informal dwellings can become taken up into the technocratic work of states and nongovernmental organizations.

Although it is important to recognize spatial practices of the poor as generative, scholarship of the past four decades, often critical of how the sector has been operationalized from above (see Elyachar 2003), has offered many valuable arguments against bracketing off informality. Three objections are particularly common, and salient in the South African case. First, categorical or ontological distinctions between the formal and informal reinscribe old colonial antinomies of the modern and the traditional, the civilized and the unruly, the cartographic and the terra incognita, which have the potential to romanticize or pathologize the urban poor and African cities. The second is that as a hard-and-fast dichotomy, it does not hold, for features of the informal sector can be found in the formal sector and vice versa, especially at a time of urbanization and unemployment in a globalized economy. The third is that there is such a multiplicity of formal and informal sectors, which remain so varied or contradictory, interconnected and coconstitutive, that the categories are too underspecified to be useful. However, rather than approaching informality etically or as an analytic, I propose to examine how both activists like Monique and state agents—particularly, vis-à-vis the social life of policy such as Breaking New Ground (BNG)—mobilize local understandings of the informal, and do so tactically, to achieve certain political ends. Informality, then, as a key discursive category and set spatial practices, becomes a staging ground for contested claims to land and housing, which map onto and contribute to the production of urban space.

"Breaking New Ground" with Old Tools: Land and Housing Policy Reform

Examining land and housing reform, with particular attention to the policy known as "Breaking New Ground," provides an instance of how informal territorial sovereignty and governing institutions interact. Since 1994, the African National Congress has aimed at dismantling the architecture of apartheid by extending citizenship rights enshrined in new legislation and national policy. The extension of these rights has included the provision of formalized housing on a mass scale and the eradication of so-called slums (Makhulu 2010). Nearly 2.4 million homes have been built, but the post-apartheid state has struggled to keep pace with overwhelming demand: in Cape Town alone, the number of families on official housing waitlists is estimated to rise by twenty thousand annually from the starting point of a half million. In no small measure, these numbers result from wageless urban migration at the fall of apartheid (Pieterse 2008), which the Breaking New Ground policy document flags as a significant challenge to national land and housing programs, and inherited from the previously race-based state. With the lifting of pass laws and other repressive legislation that restricted the mobility of African, Indian, and Coloured communities, hundreds of thousands of people moved to urban and periurban areas in search of work, education, and other previously unavailable social and economic opportunities, many joining the millions already living in shacks.

South Africa's new Constitutional Court, since its first session in 1995, has played a key role in adjudicating these new citizen claims to land and housing. The Constitutional Court is South Africa's highest judicial institution.

Any activist network recognized on the national political landscape has appeared before the Constitutional Court. Section 26 of the South African Constitution obliges the post-apartheid state to provide housing, while also safeguarding against arbitrary evictions. The section states: "Everyone has the right to have access to adequate housing. The state must take reasonable legislative and other measures, within its available resources, to achieve the progressive realization of this right. No one may be evicted from their home, or have their home demolished, without an order of court." Section 26 has been a matter of contention in court cases brought by activists. In 2000, the Constitutional Court—in a landmark case named after Irene Grootboom, a shack dweller in Cape Town—found that the national housing policy fell short of constitutional obligations. The rewritten policy (the previously mentioned Breaking New Ground policy) coincided with the construction of the N2 Gateway Project and names it as a "lead pilot project."[6] The document emphasizes that the aim is to "overcome spatial, social and economic exclusion" while advancing the "eradication" of slums through relocations to "a range of . . . housing typologies," notably including transit camps.[7] Grootboom ostensibly won her court case and contributed to a new housing vision, celebrated by activists. She died in 2008, however, while still living in a shack in Cape Town, a story often retold in South Africa's shacklands. These retellings usually are framed as a warning about the limitations of legal redress as it touches the ground of lived experience in shack settlements.

Among the limitations of post-apartheid legal interpretations of policies such as Breaking New Ground is that housing typically indexes urban space, whereas land indexes rural space. Under colonial orders in South Africa, land and housing were treated as demarcated zones of social, biological, and especially agricultural reproduction. Whereas houses were given away for free, land was classified as a currency of transaction. Broad-based post-apartheid land reform, envisioned largely as pertaining to rural farms, retained the principle of "willing buyer, willing seller," which means that those involved in the transaction enter into a voluntary contract.[8] This model of land reform, the World Bank argued at the time, was necessary to avert political and economic volatility and to stimulate growth in South Africa. Within this model, the aims were threefold. The first is land restitution, to reunite those dispossessed of land under colonial orders, particularly those forcibly removed. The second is land tenure reform, to secure rights to the land for those who previously by virtue of segregationist legislation had no such rights. The third reform, which was suspended in 1999, aimed to change race-based landownership patterns. Although some of the reforms led to credible land reclamation (Mavhunga 2014), activists have decried "willing buyer, willing seller" as market-led and antipoor. As a matter of practice, residents have been redistributing land by other means, especially informally occupying and creating homes upon it.

Although South Africa's post-apartheid reforms tend to segregate rural land (*umhlaba*) from urban housing (*izindlu*), residents such as Monique and her neighbors characterize them as coterminous. "A place to call home" (*ikhaya* in *isi*Zulu and *isi*Xhosa), a slogan used by the AEC and Abahlali, implies both land and housing. In South African languages, *umhlaba* means soil, but also more broadly earth or world. It is the current world as opposed to the ancestral afterlife. It is, therefore, at once, a semiotic and biophysical ground upon which practices and interactions in this life unfold. *Izindlu*, plural of *indlu*, in *isi*Zulu and *isi*Xhosa refers to the structures in which you dwell. *iKhaya* may or may not be home, the place of affective belonging to kith and kin, denoting neither the structure nor the land per se, but the complex interactions between the two. *iKhaya* may or may not be a place of private ownership. It is one of tenure, an ability to remain or return, wherein property is defined in terms of rights and obligations, but not necessarily individuated. Residents may experience a security of land tenure without ownership— for instance, under traditional authority—in contractual form of enclosure under systems of private property. However, even traditional authority has been long codified in colonial, as well as postcolonial, law and policy. It is the criminalized specter of urban informality captured by *umhlaba* and *izindlu* that the Breaking New Ground policy sought to eliminate. Informal territorial sovereignty, in other words, may have force, but only through circuitous channels of recognition.

The Emergence of Post-apartheid "Slums"

During the buildup to the 2010 Soccer World Cup in South Africa, informal territorial claims to *umhlaba* and *izindlu*, that is to say not regulated by state or corporate agents, came into profound tension with national efforts to build "world-class cities." As scholars elsewhere have noted (Ghertner 2011), the "world-class city" is a future-looking utopian project, whose aims and aesthetics may vary from place to place but is generally characterized by sleek modern design, high levels of state efficiency and corporate profitability, and if not the elimination of poverty, at least its orderly management. In 2008, when Monique and her neighbors occupied houses in Delft, the city of Cape Town was preparing to host the 2010 Soccer World Cup. Thousands of visitors were expected to drive along the N2 highway corridor that connected the airport to swanky downtown hotels, tourist attractions, and a stadium built for the games. On either side of this corridor are the city's most historic townships and sprawling shack settlements. These areas occupy various national and local registers in contemporary South Africa, including as heroic battlegrounds of the liberation struggle. However, in 2008, the term "slum" reemerged—in new legislation, parliamentary debates, tabloids, and television news—to describe the city's poorest quarters, earmarked for clearance or development. Shack settlements were matter-out-of-place.

Since James Mpanza's day in the 1930s, the term "slum" in South Africa has been associated with efforts to legislate racial rezoning, often under the aegis of effective policing. The 1934 Slums Act was a colonial precursor to apartheid-era law. By proclaiming black communities "slums," land was appropriated by apartheid agents, particularly on the desirable urban city center and immediate periphery. Under apartheid, with the election of the National Party (NP) in 1948, the government soon passed, and later rigorously enforced, legislation that struck out against life in shack settlements. This legislation included the notorious 1950 Group Areas Act, which led to the racial rezoning of Cape Town, and the 1951 Prevention of Illegal Squatting Act, which authorized forced evictions. Empowered by this legislation and in efforts to ruralize black workers when not on the job, municipalities enacted "slum clearance" initiatives, which residents—and especially women—fought, often militantly.

Monique, like her neighbors in Symphony Way, is a longtime resident of Delft and the Cape Flats. The most bitterly recalled removal among residents in Delft is the demolition of the iconic community of District Six, a place known as a thriving arts and cultural center, where sixty thousand people were displaced and scattered throughout townships in Cape Town. Transit camps, then, were used for the screening and repatriation of unwanted black populations. Progressive lawyers, in the ambiguous late apartheid years, used transit camp legislation to prevent the removal of people to distant sites and service areas.[9] In the 1970s, a time of intensified unrest, the camps also served to demobilize organized politics by breaking apart long-standing mobilized communities.

Although the term "slum" is still a pejorative in the post-apartheid period, it has taken on new meanings informed by South Africa's liberal democratic transition. "Slums are bad for our country," said a housing official to Parliament in 2007, speaking in support of expanding clearance programs ongoing since 2000. He continued: "We dream of a tomorrow where all of us can rightfully and proudly proclaim our citizenship. . . . We dream of a tomorrow that is free of slums."[10] In this, and similar statements, evictions—in comparison with apartheid removals—are justified under a liberal logic of citizen rights, where political belonging is materialized through formalized interactions with the state.

Yet residents in Cape Town and other cities have resisted—as many did under apartheid—using "slum" to refer to their communities, especially because the term so often has been used in the service of forced relocations to less desirable areas, and also because it suggests impermanence to longstanding residency, which in the post-apartheid period might provide viable legal standing in tenure claims. Responding to the same 2007 parliamentary debate, Abahlali baseMjondolo, a movement then affiliated with the AEC as part of the Poor People's Alliance, said in a press release:

> The word "slum" . . . makes it sound like the places where poor people live are a problem . . . because there is something wrong with poor people. . . . But it does not admit that . . . places where poor people live often lack infrastructure and toilets because of the failure of . . . the government to provide these things. The solution to the fact that we often don't have toilets in our communities is to provide toilets where we live and not to destroy our communities and move us out of the city.[11]

The press release presents a rebuttal to parliamentary debates that echoes sentiments regularly expressed by movement members at community meetings and mass gatherings, namely that the term "slum" pathologizes settlements while eliding historical struggles with the formerly race-based state over land and housing. Nevertheless, where the parliamentary debates and community meetings align is in that both invoke shack settlements with reference to forward-looking housing projects for the urban poor that implicitly tie formalized homes and land tenure to inclusive citizenship.

At the same time, the term "slum" adheres to national panic over crime, perceived as exponentially increasing since the fall of apartheid. The Breaking New Ground policy document cites "combating crime" and "promoting social cohesion" as an integral part of its "new housing vision."[12] However, crime is highly racialized in South Africa. Racialized stereotypes of shack settlements, and inner-city dwellings as the home of gangsters and prostitutes, marked by potentially polluting moral and corporeal degeneration, appear regularly in mainstream South African news and in popular media. A housing official in a representative article characterizes slums as "hives of crime" and infested with "raw sewage," combining fears over public safety with public health.[13] South African travel websites echo familiar middle-class warnings against visiting townships: "[Corrugated tin shacks] are breeding grounds for crime and violence. The majority of all crime occurs in these slum areas."[14] Residents I spoke with in Cape Town and other cities suggest, in part, their criminalization is tied to informal spatial practices, such as the building of shacks and the occupation of land, which are illicit and sometimes illegal, but they view these activities as necessary to make urban life viable and, therefore, to have political power. "The poor are criminalized for the life we are living," movement members often told me.[15]

Although the term "slum" in South Africa is stamped with its own historically located local and national meanings, its deployment during the buildup to the 2010 Soccer World Cup reflects its resurgent use in international development. In recent decades, international institutions have launched studies, projects, and programs, including the United Nations Millennium Development Goals, to combat "slum growth" on a global spatial scale (Disterhoft 2011). South Africa adopted the Millennium Development Goals with vigor, incorporating them into national policy and law. In 2009, South African officials in the province of KwaZulu-Natal passed a new Slums Act, which was expected to form a national legislative template. The act centrally featured transit camps. It aimed to "eliminate and prevent the reemergence of slums" by the year 2014. Although 2008 marked a ramping up of slum clearance initiatives, the fact remained that in South Africa there were more people living in and moving into shacks than there were formalized homes that could be built within the same time frame. "Slum eradication" would produce a population still awaiting formalized housing, but removed from their homes in existing shack settlements. For this excess population, there were transit camps.

Transit Camp Dwelling at the N2 Gateway

When the N2 Gateway Project broke ground, then housing minister, Lindiwe Sisulu—the daughter of famed ANC liberation heroes—called it "the largest housing project ever undertaken by any government." The project literature proposes that formalizing informality would result in "integrated . . . mixed income . . . human settlements"—a gateway from the apartheid city to the "World-Class City." Initially a joint endeavor by various levels of government, the management of the N2 Gateway soon was outsourced to Prince Xhanti's private company, Thubelisha. This company, in turn, worked within a network of other private-sector institutions. These include, for instance, First National Bank, one of the largest banks in South Africa, which has colonial origins and operates across the African continent. Once part of the British bank Barclays, it was sold amid 1980s anti-apartheid sanctions.[16] Along with rental and bonded units that were too costly for shack dwellers, the last and only phase of the N2 Gateway Project consisted of subsidized housing in Delft—the same houses Monique and her neighbors occupied. Seventy percent of the houses would be allocated to shack dwellers and 30 percent to backyard dwellers, populations racially coded as African and Coloured, respectively. These official designations resulted in some tensions between communities that later would at times trouble the mobilization at Symphony Way. For those who were not allocated these subsidized houses, all that remained were transit camps.

During my visits to the Delft camp in 2008, the surrounding gates were locked at particular hours, with a police trailer and armored military vehicle stationed at the single entrance. As I found in other camps, access inside is often controlled. The shelters in Delft and camps in Durban and Johannesburg usually consist of a one-room, twenty- to twenty-six-square-meter box with a corrugated tin roof and sides, which residents point out leaves little room for families to change or grow. Some structures, built in rows, share a wall made of a single piece of metal sheeting.[17] Many camps are without energy infrastructure. Cooking facilities depend upon whether residents have access to prepaid electricity or have an illicit connection (in which case kettles and hot plates are used). On special occasions, where large portions of food are required, women cook over fires outside. For those who do not have electricity, or cannot afford to feed the prepaid meters, the use of fires or paraffin stoves along with candles for light is routine, which results in occasional camp conflagrations.

Access to water is highly variable. Most camps are fitted with communal cold-running water taps, but when these are broken, residents frequently rely on neighbors outside the camps, which at times causes tensions that take the form of racialized antipathy. Water, largely gathered by women from the taps, is stored in buckets inside the home. Most camps also are fitted with outdoor communal latrines, but these very often are blocked or broken, sometimes leading residents to "privatize" them by maintaining them and charging for their use. Without functional toilets, buckets containing lime are typically used, along with other types of containers or methods. Using the "fly toilet," for example, simply refers to the practice of relieving oneself in a bag and throwing it as far as possible into the bushes.

As for work, most residents are unemployed or labor in the informal sector, for instance in construction, domestic labor, gang activities, or hawking, but some work in the formal sector. Formal sector jobs depend on where the camp is located, but across cities and regions, security work is common. Rather than individually, residents are most often moved as a "community."

Frequently they are placed in the same camp as other communities. In Delft, this has caused conflicts between rival gangs. What people do all day, of course, depends heavily on how or if they are employed, as well as on their age, gender, and other factors, but there are many communal activities in camps, including entrepreneurial projects such as *spaza* shops and shebeens (bars) that draw crowds (despite efforts to police them); active religious groups of various kinds, such as Pentecostal churches and madrasas; volunteer associations; and political organizations including social movements and political party structures, as well as cultural committees.

Camps are typically built far from where residents have lived for many years. An erosion of social networks means residents, especially women, often fear for their safety after dark. As this suggests, location matters. Many have lost their jobs, where transport costs are higher and shops less accessible. Those on HIV/AIDS medications struggle to get access to treatment at neighborhood clinics, even in short-distance moves. Unable to be accommodated in local classrooms, children in Delft have been placed in "temporary" camp schools; before this development, they were bused some twenty-five kilometers back to their previous township schools. Some post-apartheid camps have taken on the status of permanent settlements: "Happy Valley" transit camp, for instance, which was built fourteen years ago, and "Red City,"

The Delft transit camp, prepaid electricity lines, and police vehicle. (Photo by author)

which acquired its name from the rust that has replaced the shiny gleam of the original tin structures.

From Cape Town to Durban to Johannesburg, whether for reasons of livelihood, location, or autonomy, residents are protesting against transit camps through increasingly cross regional and translocal political and legal networks. Residents in the Delft and other camps would hear about a march by word of mouth from neighbors, for instance, at community meetings, at the water taps, at taxi ranks, via cell phone text messages, or literally seeing it unfold on the streets. Like Monique, those protesting have been arrested, shot at by police, and portrayed by officials as thwarting urban development. As an Abahlali press statement put it, the camps project an indefinite and precarious future for shack dwellers:

> We have a situation where people are being removed from a slum, and sent to another slum. Only this time it is a government-approved slum and is called a transit area. . . .
>
> [The state] does not give any guarantees as to where these "transit areas" will be located, what services will be provided there, if communities will be kept together or broken up . . . or how long they will have to live in these places.
>
> We know that all through history and in many countries, governments have put their political opponents, the very poor, people who were seen as ethnically, culturally and racially different, and people without I.D. books in camps. These camps are always supposed to be temporary—a "transit" between one place and another. But very often these camps have become places of long and terrible suffering.[18]

Here, movement members posit equivalence between their self-made shack settlements and government transit camps as informal dwellings. However, they reject the N2 Gateway's promotion of transit camps as formalized temporary infrastructure in anticipation of brick-and-mortar homes.

Inhabiting "Formalized" and "Informal" Housing

Complicating the spatial futures projected by the N2 Gateway are the many practical ways that residents inhabit housing in Delft. Sitting with Monique on Symphony Way, outside the makeshift AEC office, we talked about how she came to reside there. For her, the story of the Symphony Way begins, years earlier, with her days spent cleaning homes in the city's luxurious suburbs. She lived in a backyard shack made of wood and scrap metal, which she rented from a couple—themselves barely making ends meet—who lived in a formal, state subsidized home. When the electricity worked at all, it could be switched off by her landlords, which left her reliant upon candles and paraffin, both hazardous and expensive.

Seeking better conditions, she moved into a Delft council house of her own. The owners, who rented it, lived in another area of the Flats. After local officials learned of this (entirely common) "gray market" rental of state housing (an arrangement also common with transit camps structures), the owners, under threat of legal action by the council, arrived at 3:00 in the morning to evict Monique and her daughter, carrying their belongings onto the street. She appealed to the Delft police, explaining that she had lived in the house for more than a year, had no notice of eviction, and had no place to go. The police told her that she could not take the matter to court, given that she was not the rightful owner of the house.

Following this eviction, Monique and her daughter lived on the street in the back of a bakkie (pickup truck). When her employers at the cleaning company learned of her situation, they helped her access accommodation in Delft through their connections at the N2 Gateway Project. Along with victims of a massive 2005 shack fire in the Joe Slovo shack settlement, Monique moved into a Delft transit camp called Tsunami. During her time in Tsunami, local experts discovered the walls of the temporary structures had been made with asbestos, a matter of criminal investigation.[19]

After her daughter developed a bronchial and skin condition, which required full-time care, she left her job. By the end of the year with doctor fees mounting, Monique began work for a building contractor hired by Thubelisha, laying the foundations and fitting the plumbing for the N2 Gateway houses. She, along with other temporary workers, eventually went on strike, saying they were never paid for this work. Unable to sustain basic subsistence, Monique moved with her neighbors into the unoccupied N2 Gateway houses, with official but fraudulent allocation letters issued by their DA local councillor, who was later arrested.

Thubelisha and state agents quickly sought and secured their eviction through the courts. Monique was a respondent in the failed appeal. Judge Van Zyl, who granted the order, echoing other officials said that residents cannot "take the law into their own hands. There would be anarchy in the country if this were allowed."[20] Monique and other residents inferred that "anarchy," here, played on racialized fears of crime. As the judge stood to leave the packed courtroom, Delft residents shouted, "Ons gaan nêrens!" ("We are going nowhere!" in Afrikaans).[21] Land occupation, even as a semiotic threat, carries force.

On the day of the eviction, Monique's elderly neighbor recounted that after being shot in the side with a rubber bullet and falling to the ground, a police officer kicked and swore at her. The same day, Housing Minister Si-sulu's office issued a statement containing no mention of the injuries or of the police violence captured by news cameras. The official version of events again cited the dangers of anarchy at the center of progressively realized rights: "This morning at dawn, the Sheriff of the Court moved into Delft, supported by police. . . . The rule of law must prevail. . . . [The] government has built . . . more houses than any other country in the world. . . . The N2 Gateway . . . is a project that should be nurtured and guarded by all South Africans."[22] While state agents emphasized law and order, the national news framed the scenes of the eviction as harkening back to unrest of the mid-1980s. Moreover, the eviction suggested how responsibility was vacated for housing demands newly legitimated by post-apartheid law. When public criticism mounted over the eviction at the N2 Gateway, Sisulu said she instructed Thubelisha to do "everything in their power to assist the people of Delft . . . to move back to their previous places of accommodation" and to provide them with transport for that purpose.[23] Thubelisha's project manager denied receiving any such directive and said that the sheriff or the court was "solely responsible" for the eviction.[24] The sheriff also denied responsibility, saying, "The order [from the court] says I must evict the people and remove their belongings to a place of safe custody and that is what I did."[25] Monique and other residents, having given up their former shacks and backyard dwellings, had nowhere to go after the eviction. The police spokesperson said this too was illegal: "The court order instructed the residents to leave the entire area . . . [I]t was illegal for them to remain on the street." He added that a "[private security] guard was posted outside each empty house to prevent people from returning."[26] Here, the sovereign power to evict is authorized by dispersed governmental modes of managing "slum populations," which may aim at control but instead occasioned a two-year-long protest that began and ended in periurban precarity.

Conclusion: Spatial Futures of Informality

By using the land to collectively identify and transform housing infrastructure, residents deploy informal spatial practices from movements such as James Mpanza's Sofasonke. They also transform these practices by using post-apartheid law and policy in the recently desegregated courts. Cassim told me the origin story of the AEC, which began in 1999 on the Cape Flats. After dabbling in gang activities, Cassim worked for a printing company responsible for typesetting pocket compendiums of the new South African Constitution. There he said he learned of Section 26 and post-apartheid protections against arbitrary evictions. From the vantage point of his mother's council home—amid aggressive cost-recovery measures—he watched as removals intensified on the Flats. An elderly man, his mother's neighbor, was among the first to be ejected from his home. In response, residents orchestrated a mass gathering, referred to as a "blockade," that overwhelmed security forces and prevented the delivery of an eviction notice, which is required by law.[27] The police returned the next day with military personnel and with state agents who told the press that the AEC was a front for criminal gangs. Cassim, identified as a leader by security forces, was beaten bloody. He claims—supported by others who saw media coverage of the beating—that his front teeth were kicked in by a steel-tipped police boot.[28] The blockade, however, held ground and the elderly man remained in his home.

These informal spatial practices that claim territory, in spite of racialized policing, are not only composed of street protests, but also activities that arise from daily life in townships and shack settlements, such as building without a permit, or disabling state electricity meters. In this way, Monique and other residents characterize living on the pavement of the N2 Gateway—what would prove a long, hard time for many—as a mode of representing themselves in their appeal for land and housing in the city. Monique lived on Symphony Way in a two-room shack, which she constructed from collected scrap materials: cloth advertisements, a plastic sail, wood planks, and a patterned linoleum floor. Inside was a kitchen and sitting area, carefully fitted with Styrofoam countertops, a bakkie (pickup truck) seat couch with mauve and green ruffled pillows, and window curtains.

From the early weeks, men and women built tire blockades, sometimes burning, on either side of the settlement so that police vehicles could not enter. A day care center, community kitchen, vegetable garden, and children's day camp was launched, run by volunteers. A night watch patrolled until the early hours, serving as protection, especially from the hazards of unattended fires or candles. Residents religiously held mass community meetings every night. In addition to street marches in the Cape Town city center and to the steps of the High Court, residents organized soccer tournaments and informal theater about pavement life. As word of their land occupation spread, they hosted journalists and activists from across South Africa and the globe, and their story was broadcast by international print, radio, and television news. Through these informal spatial practices, Symphony Way visibly asserted, from the "slums" hidden from view in the city, struggles over urban space between the urban poor and South Africa's public–private partners in development of land and housing. Living politics, then, suggests how residents appeal to formalized institutions, for instance, through constitutional clauses and existing housing policies in the courts, as well as to informal activities conducive to particular infrastructural norms.

By examining Symphony Way and the Delft transit camp at the N2 Gateway Project in relation to each other, I have argued that the informal spatial practices of the poor produce infrastructure that has long shaped, and continues to shape, urban space (*umhlaba* and *izindlu*) in contemporary South Africa. Living politics, by melding practices that make the urban poor seen and heard in the city, does so not toward the ends of effective policing, but toward the ends of establishing a home (*ikhaya*). In the post-apartheid period, "slum elimination" in Cape Town and elsewhere has meant the eviction of shack dwellers close to urban centers and their relocation to undesirable sites on the periphery, which they cannot afford or where they have little incentive to remain.

Since 2012, the government has secured the eviction of twenty thousand families from the Joe Slovo shack settlement in Langa for relocation to Delft. At times, including in court cases, Joe Slovo residents have joined forces with the AEC in Delft. Residents (some of whom have lived in Joe Slovo for more than two decades) appealed their removal in the Constitutional Court.

An Anti-Eviction Campaign activist gazes at the construction site of the Delft transit camp. The transit camp is on land owned by South Africa's electricity parastatal, Eskom. (Photo by author)

The court called for negotiations. After many years and street protests—
including renewed violent clashes with police—these negotiations are still in
progress.[29] As for Monique and her neighbors, following another protracted
legal battle they were removed from Symphony Way. Some scattered to other
townships and shack settlements on the Flats, while others were placed in
transit camps. Those who remain are still collectively demanding permanent
residence in Delft, though the AEC has largely demobilized. Thubelisha has
been declared insolvent, after facing corruption charges in the Western Cape
and other provinces. However, some officials report that transit camp construction has been scaled back amid the public pressure exerted by residents
like Monique and her neighbors.

Contrary to utopian or apocalyptic representations of "slums," for instance, in the "Slums Act," which cast residents as lying in wait for the de-
velopmental state or undermining it, I have demonstrated how these are
places of thriving political and legal life, with complex histories that reveal
the contradictions of lived experience when juxtaposed with neat distinctions
between formal and informal space. As Monique said the last time I saw her
before she disappeared from Symphony Way, "The reason I think I should
stay [on the pavement] is because I am a citizen and have a right to a home.
Also, it's about the future of my child . . . I never want her to live in a shack
or any such structure again." Only by establishing and maintaining a home,
Monique suggests, may she and her neighbors claim land and belonging in
the city. However, as the next chapter examines, belonging remains fragile in
shack settlements when met with routine episodes of violence. As xenophobic pogroms leap to the headlines of South African news during the buildup
to the 2010 Soccer World Cup, settlements become scrutinized not for their
protests or living politics of "the poor," but as sites of what Abahlali members
call "a politics of death."

Modular Elements

Dispatch

Our Movement Is under Attack
Submitted by Abahlali on Wed, 2009-10-07 04:24
OCTOBER 6, 2009

We are under attack. We have been attacked physically with all kinds of weapons—guns and knives, even a sword. . . . We have been driven from our homes and our community. . . . We are a movement of the poor and that means that we do not make divisions between the poor. We have always been clear about this. This is our politics and we will stick to it. . . . Every life counts and every death is regretted. There is a long and terrible history in our country of the poor being made to fight each other so that they do not see who the real enemy is. Once again people have died and killed without really knowing what they have died and killed for.

5

"The Anger of the Poor Can Go in Many Directions":
Rematerializing Identity and Difference

On September 26, 2009, an armed group ignited a nightlong pogrom that left two men dead in the Kennedy Road settlement. Over a thousand residents were displaced, including Siboniso, his wife, Nombeka, and their children. The armed group destroyed homes and set shops on fire. Mobilizing ethnicity and political party affiliation, they chanted Zulu-nationalist ANC slogans.[1] Many residents fled to a local church and a Red Cross shelter. Some slept in public parks. Others sought refuge as Busisiwe did with kith and kin in other shack settlements, carrying news of ethnonationalist pogroms in the city. Abahlali leaders and their families—fifty-seven parents and children in total—also were left homeless. They went into "hiding" in safe houses in Durban offered by a London-based human rights organization. The national headquarters of Abahlali in the settlement was dismantled, and then ransacked.[2] For nearly a year, Abahlali's activities—along with Siboniso, Faku, and Busisiwe—operated "underground."[3] This pogrom brought home to Abahlali members that, though elements of living politics can be used to construct a collective self-identification through shared practices and interactions, this identity could also violently break apart through countermobilizations that serve to differentiate the poor.

Through an event history of the pogrom in the Kennedy settlement, this chapter analyzes countermobilizations premised upon ethnicity, policing informal trade, and access to basic infrastructure. The event history focuses on the night of September 26, 2009, when the pogrom—in its most violent manifestations—began. The account is centered upon the Community Hall, the only electrified, formalized structure in the Kennedy settlement. As previous chapters have suggested, the Hall until the pogrom was a locus

Former Abahlali national headquarters, a modest "Wendy house," next to a day care center and the Kennedy Road Community Hall with the city in the background, 2008. (Photo by author)

of day-to-day activities in the community. It was the national headquarters of Abahlali. Importantly, it also was an expressed target of armed men that night.

Although Abahlali was a target in the pogrom, thirteen of its members were arrested. These Abahlali members languished in prison for nearly two years awaiting trial. The courts found them innocent of all charges that included murder, assault, and robbery. At the court hearings, the prosecution's own witnesses reported a frame-up on the stand, claiming that their testimonies were coerced by local police. ANC supporters, wearing party paraphernalia, arrived at the court in two commercial buses, raising speculation that they were a rent-a-crowd. Some carried traditional weapons. They told me they carried guns. Some issued death threats to Abahlali and the church leaders gathered at court.[4]

Abahlali's founding president, S'bu Zikode—who remained in safe houses for over a year—said at court, "[We] have been made refugees in our own country, in our own province, in our own settlement" (Zikode 2009). Abahlali alleged that the pogrom was carried out by an "ANC militia" and was backed by police and other state agents. As national and international news spread about the pogrom in Kennedy Road, protesters gathered at local universities and at South African embassies from London to New York to Moscow under Abahlali banners. The South African president, Jacob Zuma, was picketed during speeches. Church leaders and academics from the archbishop of Cape Town to Noam Chomsky condemned the attacks, as did Amnesty International, Human Rights Watch, and other prominent civic groups in South Africa.

In the days and weeks that followed September 26, 2009, however, state agents told an altogether different story. Local, municipal, and provincial state agents circulated public statements in the news and online claiming that violence at Kennedy Road was not political or ethnicized, but criminal, and perpetrated by an Abahlali-affiliated "vigilante group." State agents claimed that the vigilante group—allegedly the thirteen Abahlali members arrested—held Kennedy under a strict curfew, barring residents from cooking, watching television, or walking outdoors after 7:00 p.m. A provincial minister announced that the settlement, therefore, had been "liberated," and that a resolution had been passed "to dissolve Abahlali baseMjondolo."[5]

Two days after the pogrom on September 28, 2010, state agents hosted a meeting and press conference at the Kennedy Road Community Hall, with eighty-eight "stakeholders," all government or ANC affiliates.[6] Although residents continued to flee during the meeting, a police representative announced that authorities had "no knowledge" of displaced persons. In an official press statement issued the day of the press conference, the spokesperson for the provincial minister further claimed: "For the records [sic] there are no xenophobic or ethnic politics at Kennedy Road." Instead, the minister said, "Criminals would soon be brought to book, which may or may not include [founding Abahlali president S'bu] Zikode."[7] A representative of the Durban Housing Department at the press conference further warned that the *imfene* dance group—in which some of the thirteen arrested were performers—"in our culture is associated with *muthi* [witchcraft]."[8] He stated that Abahlali and their affiliates stood in the way of infrastructural development projects in Kennedy Road, such as electricity. A new ANC-aligned community committee, which then took the former Abahlali national headquarters, was soon elected.

To this background, a further note on method: this account draws from approximately one hundred group and individual interviews with those present during the attacks, both men and women, young and old, across a range of affiliations or lack thereof to Abahlali, to political parties, to various ethnic self-identifications, those remaining in Kennedy Road, and those who fled.

Interviews were conducted from September, within the first days the pogrom began, to December 2009, with staggered follow-up until August 2013. I was present in the settlement during the buildup to the armed attacks and its immediate aftermath. From these and other archival materials,[9] I examine how the elements of fire, water, air, and land are mobilized to the ends of ethnonationalist violence. Time headings err on the side of sequence, as well as mean consistency between separate witnesses, though variation also is noted. It is not a close textual reading of individual testimonies, about which much could be said, but here, instead, aims at temporally moving event history of a twenty-four-hour period.

I propose viewing the pogrom—and the elements the armed group deployed—on an existing terrain of interactions with state agents, especially local government, police and private security forces, and provincial legislature. When recounting that night, residents speak to three relevant shifts in these interactions leading up to 2009—which, notably, was an election year and mere months before South Africa hosted the 2010 Soccer World Cup. These are: (1) the mobilization of an ethnic and national other in party politics; (2) a police crackdown on the informal liquor trade and organized crime; (3) contested claims to territorial sovereignty over new election-time infrastructural projects. Ultimately, residents claim that an armed alliance formed between ANC supporters and local entrepreneurs, including taxi bosses, shebeen owners, and gang members, who viewed their targets as depleting their political and economic power in the settlement. Post facto, state-sanctioned officials, again local and provincial, stepped in and cemented the hegemony of these groupings in the settlement.

Some commenters described the pogrom accurately as "coup," organized to dismantle Abahlali in Kennedy Road, and, by extension, in other historically ANC-voting settlements.[10] However, often overlooked in the commentary is that the pogrom also targeted especially female, and Xhosa-speaking entrepreneurs. These women presented competition in the informal economy. But they also had aligned themselves politically with Abahlali and a new ANC-breakaway party called COPE (Congress of the People), led at the national level by liberation struggle stalwarts. The pogrom illustrates the fragility of living politics and the platforms for life that residents build, yet also their complex resilience across time. To explore this tension between fragility and resilience, I first pair elements—such as fire (ungovernability) and air (effervescence)—to illustrate how they interact with each other during the buildup to the pogrom, and then how all the elements volatilely come together in the violence that unfolded on September 26, 2009.

Fire and Air: Ethnic Modularity and Unmaking the Urban Poor

The urban poor use the ungovernable properties of fire (*umlilo*) and effervescent properties of air (*umoya*) to construct a collective identity that cuts across
lines of difference. Practices such as burning barricades or singing liberation
songs at mass gatherings produce transformative solidarities across historically African, Indian, Coloured, as well as some white communities. However,
these practices do not presume to destroy ethnic and racial differences. Practices such as burning down homes or chanting ethnonationalist slogans re-
ignite tensions within networks of a collectively self-identified "poor." Abahlali members generally oppose ethnonationalism, referring to it as a "politics
of death." Yet living politics and this politics of death also share certain ungovernable, effervescent features. Like living politics, ethnonationalism draws on
the elements at hand—such as the combination of *umlilo* and *umoya*. Both
reach back to past political mobilizations in townships and shack settlements.

To analyze the combination of *umlilo* and *umoya*, I begin at 9:00 a.m. on
September 26, 2009. Already, it was no ordinary day in the Kennedy settlement. Abahlali was hosting a weekend-long Heritage Day mass gathering at
the Community Hall. I went to the Hall with Siboniso's neighbor, Lindani,
to watch some of the performances. Heritage Day is a South African public
holiday. Under apartheid, it was an ethnonationalist celebration, known as
"Shaka Day," after the famed unifier-king of the Zulu nation. In 1995, Nelson
Mandela rebranded "Shaka Day" a celebration of pan-African nationalism.
In a not-so-veiled comment on apartheid-sympathizing ethnonationalists,
he said that Heritage Day celebrated pan-Africanism rising "like a phoenix"
from "the ashes of conflict and division" sewn by colonial rule.[11] Heritage
Day, then, became emblematic of the ascent of nonethnic liberation move-
ments, such as the ANC.

Yet ethnic and racial violence forcibly persisted after apartheid. In the
city of Durban, the most markedly unequal categories remain "black" and
"white," the former that typically includes African, Indian, and Coloured
communities. In Durban's periurban periphery, race-based tensions arise between neighboring African and Indian residents: on Kennedy Road, between
shack dwellers and formalized homeowners, respectively. However, inside
Kennedy and other Durban settlements, among the most charged relational
difference is between Zulu and Xhosa.[12] These are ethnic groups classified
under apartheid as belonging to separate "Bantustans" and, thus, distinct regions of racial belonging under apartheid.

Any Kennedy resident will be familiar with the finer points of Xhosa–

Zulu tensions, even if they actively taboo or reject them. Abahlali members commented that among the strengths of their mobilizations is that they cut across this divide. In KwaZulu-Natal, Xhosas—like other foreign national migrants and refugees, such as Zimbabweans or Malawians—are said to be exogenous, and therefore without claim to local land, sexual partners, or state infrastructure. Xhosa-speaking *ama*Pondo were particularly derided. For many residents I spoke with, breathing the same "ghetto" air can take primacy over ethnic or national identities. One Abahlali member, whose own shack had been burned down in an ethnic pogrom, explains: "Apartheid told us we are Zulus or Xhosas. I grew up in the Eastern Cape [where Xhosa homelands were located], but I speak *isi*Zulu. My wife grew up in KwaZulu-Natal [where Zulu homelands were located], but she speaks *isi*Xhosa. Our children and us, we are South Africans. We are Black people. We are all living in this ghetto." Here, the Abahlali member points to national liberation, geographic mobility, and marriage to capture the instability of apartheid-era ethnic categories. Although other identities Zulu/Xhosa, urban/rural, male/female are not shut down, the primacy of identification falls at the intersections of race and class: with living in a poor black community.

Yet "nonracial" citizenship constructed upon highly racialized urban poverty is only partly resolved by the "social glue" of living politics. Sections of the Kennedy Road settlement are associated, loosely, with Zulu and Xhosa groups, both spatially and temporally. The oldest section near the Community Hall, for instance, which dates back to the community's founding in the 1970s, is said to house elderly and established Zulus, such as Siboniso's family. Xhosas, such as Lindani's family, are associated with the comparatively youthful and less desirable outer perimeter near Bissar landfill. Another ethnic group, said to be "neutral like Switzerland"—and, generally lacking numerical power in the settlement—are the *ama*Bhaca, who populate the territorial buffer space in between Zulu and Xhosa sections. These ethnic enclaves have shared kith and kin networks, which extend to corresponding rural ex-Bantusans and across urban shacklands.

Residents explain that ethnicity—perhaps especially in robustly diverse urban shack settlements—is highly modular. At salient moments, its components are detached, rendered mobile, and recombined. In Kennedy, a Zulu resident might be called "Xhosa" to delegitimize his claims to electricity. Or a Xhosa resident might claim "Zulu" identity to authorize his informal economic activities in the settlement. Multiethnic groups might identify as Zulu, or Xhosa, or both on different occasions, as some Heritage Day performers—such as the Dlamini King Brothers—in Kennedy Road do. These are ethnic performances that produce effects of stable identity, while eliding the contradictions of its mobility once it is lodged inside an actual body, collective, or perceptibly ethnicized gesture.

As Lindani and I found at the Hall, Abahlali's Heritage Day performers were acting out this ethnic modularity. Through combined speech, song, and prayer (*ukubhodla*), they sought to direct collective effervescence toward sustaining an identity as "the poor." Faku, who served as MC, roused the crowd in a costume of discordant ethnic components: traditional Zulu fur accessories, a Union Jack T-shirt, a belt painted with Shepard Fairey's iconic Obama "Hope" design, and a drab brown pantsuit flecked with bright pan-Africanist colors known as an *umblaselo*. Faku called it "dressing against tribalism." By recombining racial and ethnic markers, he invoked urban workers uniforms and rural ceremonial dress, his own royal Xhosa-speaking ancestor's well-known military battles against British colonizers, as well as Abahlali's claims to global networks. In contrast to bricolage, pastiche, or hybridity, these ethnic performances stabilize identity, rather than destabilizing it.

To produce a standard interface of a pan-African "poor," these mobile ethnic components interact to share and exchange ritual energy. The eight-hour Heritage Day program, as Faku did as MC, used effervescent performance to project a pan-African history of Abahlali, and as an extension of the liberation struggle. Lindani and I watched gospel singers, whose songs pleaded to the sovereign Holy Spirit (*umoya*) to intervene in earthly matters. We saw *pantsula* dancers, whose intricate footwork—developed in the urban townships of the 1960s—was said to ward off forced evictions. There were child gumboot dancers, ubiquitous in South Africa's tourist haunts; whose mechanized slap-step against their tall rubber boots is fabled to be code secreted from white bosses. Aside from the *isicathamiya* group, the Dlamini King Brothers, the most popular crowd-pleaser was an ornately costumed *imfene* dance group. *Imfene* is a Xhosa traditional dance, said to be provocative because of its "twerking" pelvic gyrations and invocation of suggestive witch familiars—notably, the virile snake and, as its name suggests, the baboon.

Abahlali devised their Heritage Day program to diffuse ethnonationalism percolating in the settlement by seemingly presenting a unified pan-African urban poor. Abahlali members perceived ethnonationalism as intensifying, as necklacing, as well as the torching of shops and homes spread in Durban, Cape Town, and Johannesburg. Residents in Abahlali-affiliated settlements frequently blamed unmarried and unemployed, and, therefore, liminal and socially ambiguous young men for the violence. Bereft of status or mobility, said residents, young men were alternatively employed in crime or political patronage: in the organized extraction of informal capital in the settlement, or the organized extraction of electoral votes. Especially elderly women in

Kennedy said that work in gangs or political parties tore at the social fabric of the settlement and divided a collectively self-identified poor. Gangs and political parties also sapped Abahlali's membership and contested the authority of its leadership in settlements.

Although even residents perceive shack settlements as the periphery of the city, national political winds—such as changes in the ruling party—continually sweep through them. Often, these forces sweep more intensively than anywhere else because shack settlements are so much engaged with state agents, whether as policed subjects or development populations. Among them was a rapid reorganization of political party affiliation prior to the 2009 national elections. This reorganization, in turn, became refracted through a Xhosa–Zulu divide and hence onto regional geographies and their reproductive resources.[13] The charismatic rise of President Jacob Zuma is iconic of this reorganization and of ethnic modularity. His rise correlated with the founding of ANC-breakaway party COPE by those who rejected Zuma's takeover.

The effervescent mobilization that carried Zuma's ANC faction to power became known nationally as "Zumania." A combination of "Zuma" and "mania," the term implied an infectious populist energy. Zuma, modestly born and raised in KwaZulu-Natal and dubbed a "100% Zulu Boy" by his supporters, ousted former president Thabo Mbeki and a predominantly Xhosa ANC leadership faction. These internal ANC factions, while refracted through a Xhosa–Zulu divide, were nevertheless made up of wholly multiethnic constituencies. Zuma's most prominent supporters were not themselves Zulu, and, locally, Xhosa residents in Kennedy were not immune to Zumania. In the Kennedy settlement, signature red Abahlali T-shirts that once could be seen awash on clothing lines slowly were replaced by smiling yellow Zuma tees flapping in the wind. It suggested a waning influence of Abahlali in the settlement, as well as a hardening of lines between ethnically modular factions of the ANC.

Ethnic modularity, and the ungovernable effervescence it can stimulate, reaches beyond the Xhosa–Zulu divide. It extends to xenophobic pogroms against African migrants and refugees in South Africa, whom, like Xhosas, some residents regard as encroaching outsiders.[14] At an antixenophobia gathering in a Cape Town township in 2009, attended by a ranking United Nations representative and local police, an interim committee—supported by Abahlali's affiliate the AEC—was elected to address community tensions. These tensions largely were between local entrepreneurs, who were battling over price-fixing in *spaza* shops (informal convenience stores). An hour after the meeting, I received a call that a Somali man on the committee was murdered, his shop burned to the ground. This meeting came in the wake of the 2008 xenophobic pogroms, during which sixty-two people were killed. A third of the dead were South African citizens. AEC members I knew were targeted—including being chased by armed groups and shot at with live ammunition—for sympathizing with African migrants and refugees. In this case, rather than the Xhosa–Zulu divide, violence is directed between a multiracial and multiethnic group identified as noncitizens and sympathizers.

Across regions from Durban to Cape Town to Johannesburg, the first winds of an impending ethnonationalist pogrom usually took the form of rumor. Months before Heritage Day at the Hall, rumor of a Xhosa plot to take over Abahlali swept through Kennedy Road. At a mass gathering to elect new leadership at the Community Hall, a local ANC official caused a scene by seizing the microphone to warn of this Xhosa plot. Before the audience booed him off stage, he shouted, "Now, is the time of the Zulu!" The next speaker at the microphone was Faku, who responded with what would become an opening invocation for mass gatherings thereafter: "We Are All Mhlali, no matter Zulu, Xhosa, Indian, Coloured, and no matter ANC, DA, COPE, IFP, or what-what." Faku's injunction endeavored to reclaim collective sentiment for Abahlali. But after the gathering, some residents worried that it might be steered in ethnonationalist directions. Increasingly, some residents viewed Abahlali as aligned with Xhosas, elderly women, and other African migrants against Zuma's homegrown ANC—who were marked as Zulu, young, and male.

Slowly, then, ethnonationalism rose like a lapping fire in the Kennedy settlement. The founding president of Abahlali, S'bu Zikode, a well-known public figure, was attacked with a knife and broken bottles at the entrance of the Hall in the middle of the day by three young men—two identified by their own elderly female kin as hired gang members from outside the settlement. Zikode was beaten all over his body, smashed glass lodged in his face, ears, and head. Zikode self-identifies as Zulu, having grown up in rural KwaZulu-Natal. But he married and had children with a Xhosa woman, who grew up in the city of Durban. While recovering with his family in their Kennedy Road shack, where I visited him, Zikode learned that five young men shouting ethnic slurs also attacked Abahlali's Xhosa-speaking vice president outside the Hall.

Though often the perpetrators and victims of these and other attacks were multiethnic, the violence was refracted—in enactment and subsequent interpretations by residents—through an ethnicized party political divide. In response to rising Zulu-nationalism, Abahlali held mass gatherings at the Community Hall, speaking against dangers of arbitrary divisions among the poor, and held family mediations, drawing in mothers and grandmothers to quell further violence. In the manner of traditional courts, they negotiated settlement agreements between injured parties and their families, in which small sums of money would be exchanged or animals would be slaughtered to heal relations.[15] Online and in the local news, Abahlali issued strong statements against xenophobia and ethnonationalism, and organized public marches with refugee groups, such as the Congolese Solidarity Campaign.

Responses by state agents to ethnonationalist violence in Durban varied. However, the predominant response by security forces and local and provincial government officials was to say the pogroms were orchestrated by criminals aimed at making the cities "ungovernable." In effect, the work of activist networks, gangs, and ethnonationalists were conflated. The bodies of the two men killed on September 26, 2009, during the pogrom in Kennedy Road fell into this nexus of criminalization. The provincial ANC publicly claimed that the men had been killed in a brawl between criminals. COPE and Abahlali, meanwhile, claimed that the men killed during the 2009 attacks were their own supporters targeted by ANC cadres.[16] I could not confirm whether the men were COPE supporters from their neighbors or by those who knew them. Both were steadily employed, living in separate areas of the settlement. Both were Xhosa speakers. Neither attended regular Abahlali meetings. However, competing claims made upon the bodies of the dead speak to the politicization and criminalization of the settlement, not least through the elements of fire (*umlilo*) and air (*umoya*).

Air and Land: Popular Policing and Securitizing the Urban Poor

Instead of effervescence unifying residents, ethnonationalist fervor produced fragmentation, which split claims to territorial sovereignty in the Kennedy settlement. At stake, in particular, was policing the informal liquor trade. The question—at mass gatherings, in meetings with local police, and at the communal water taps—was: To what extent did Abahlali, local entrepreneurs (including gangs), or the police hold the power to secure territory in the settlement?[17] To examine these competing claims to territorial sovereignty, I return to Heritage Day at the Kennedy Road Community Hall. By 5:30 p.m., the performances were winding down. The *imfene* dance group went outside to a bustling taxi rank, headed for an overnight dance competition. Brightly costumed in crisp white T-shirts and green-and-red trimmed pants, the choir cut a distinctive figure at the taxi rank. To perform, the choir leader usually wore a fur and metal headdress with polished bull's horns protruding from either side. He was one of the albino residents in the settlement, said to have spiritual powers. Many suspected him to be a witch.

The *imfene* dance group was uneasy at the taxi rank. During their performance at the Hall, they had been jeered and physically disrupted by a few, evidently drunk, young men. The provocateurs were seated with the settlement's shebeen owners, who made their presence felt in the audience. Shebeen owners, along with taxi bosses, were the most powerful informal entrepreneurs in Kennedy. The liquor they sold or transported, in turn, materialized kith and kin networks, debts, and citywide exchanges. The shebeen owners, at the time, were said to have been cultivating their existing patronage ties to the local councillor and to the gangs. The *imfene* dance group seemed an unlikely target of such powerful men, but they were symbolically aligned with a rival trifecta of Abahlali, elderly women who viewed the shebeens as a social ill, and a brand new community-policing forum. Two members of the *imfene* dance group also were members of what became simply known in Kennedy as "The Forum."

At an Abahlali mass gathering a few months before Heritage Day, women in Kennedy—most of them churchgoing matrons—called for the establishment of a full-time community-policing outfit. Violent crime, said the women, was rife and intensifying, particularly around the shebeens: murder, rape, assault, and robbery. These crimes, they said, were committed by known gangs and posed a particular threat to young women. Virginity tests were called for around the same time, particularly by respected elderly women in the settlement, as a measure against HIV. At the mass gathering, the congregation nominated, and later elected, twelve young men. All were Xhosa speakers. Some Abahlali members noted to me at the time that the lack of ethnic representativity in the Forum could raise tensions, but they did not intervene in the popular public vote.

The support of the Forum by local police ushered in a period that residents called *ukubambisana*, hand-in-hand cooperation, a term used in Dlamini King Brothers' anthems. An official launch was hosted at the Community Hall, attended by the police superintendent, a provincial crime intelligence officer, Abahlali leadership, and Kennedy residents. Photocopied flyers were distributed around the settlement with photographs of the Forum, and their cell phone numbers. Following the launch, residents reported suspected crime to the Forum, which, in turn, handed apprehended suspects over to the local police. Each crime and its manner of response were recorded in a logbook. The logbook I saw detailed crimes ranging from late-night music to the attempted rape of a young girl on Kennedy Road. *Ukubambisana*, drawing upon effervescent gatherings mobilized at the Community Hall, effectively claimed all territories in the settlement under the Forum's jurisdiction.

The establishment of the Forum, for that reason, threatened gangs and local entrepreneurs. They viewed Abahlali as extending their political and economic power in the settlement. Meanwhile, women expressed a growing demand that the shebeens—as havens for gangs—be shut down entirely and their owners be forcibly ousted from the settlement. Shebeen owners, however, wanted their businesses to remain open twenty-four hours. They said liquor sales were their primary means of supporting their families. Abahlali's branch in Kennedy—that is to say, not its national leadership, but its local one known as the Kennedy Road Development Committee (KRDC)—entered into negotiations with the shebeen owners to close their doors by 10:00 p.m. The local police publicly endorsed the proposed closing time. Abahlali leaders in Kennedy told me that they thought a compromise was on the horizon. Abahlali always had tread carefully with the local entrepreneurs and the gangs, and in previous moments maintained mutually amicable interactions—far more amicable than with the local police. However, some residents viewed the Forum as overstepping by interfering with businesses.

While setting rival groups on edge, the establishment of the Forum also had the effect of fragmenting—by virtue of multiplying and realigning—policing authority in the settlement. Abahlali and the local police routinely came to conflict since the movement's emergence in 2005. Many, such as Lindani, found *ukubambisana* with the local police an unexpected and undesirable development, and contrary to the principles of living politics. Since 2005, the local police response to Abahlali's mass gatherings and street protests was arrests and brutality. In 2013, Abahlali won a civil claim, supported by Amnesty International, against the police superintendent and the minister of the police for the 2006 torture of the movement's president and vice president. Even during this period of *ukubambisana*, interactions with police could be a tense affair. On one occasion, the superintendent handing Zikode's child a blue plastic police ruler, said, chuckling, "Now don't act up, or I'll slit your throat like I did your daddy."[18]

The fragmentation of policing authority quickly emerged. Soon after the Forum was established, there was an altercation between two young men suspected of robbery and three members of the Forum. The local police arrested not the suspects, but the Forum, including those who were not present and had no knowledge of the incident. Then it was said by residents that *ukubambisana* was not possible with the police who had beaten shack dwellers in the past.[19] Abahlali leaders, some nervous of the power unleashed by the Forum and seeing it as not entirely within the movement's control, organized a series of training workshops with experts on human rights and community-policing from the local university.

While the parameters of *ukubambisana* were under consideration in Kennedy, it was a time of national public anxiety over policing and vigilantism, and especially by what criteria the two might be distinguished. In the post-1994 period, as part of an effort to integrate security forces, the former apartheid police and military were cojoined with the MK, the ANC's military wing. Community policing was popularized during this period, as part of a broader effort to shift relations between police and African, Indian, and Coloured citizens. Across South Africa's urban townships and shack settlements, there are community-policing bodies like the Forum. They come in all shapes and sizes: many are official structures of local government, whereas others such as the Forum are self-organized and supported by police. Some model themselves after pan-Africanist traditions from King Shaka's mythic Zulu regiments to the Black Panthers' armed citizen patrols.

National anxiety over policing was exacerbated in early July 2009, a few months before the pogrom in Kennedy Road, when the government announced "a new war on criminals." This war echoed, and in some cases borrowed directly, from American police reforms of the 1980s, which included the controversial "Broken Window Policy." In such reforms, crimes such as drinking liquor in public would be treated as a serious offense to routinize, internalize, and generalize law and order. It refers back to British colonial principles of modern law enforcement outlined, for instance in 1929, by famed police reformer Sir Robert Peel. The central principle is that to police effectively and efficiently, the authorities must gain willing cooperation from the public, and, ideally, have the public police themselves (Steinberg 2009). In South Africa, as in the United States, these reforms historically were used to target black and poor communities with undue arrests and harassment.

The result of these police reforms—borrowed at once from the United States and British colonial policing—as well as traditional authority, culminated in "Operation Wanya Tsotsi." Loosely translated as "criminals you will shit," the operation was a popular mobilization program against crime. The Forum, by detractors, was called Wanya Tsotsi. The operation was part of a broader intensification of policing announced before the 2010 Soccer World Cup. Among the most controversial of these reforms was the national "shoot-to-kill" policy.[20] The policy authorized police to shoot with the intention of killing suspected criminals. The deputy police minister described the operation as: "A weapon to instill fear and respect from one's strategic opponent. It is an expression of readiness of one's forces of war. It is a strength exhibition! It is a war cry!"[21] The enemy constructed by the operation presupposed criminals housed and hidden in the city's historically race-based townships and shack settlements.

Official national statistics during this period suggested an increase in police violence, but regardless of the number of incident reports, there were a slew of local, national, and international news stories—circulated on Facebook, Twitter, and blogs—which turned an international media spotlight on the grisly shoot-to-kill policy.[22] Abahlali members, such as Faku spoke about this policy frequently, in settlements and Abahlali meetings. There was the death of a young black law student, the shooting of a toddler holding a metal pipe construed as a gun, a carful of women partygoers, and a long list of others who could in no way be construed as criminals. Those without citizenship papers, such as migrants and refugees, were particularly vulnerable. At the same time, "mob justice" in the form of necklacing and other punishments compounded middle-class fears of ungovernable "slum populations."

Looking to Brazil, experts on policing wondered whether the state-backed crackdown on supposed criminals and an expansion of crime intelligence operations would "cleanup the streets," or mobilize the retribution of criminal gangs in their unwillingness to cede territorial sovereignty or the unrequited memory of fallen comrades. A national debate erupted about the dangers of a slowly "remilitarizing" police force, a proposal, which had been forwarded seriously in policy circles. The shoot-to-kill policy had been practiced in a de facto manner in townships and shack settlements such as Kennedy Road since the apartheid era. I had witnessed two such incidents, one with Busisiwe. Now, however, making an appearance on the middle-class streets, literally and via the news, suggested that the walls between "slum" and suburb were becoming porous, such that experts also feared gangs would strike back in indiscriminate locales.

Amid these policing reforms, state agents often conflated criminal and political activities. At the ANC Regional Conference, one week prior to the Kennedy pogrom in 2009, the chairperson warned against "counter revolutionaries . . . colluding with one mission to weaken the ANC." Under the bold heading "CRIMINAL" in his speech, he proposed that "criminal elements" had gone undercover as COPE members in Gleblands hostel, where ethnonationalist violence had taken place, to provoke the ANC. He added, referring to Abahlali by name, "The element of these NGO who are funded by the West to destabilise us, these elements use all forms of media and poor people [sic]." His speech echoed public statements between 2005 and 2010 by various officials positing that Abahlali is not a legitimate activist network, but a dangerous "criminal" force—often imagined to be supported by foreign agents—bent on disrupting elections by undermining ANC structures.

These months of community-policing *ukubambisana* came to a definitive end when the local police and provincial crime intelligence officer, as principal investigators into murder of two Kennedy men on September 26, 2009, arrested the *imfene* dancers and the Forum. The arrests revealed the multiplicity of agents seeking to claim territorial sovereignty over the settlement through mobilization around community policing. Along with the rise of ethnonationalism, the fragmentation of policing that resulted in a crackdown on the informal liquor trade set constituencies within the settlement against each other, and exacerbated historically tense interactions with local police, setting the stage for an ensuing pogrom.

Land and Water: Election-Time Toilets and Developing the Urban Poor

While territorial power can be produced out of effervescent mobilization, whether as "the poor" or an ethnonationalist grouping, territorial power also can be produced out of control over infrastructure. Since 2008, day-to-day interactions between Abahlali and state agents had moved from "the street" into "the boardroom" and "the courtroom." Abahlali, at the time of the 2009 pogrom, was engaged in boardroom negotiations with state agents at the municipal and provincial levels over the installation of infrastructure in Kennedy and other movement-affiliated settlements. Before these negotiations, Abahlali's activities—and the ways members characterized living politics—were largely defensive: when the municipality banned street march, when its members were arrested, or when a settlement was to be unlawfully evicted.

After several years of street confrontation, Abahlali met these boardroom negotiations with a degree of caution. At regular Abahlali meetings, and mass gatherings at the Hall between 2007 and 2009, members debated, often heatedly, the potential for negotiations to lead not to the installation of water and toilets, but to political demobilization or co-optation.[23] As Faku put it, "[they keep] us busy in boardrooms with paperwork, in order that we're not busy in the streets with the people." However, by 2009, architects already had produced topographic surveys for the settlement-upgrading project in Kennedy. Plans, including unit designs, were presented at mass gatherings at Kennedy Hall and collectively discussed. For the first time since 2001, shacks had been numbered with neon orange spray paint. Residents previously had prevented the municipality from counting the shacks in Kennedy, as these orange numbers typically signified impending eviction. Still, some residents were wary—numbering the shacks also meant counting who belonged in the community, and who did not. Having a number meant having a place in the promised upgrading project.[24]

Along with municipal and provincial state agents, Abahlali was in the most unlikely negotiations of all: with the local ANC councillor. The local councillor had been unwelcome in the Kennedy settlement since 2005, when he "was buried" in a mock funeral. Over time, Abahlali had taken over bureaucratic state functions in the settlement—notably, issuing letters of residency—needed for shack dwellers to access bank accounts, jobs, IDs, social grants, and subsidies. In the exclusive hands of the local councillor, residents claimed that these letters were issued on the basis of his allegiance, the currency of an entrenched system of political party patronage in the ward.

When the local councillor initially launched the toilet project, it was without consultation with Kennedy residents or elected Abahlali leadership. The councillor appointed, as head of the project, a woman known to be active in local ANC branch structures, who lived in a formalized house adjacent to the settlement. Various residents lodged complaints at the Abahlali Office in Kennedy that the councillor yet again was unfairly doling out jobs. The project was seen, at its inception, by Abahlali members as a means of undermining existing community structures and, at the same time, an effort to garner votes for the upcoming local elections. Candidates in these elections, before they even run, are required to first establish that they have an acceptable voting base. The time, in other words, for electioneering in Durban was during the buildup to the September 26 pogrom.

The toilet project represented a shift in relations with the councillor, who since the boardroom negotiations of 2008 had been quietly cooperating with Abahlali. Members of Abahlali were not in principle opposed to toilets. The demand for toilets—in Kennedy Road, for instance, where the ratio in 2005 was estimated at six toilets to seven thousand households—was central to Abahlali's founding. However, construction at election time, without consultation and entailing an allocation jobs on the basis of party affiliation, was talked of as a "dirty politics" in the settlement.

Following the pogrom in 2009, the politically connected woman who ran the councillor's toilet project also became head of the ANC committee that took over Abahlali's national headquarters in the Community Hall. The day care center and the health clinic, previously run by Abahlali members, were closed to deleterious consequences to those who were HIV/AIDS positive and received treatment there. Toilets at the Hall, previously maintained by Abahlali members, began leaking raw sewage into the shacks below. On October 11, 2009, a new community policing forum of eleven men was nominated at a "stakeholders" meeting at the Community Hall. The new policing forum was listed as an objective of the provincial government Task Team mandated to address the "Kennedy situation." The provincial minister for Safety and Security added that a housing project, another of these objectives, would be built in the settlement by February 2010.

The housing project, and the councillor's toilet project never transpired. However, what these projects suggested was how infrastructural projects could mobilize political belonging not only in the form of votes or claiming informal territorial sovereignty over electoral zones, but also through infrastructural projects. Infrastructural projects are never a neutral political process, but through the pouring of concrete, the laying of brick, the connection of water, they are an exercise of sovereignty over the settlement, the city streets, and the region as well. Land and water are two elements that make these powerful connections.

Fire, Water, Air, and Land: The Making of a Pogrom

In preceding sections of this chapter, elemental combinations touch upon relevant shifts in interactions between residents and state agents that led up to 2009 pogrom. I now seek to show how these elements combine—recalling the significance of their properties from the mid-1980s—in ethnonationalist countermobilizations. Returning to Kennedy Road on September 26, an Abahlali Youth League Camp, an overnight mass gathering for young members, was scheduled to begin around 8:00 p.m. at the Hall. By that time, the Kennedy settlement was bustling with activity. It was a Saturday night, the first clear weather in weeks, and, not least, the end of the month when work paychecks and social grants were issued. Young people were headed to downtown Durban, or to see friends in other settlements. They departed with the taxis in front of the Hall.

Next to the main taxi rank, about twenty to thirty men were gathered, and had been from 6:00 p.m., talking to two members of the Forum. Onlookers, passing by or from the Heritage Day performances and soccer practice, milled around. All were waiting for the local police and provincial crime intelligence officer to arrive. A man stood accused, by the residents who had apprehended him, of killing another man while drunk; although the man himself said he had no memory of the earlier parts of the day. The accused stood sheepishly, hands in his pockets, but was not being restrained, nor was he injured. By 8:00 p.m., a local police car and provincial crime intelligence officer in his unmarked vehicle arrived, spoke to the Forum members, and took the accused into custody before departing.[25]

As the hours passed, between 10:30 p.m. and 12:00 midnight,[26] members of Abahlali's local branch area known as the KRDC (Kennedy Road Development Committee), and their families, were asleep in their homes. Suddenly, they were awoken: armed men were banging on doors and walls of shacks with their weapons, breaking windows, shouting, "Come to the Hall! We don't need Abahlali anymore! We don't need the Forum in Kennedy anymore!" Situated in different sections of the settlement, separate witnesses saw members of the armed group rousing men from their beds, ordering some, at weapon point, to join their march. Some said it was reminiscent of Zulu regiments. One man said that "a mob," banging on his door, called him to the Hall. When he looked outside, he saw a teacher, an ordinary resident whom he knew, already seriously wounded, stabbed and bleeding. Neighbors were carrying the teacher to the top of the road for medical attention. He and others repeatedly called an ambulance, which he said did not arrive until daybreak.

In a case of misidentification, armed men, striking the walls of one family's home with blades and sticks, switched off the electricity. They demanded that a member of the Forum come outside, shouting that they intended "to kill." When the man of the household confronted "the mob," one among them shouted, that he was not "of the Forum," and they left. He and his family, packing their belongings, fled Kennedy the following morning. A woman, alone in her shack at the time, heard the shouts, then banging at her door: members of the armed group forcibly entered, looking for her husband, who was among the ten members of the Forum. They swore and threatened her, calling her a "whore" and "bitch wife of *Wanya Tsotsi* [Kennedy Road's community policing forum]." One man said, "We will kill you, instead." They left, but promised to return. She ran from the settlement to family in a nearby settlement, where she remained overnight.[27]

Now, by 12:00 midnight, an estimated hundred men in throngs were seen running through the settlement, moving toward the road and the Hall.[28] They shouted: "We don't need those red [Abahlali] T-shirts in Kennedy anymore! We only need the ANC!" From what can be gathered by separate witnesses accounts, early in the night from 10:00 p.m., armed men centered around two sites in the settlement: in front or behind the Simunye shop, a liquor store on Kennedy Road affiliated with shebeen owners, and in front or behind the Community Hall. Abahlali leaders, named targets of armed men, reside around these two sites. It is near these sites that one of the two men was killed. Later, after 3:00 a.m., members of the armed group were seen elsewhere in the settlement, farther within the interior below the primary sites, where the other man was stabbed to death and several injured.

While other Abahlali members silently waited for "the mobs" to leave their homes, the movement's vice president was at his shack in Kennedy, asleep after working a full shift as a security guard. His wife and three-year-old daughter were also sleeping. Around midnight, they heard a crowd of what sounded like drunken men gathered around their home. They were beating the walls of his shack with some kinds of weapons, repeatedly shouting, "We will kill you *im*Pondo! We will kill you!" The vice president covered the mouth of his child, as she began to scream. The family stayed quiet, pretending not to be inside. Several hours before, he was warned by a family member and friend, whom he trusted, that ANC factions in Kennedy had resolved to remove him as a leader of Abahlali and the KRDC the following day. It was rumored that his head was to be cut off and thrown into the Hall, and his body into a nearby river. The family member and friend advised him to flee. Fearful, though skeptical of rumor, he locked his door from the outside, to leave the impression that he was not at home. He said that the ruse worked, the men departed. The family then fled the settlement. His home was later looted and demolished.

Not far behind the Simunye shop, though not visible to the vice president's shack, S'bu Zikode's wife and children were asleep in their shack. Zikode, at the time, was visiting his ill mother in northern KwaZulu-Natal. His wife awoke to hear the sound of chanting: "*Phansi* [down with] S'bu Zikode! *Phansi* the KRDC! Zikode is selling us to the *Ama*Mpondo! Kennedy is for the *ama*Zulu!" The slogan linked the attacks on Abahlali with Zulu-nationalist rhetoric. Once the men retreated, realizing that Zikode was not at home, his wife fled with their children to the home of a neighboring woman, waking her. They all hid in the bushes with the children through the night after it started raining again, fearful that they would be targeted. From the bushes, later, they saw some armed men go toward the Hall. They saw shadows of figures running between the shacks. They saw young men in the street. Some went to the *spaza* shop owned by a Forum member, on Kennedy Road. Zikode's wife and children saw the men hitting the walls of the shop, removing items from it, and then trying, unsuccessfully, to burn it.[29]

Now, by midnight, armed men were exiting the settlement. They were gathering at the main taxi rank next to the Hall. Identified among them by separate witnesses were shebeen and taxi owners, taxi drivers, "shack lords," "thugs-for-hire," and some associated with well-known gangs[30]—all, in some form, local "businessmen"—as well as the predominant composition, drunken young men. Some members of the armed group were from Kennedy Road; others were recognized from neighboring townships and shack settlements. Once the armed group arrived at Kennedy Hall, a small number of women, approximately five, including the woman who was the head of the ANC ward councillor's toilet project, were identified among the men.[31]

Between 11:00 p.m. and 11:30 p.m., the Abahlali Youth Camp participants said that they heard chanting, and beating upon the plastic pit latrines on Kennedy Road next to the Hall. Following the noise outside, participants saw what they referred to as "a mob," an estimated forty men, wielding machetes, bush knives, and knobkerries (traditional weapons)—later, with guns, broken bottles, and other makeshift weapons. The armed group passed the Hall, marching down Kennedy Road toward Umgeni Road and the grounds, singing "The Struggle Allows It,"[32] before entering a wide pathway into the settlement. Abahlali Youth Camp participants were wary, some fearful, but they continued, set to discuss impending evictions during the 2010 Soccer World Cup. That the armed men were beating on the toilets led some participants of the Youth Camp to conclude that the mob had to do with a toilet project, launched in the preceding months by the local councillor.

Phoning, and furtively moving through the bushes to each other's homes, members of the KRDC rushed to the Hall together, before midnight. Two members of the Forum, who earlier had addressed the citizens' arrest, already were there, inside the fence, now locked, which encircles the Hall. Upon their arrival at the Abahlali Office, across the courtyard from the still ongoing Youth Camp, they say that they dialed the provincial crime intelligence officer on his cell phone and the local police. They discussed the violence unfolding in the settlement. From inside the Abahlali Office, they heard heavy footfalls on the narrow pathways behind the Hall. They heard the scraping of weapon blades against the ground; one said he heard the loading of a gun.

Around midnight, a dog unit police van came to the Hall.[33] The officers, speaking to members of the KRDC and the Forum refused to "go into the darkness," inside the settlement, and left shortly thereafter.[34] The provincial crime intelligence officer also arrived. Parking his car, he walked up the road to address the armed men, gathering at the taxi rank outside the Hall. Armed men reportedly surrounded him. He left the settlement, telling KRDC members he would return with backup security forces.

Reports on when the police arrived and departed during the night vary widely, as do the accounts of what they did when they got there.[35] At certain hours, police were said to be absent. Phone calls to the local security forces between 11:00 p.m. and 3:00 a.m. by ordinary residents inside the settlement and the Abahlali Youth Camp participants inside the Hall elicited no response evident to them; some were told that there were not enough vehicles to send.[36] At other hours, however, and especially in the days that followed, various witnesses said that beatings, stabbings, and shack demolitions happened in their presence. One witness said that armed men assaulted him as police stood by. Another said that he saw members of the armed group chasing a man whom he knew and had been previously hiding with in the bushes. He ran to the police officers for help; they reportedly asked, "What are you running for?" He answered, "I am running from the mob; they're chasing that guy there." The armed men ran past the police, he said, but they did not respond. The man chased was stabbed and was later taken to the hospital.

Around 1:00 a.m., armed men, an estimated fifty at the time, descended upon the Hall outside. The Abahlali Youth Camp participants were uncertain whether it was the same group that marched down Kennedy Road, or a "second mob." The armed group was no longer singing, but throwing objects, and hitting the plastic toilets, each strike getting louder. The men reached the fence, now locked, that separated Kennedy Road from the courtyard of the Hall. They were shouting.

The Abahlali Youth League president, leaving the camp, approached the armed men from between the fence. Getting closer, he could see that the men were carrying guns, in addition to broken bottles, sticks, and bush knives.

He spoke with a few of them: "What do you want?"

They shouted back: "Where is Zikode?"

He responded: "He's not here—why do you want him?"

"Because Zikode is letting the AmaMpondo do as they please in Kennedy!" they said. Those in the armed group demanded keys to the Hall. The Abahlali Youth League president responded that the Hall was for everyone, and there was an Abahlali meeting in progress. They said, "No, for ANC meetings, not COPE [a new breakaway ANC party] meetings." He said, "We are Abahlali, we are not COPE."[37]

Inside the day care center, the Abahlali Youth Camp had stopped. Participants, fearful, moved from sitting in a circle to alongside the wall, protecting themselves from gunfire, looking outside the windows. They locked the security gate to the day care center, so that the men could not get inside. Listening to the shouts and banging outside, they discussed what was happening in the settlement. Shortly before 3:00 a.m., again, the road went quiet.[38]

Still sitting tensely, at about 3:30 a.m., the armed men jumped the fence, and broke inside the Hall above the day care center. They were throwing rocks through the windows and throwing plastic chairs. The mob in front of the Hall chanted for "Zikode," and other known Abahlali leaders.

The Youth League president said to camp participants, "We are easy targets now," and asked what they wanted to do. They were presently inside a small room that functions as a day care center beneath the main section of the Hall. They decided to pray first, and then to try to escape. They prayed, and piled into a van belonging to an Abahlali member from a nearby transit camp, and departed, with two young women from Kennedy staying behind with the KRDC at the Hall. The KRDC remained locked and hidden inside the Abahlali Office on the floor, the lights switched off. According to the KRDC, after 3:00 a.m., the provincial crime intelligence officer returned. He told them that some people had been injured, and at least one person had died in the shacks. Early reports were as many as eight dead.

Between 2:00 a.m. and 3:30 a.m., "noise" resumed inside the settlement. Men were again running between shacks, banging on wood plank walls. KRDC members could hear: "They are not here! They are not here!" And then, "They are here, let's face them!" Several reported in separate areas of the settlement hearing men shouting, "Shoot! Shoot!" One man said at 3:30 a.m., a "crowd" came back to the shack that he shares with his wife—who was affiliated with the KRDC—and three teenage children. His family was already hiding in a neighbor's shack. He managed to flee, but his head was injured badly. Their shack was later demolished. Another man returned to Kennedy Road around 2:00 a.m. Seeing "people running up and down" and "a lot of violence," he called his wife at their shack in the interior of the settlement. She told him not to return, that she was locked inside with the baby and that his sisters were hiding "in the bush[es]."

From what can be gathered from separate accounts, attacks that began with expressed targets, mobilizing party and ethnicity, fanned out into a series of brawls and extenuating attacks in various sections of the settlement. Some said that perhaps those perceiving themselves a target—whether for the ethnic garb they wore that day, their accent, or political affiliation—confronted roving armed men in self-defense. As people fled, hid in the bushes, and made cell phone calls to friends and neighbors, word spread of an ensuing "war." Some said, "The Zulus are killing all the Xhosas," others said, "The Xhosas are killing all the Zulus." Still others said no one was certain who was attacking whom. That both isiXhosa and isiZulu speakers reported threats was noted in early news coverage.

Between 4:00 a.m. and 5:00 a.m., a police helicopter flew overhead. Residents, at daybreak, had begun to flee on foot or in taxis, children and parcels strapped to their backs, some carrying mattresses, others packing their belongings, a procession that continued through the evening and for at least the following two days.

A domestic worker with her four-month-old child, living in a two-room shack, slept through the night, but at around 6:00 a.m. saw a crowd of people near the Pentecostal Nazareth Church, "looking for a body on the floor." She said it "felt like a movie." Men armed with sticks and bush knives soon came to her home, looking for her boyfriend. By 6:00 a.m., homes including of the Forum and KRDC, had been demolished. Three police vans returned to the settlement, with officers taking statements, asking who had killed whom—this, only hours before the state press conference in the Hall. The KRDC, who gave statements to the provincial crime intelligence officer, told him then that they thought the local ANC was behind the attacks.

Those with jobs in the formal sector—in security companies, construction, factories—or with work in the settlement—a woman working in the health clinic, a woman who sold plastic containers of water—and shopkeepers, in particular, appear to have been targeted in these hours and in the days that followed. Those with jobs and shops were known to have belongings to loot. Perhaps more importantly, they—like the Abahlali leaders and KRDC—were recognizable figures in the settlement. They represented a different sort of work than that of the masculine "entrepreneurs" who joined forces with ANC supporters. They also, unlike unemployed young men, had work—even if it was of the wageless, informal, or casual kind. The attacks meant the loss of employment for those displaced, and the breaking of social networks that provided a modicum of viability to their lives. This continues to be true years later.

A young woman living in a shack divided into two rooms, one a *spaza* shop, the other her living quarters, slept through the night. At about 9 a.m. a mob came to her home with sticks and bush knives, asking her to produce a husband or a man. She replied that she had neither. The police were outside. The men left, but returned later that day to say she was lying, she "should have a man." They told her to move, or they would rape her. She ran. Her belongings were stolen, her home and shop demolished. Previously supporting her family in the Eastern Cape, she was left without income.[39] Some men in the settlement deemed women's work in the informal economy unsavory. The attacks stripped several women of this livelihood.

By 7:00 a.m. in Kennedy Road, emergency medical staff were tending to the wounded and loading several injured people into ambulances. KRDC members, still at the Abahlali Office, were told another person had been killed in the upper section of the settlement. At around 9:00 a.m., a group of residents, predominantly young and elderly women, all unarmed, came to the Hall. They demanded to know who had been killed and what had happened during the night. The women said rumor had circulated that the Forum were to blame. The KRDC told them they did not know who had been killed—initial reports were eight people. Family members could not locate each other, as some residents had hidden during the attacks.

Early in the morning, there was a heavy police presence. At least ten vans with officers were seen at the Hall. Some witnesses said they saw men still milling around at the top of the settlement with weapons, identified as members of the armed group the night before. Some among them were talking to the police. On Sunday morning, armed men were still looking for KRDC and Abahlali members, some chanting, "Down with Abahlali! Down with the KRDC!" That day, the shacks of Abahlali members were demolished. During the night that followed the state press conference in the Hall on September 28, 2009, armed men demolished more homes. The following morning and days, some left the settlement, so fearful that their bodies shook, trembled, mouthing words that could not be spoken. One of those who could not speak was Siboniso's wife, Nombeka.

Conclusion: Criminal Elements

Days after the attacks in Kennedy Road, I read aloud Abahlali's online press statement about the pogrom. The mention of fire made Nombeka shudder. The safe house, where Siboniso's wife, Nombeka, was hiding, was a non-descript apartment on a nondescript apartment block in a historically white middle-class South African suburb. The garden was lush and leafy, with a razor-sharp security fence encircled with electrical wiring. "Enough to kill a man," a police officer once told me of this wiring. Not true, but it was the thought that counted. Outside was a French-speaking car-guard, who as an additional measure of security watched the street to ward off possible criminals. He told me he was from West Africa, an economic refugee and like many looking for new avenues of employment in South Africa, and trying to start an NGO. The London head office of an international human rights organization facilitated negotiations for all the safe houses, including the one that Nombeka now found herself in. Unlike aid workers who traveled fly-by-night for brief periods of research, the organization's emissaries had intimate local knowledge of the region, having worked with activists during the liberation struggle. For Nombeka, the few days before were a blur: offers from foreign embassies extending refugee status for Siboniso, interviews with human rights workers, and secret gatherings held in a park downtown.

Inside the small room of the safe house, Nombeka sat on the edge of the bed. Ear pressed to a cell phone, her eyes reddened and her torso shook. Her pregnant cousin, glazed still, sat behind her. Word had reached the safe house that Nombeka's shack in the settlement of Kennedy Road—a generous home made largely of packed mud—was about to be destroyed by armed men. She could see the interior of the shack in her mind's eye: three large immaculate rooms, a refrigerator covered in crayoned children's drawings, and an over-sized, thrift shop painting of the biblical lion laying down with the lamb. The mud walls, like the "rondevels" or rounded huts found mostly in rural areas, kept the sun's heat in the winter and provided cool shade in the summer.

Nombeka gestured to me. I sat down next to her, my ear now also pressed to the receiver. On the other end, we heard muffled shouts and chopping. The chopping: was it the skeletal wood planks or the tin roof? The woman on the other end of the line said that men, wielding *pangas*—a type of machete used equally for labor as for war—had broken inside and were looting the place. Nombeka let out a reversed gasp, exhaled shock, which would be the last sound I would hear from her for days. She, thereafter, only communicated by pen and paper and, then again, only when necessary. Her cousin and I tried comforting her to no avail. We read to her. The only book in the apartment, of all things, was American poet Walt Whitman's *Leaves of Grass*, a meditation on life and death: the first stanzas provided, at least, distraction. But the mention of fire brought on sobless tears: "A Phantom rose before me with distrustful aspect . . . As to Me Directing Like Flame to Its Eyes."

Nombeka was never an activist, nor ever wanted to be; her husband, though, had become a prominent movement leader. She worked in data entry at an office. Nombeka's mother had been a domestic worker in the same white suburb where we now sat. Like many young South Africans I knew, Nombeka wanted to see her children off to university, and for them to live the "better life" promised by the liberation struggle. In the years I had known her, though supportive of her husband, Nombeka did not much care for the movement politics that surrounded her: the constant phone calls, the endless meetings, the lack of income, the arrests, and the injuries. Local tabloids had called her husband "Robin Hood," a witch, and the secret owner of a mansion in a posh coastal resort. However, this moment in the safe house was different. She never had to flee her home before, kids in hand, with a few bags of belongings. The ground beneath her feet shifted; permanently, it had seemed.

With her and other residents, I spent about three months in and out of various safe houses during the end of my research in Kennedy Road, while leaders of Abahlali and their families were "underground." The safe house put into relief the suburban apartment enclave and Nombeka's shack settlement. The apartment had running water, flush toilets, limitless electricity, and fresh air in an open garden. Her stay there, moreover, was qualified, lived differently than the middle-class tenants, going casually to and from work and about their day. For Nombeka, that apartment was a place of anxious waiting, away from family and friends and her mobility largely restricted. The conditions of shack settlements reached into Nombeka's safe house, even as they seemed worlds apart.

Conclusion: Liberal Governance and the Urban Poor Revisited

The previous chapter centered on how elements of life in urban shack settlements can fracture communities and activist networks of the poor. I conclude by exploring how Abahlali-affiliated settlements endeavor to rebuild institutions of living politics, both in the aftermath of the 2009 pogrom in Kennedy Road and in the context of police violence. Nqobile Nzuza was considered a "born free." With her birthday on the cusp of Nelson Mandela's 1994 election, she grew up in a democratic South Africa. At seventeen, Nzuza lived with her parents in the shack settlement of Cato Crest while attending a nearby primary school. The settlement is eight kilometers from downtown Durban in the hidden quarters of the city's leafy middle-class suburbs. Nzuza was an active member of Abahlali. On September 30, 2013, just before dawn, Nzuza was killed during a street protest over land and housing in the city. She was shot twice in the back with live ammunition. Witnesses say Cato Manor police fired the shots. The police do not deny this fact but say they feared for their own safety.

After receiving frantic calls from members, Abahlali's general secretary rushed to the scene. Upon arrival, she was arrested as an instigator and accused of "public violence," a vaguely defined charge frequently attributed to activists. Siboniso, Faku, M'du, and many other Abahlali members had been arrested on similar charges, which never once held up in court. After two weeks, with the general secretary in prison and Nzuza buried, city officials called a press conference, declaring Abahlali a "criminal" force bent on "making the city ungovernable."[1] However, news of Nzuza's death and the secretary's arrest stirred protests in Durban and at South African embassies from London to New York building upon networks forged in previous years of mobilization. Prominent academics—including Slavoj Žižek,

V. Y. Mudimbe, and Judith Butler—issued an open letter condemning the Cato police and city officials, echoing press statements by human rights groups and church leaders.[2] In mourning and anger, residents of Cato Crest and other settlements called Nzuza's death a "sacrifice."

The works of several Cato Crest letter signatories (Butler 2002; Mudimbe 1994; Žižek 2004), along with a growing body of literature in Africanist anthropology (Ferguson 2013; Graeber 2011; Mbembe 2003; Obarrio 2004; Ralph 2015; Smith 2008), explore the distinctions and complex relations between gift giving and commodity exchange in political life. Following Marcel Mauss (1954), who differentiates *homo economicus* from other forms of debt and social obligation, anthropological writing has emphasized "the gift" as a space and set of relations not wholly determined by the profanity of the market, thereby holding the potential for collective justice (Obarrio 2004), political autonomy (Graeber 2011), or economic redistribution (Ferguson 2013).

"Sacrifice" happens, according to Hubert and Mauss ([1899] 1981), when one destroys something sacred or, in extreme cases, gives one's life in exchange for a communion with the divine. Later debates locate sacrifice within specific emergent social, historical, and, I will add, biochemical processes (Appadurai 1988; Bourdieu 1977; Parry and Bloch 1989). At a time in South Africa when Pentecostal churches and political parties remain promised refuges of spiritual salvation—as well as civic engagement and economic mobility (Comaroff 1985; Comaroff and Comaroff 1991)—it might therefore be perplexing that so many men and women, like Nzuza and other activists, are prepared to lay down their lives, in respect to neither God nor nation, especially when there seems to be no common political enemy, no repressive laws to overturn, and no unified organizational banner under which to imagine a certain future.

However, Abahlali's positing of sacrifice as central to living politics suggests a rich political theology looking backward to liberation movements and forward to an emergent critique of twenty-first-century political economy. Abahlali's idiom, "sacrifice," is neither reducible to the paradigm of "the gift" (i.e., pertaining to relations either outside or prior to the market), nor to the paradigm of economic exchange (i.e., pertaining to relations inside the market). On the one hand, "sacrifice" is entangled with the market by virtue of a blurring between public and private institutions in South Africa under economic liberalization. For members, Nzuza died because of the securitized defense of elite networks of formal and informal political patronage in Cato Crest. On the other hand, "sacrifice" in Abahlali's idiom is understood as giving over one's body to a sacred collective politics outside of formal state structures and against the privatization of governance. For members in Cato

Crest, Nzuza died for a politics whose aim is to secure communal land and housing in the city, outside and against the contractual logics of elites.

Living Sacrifice: A Branch Launch in Cato Crest

An Abahlali branch launch on a sun-soaked afternoon in Cato Crest is emblematic of how Abahlali's idiom of sacrifice is instantiated through ritual practice. The launch, on July 21, 2013, was less than two months before Nzuza's death. It was held near Nzuza's family home in the "Marikana" section of the settlement. Residents named this section "Marikana" to honor the thirty-seven strikers killed by police in 2012 at the British-owned Lonmin mine about three hundred kilometers outside of Johannesburg. The name "Marikana" linked racialized endangerment in the mines to that of everyday life in shack settlements.

At the Cato Crest launch, residents were tasked to elect their neighbors to leadership positions in a branch area committee. As discussed in chapter 3, Abahlali's branches represent each territorial locality under a "National Executive," which mirrors the organizational structures of the ANC. I have attended dozens of Abahlali branch launches since 2005. On some occasions, these launches have been disrupted by groups who view Abahlali as encroaching on turf in settlements, such as members of political parties or local gangs. This time, at the launch in Cato Crest, the dangers of forming a new branch were known beyond Durban's shacklands.

As the national news in South Africa reported, Abahlali claimed that its members had become targets of local "hit men." On June 26, 2013, Abahlali leader Nkululeko Gwala, a vocal critic of housing corruption, was shot dead. Gwala had attempted a branch launch in Cato Crest. On March 15, 2013, another Cato Manor community activist, Thembiknkosi Qumbela, was killed. Rumor of a "Cato Manor hit list" circulated throughout the city of Durban, and became the subject of a highly publicized criminal trial. A year later outside of Durban, on September 29, 2014, Abahlali leader Thuli Ndlovu was shot dead in her home while watching television. Two ANC councillors were arrested, and eventually convicted, for Ndlovu's murder.

At the launch in Cato Crest, police stood, weapons ready, atop a hill. Below them were some hundred red-shirted activists. They were mostly women. The women sang, made speeches, and *toyi-toyied*. The structure and content of the launch was standard fare: a rehearsal of movement history, nominations for each elected position by a show of hands, and a swearing in ceremony. The hypervisibility of uniformed officers at such a gathering might appear as heavy handed, over cautious, or innocuously protective. Yet, with a

Mass gathering at Nqobile Nzuza's former family home, 2013. (Photo by author)

history of militant protests in Cato Manor (locally known as *Umkhumbane*), authorities took mass gatherings, be they funerals or women's elections, as potentially provocative.

In part, authorities view these events as dangerous because of their location in historically racialized—and still criminalized—geographic zones in the city. But also, in part, because authorities see danger—and power—attached to black mass gatherings outside of formal state or party structures, even today. Popular mobilization in shack settlements of the city is locally understood as contributing to the fall of apartheid. Cato Manor is the site of a notorious forced removal in 1959, a period when thousands were scattered to segregated townships on the urban periphery—where many Abahlali members live today. Resistance to removals in Cato Manor culminated in the killing of eight police officers in 1960, their bodies dragged through the streets.

At the launch, the police were on edge. So were residents, who whispered among themselves during the swearing in ceremony. For them, scenes of encounters with security forces represented the murky and always potential breakdown between the world of policing and the world of vigilante crime. This was a police force, according to residents, known for its ability to inhabit and exploit the profitable interstices of the underworld in *Umkhumbane*. Residents associated the expansion of entrepreneurial practices of police with liberalization.[3] "*Haiybo!*" (an *isi*Zulu expression of surprise and exasperation), exclaimed an Abahlali official half-ironically, half-seriously at the launch as women directed anti-apartheid anthems toward the hill: "The people, they are *teasing* the police, who are meant to protect them. They should be careful." His comment suggested that the post-apartheid security forces might have been reimagined and rebranded as protectors, but they remained figures to regard with suspicion.

Those elected at the branch launch that day—as is typical—had "sacrificed" directly or indirectly through close kith and kin. During the late liberation struggle in South Africa, being imprisoned or marked by police violence were rites of passage designating leadership.[4] In *A Long Walk to Freedom*, Nelson Mandela writes that sacrifice is not a passive activity, but at the core of mobilization: "[S]truggle was not merely a question of making speeches, holding meetings, passing resolutions and sending deputations, but of meticulous organization, militant mass action, and above all, the willingness to suffer and sacrifice" (Mandela 1994, 104). Abahlali members view mobilization and violence intertwined with sacrifice as grounded in shared material conditions in shack settlements. As one member said, when your "life is illegal"—living on occupied land, hawking without a permit, illicitly connecting water supplies, and protesting on city streets "where the poor are not meant to be seen"—violence is "part and parcel of struggle."

Symbolic Lineages of Sacrifice: Mandela and His Heirs

Although Abahlali members do not posit equivalence between democracy and "the dark days of apartheid," they do emphasize certain symbolic lineages, as they did the day of the Cato Crest launch. For instance, the leadership origin story told of founding Abahlali president S'bu Zikode concerns his brutalization in police custody by the son of an infamous apartheid-era torturer (Pithouse 2006). These lineages, in spite of the extraordinary violence represented, often are framed in creative, resilient, and playful ways with humor that, at times, disguises a more serious political message. In songs and slogans, for instance, members refer to Zikode as "the next Nelson Mandela." In turn, they refer to Mandela as "the second Jesus Christ," who suffered so that all could have "a better life." The message, here, is that Abahlali members see themselves as "carrying forward" the messianic project of liberation. The implication is that the anti-apartheid struggle has not been realized through the ascent of the ANC. Abahlali members "carrying forward" liberation harkens back to an ANC—as a liberation movement—under Nelson Mandela prior to its becoming a ruling party. Abahlali members, therefore, emphasize not formal institutional politics, but connections between sacral figures in informal domains.

These symbolic lineages are enacted through ritual practice and spatially assertive performance, particularly through mass gatherings. For instance, following the death of Nelson Mandela—by word-of-mouth, WhatsApp, and Facebook—Abahlali called a meeting to discuss "our own" interpretation of what his passing meant to the country and its members living in townships and shack settlements. Their answer was to hold a street march under the banner, "In honour of the father of the nation uTata uNelson Mandela."[5] Here, and during meetings, Mandela is invoked as "father" (*uTata* in *isi*Xhosa) as the nation's first black president, but also as an icon of a particular brand of street politics popularly imagined to have birthed the nation. Abahlali, by marching, views itself as confirming that lineage, precisely not by seeking state office, but by taking to the streets.

I will return to some of the representational complexities of sacrifice within and beyond the movement. But it is important to grasp that the invocation of Mandela as "father" in mass gatherings, in addition to inspiring collective feeling among members, has the ritual efficacy of addressing multiple publics beyond the movement and beyond South Africa. On December 9, 2013, only days after Mandela's death, Abahlali branches gathered not far from Nzuza's family's home in the "Marikana" section of Cato Crest. They marched carrying signs in both English and *isi*Zulu, onto a major roadway flanked by Cato Manor police and an ominous water cannon.[6] Members openly snapped photographs and shot video on camera phones for upload onto their website.

By invoking Mandela, an icon globally and locally, Abahlali endeavors to speak to those watching Cato Crest from afar, including academics and activists like Butler and Žižek, or the Chicago Anti-Eviction Campaign, as well as the middle class in South Africa like students who protested on their campuses against Nzuza's death. But the primary public for Abahlali are those in townships and shack settlements for whom Mandela's ANC remains a revered symbol of liberation. At the Cato Crest branch launch, by contrast, cell phone cameras were discouraged for fear of spies (*izimpimpi*) reporting to the local ANC. A brief controversy emerged—marked by whisperings and many pointed sidelong glances—when a young woman unknown to area members began recording the proceedings. It turned out that the woman taking video was a particularly enthusiastic new member, who had yet to understand the subtleties of distinguishing one public event from another within the movement.

By claiming Mandela as "father" to internal and external publics, Abahlali members seek to conjure his moral authority and that of the diverse movements that made up the liberation struggle. In a press release, circulated widely beyond Abahlali's own website on local and international blogs, the movement announced their march in Cato Crest with reference to his legal defense of a shack dwellers' movement in Johannesburg. Mandela's support of Sofasonke ("We Die Together" campaign) and their illegal land occupations during World War II "helped radicalise . . . the struggle against evictions in *Umkhumbane* [Cato Manor]."[7] Abahlali's press release, in this instance, emphasizes political inheritance, noting the arrest of their general secretary, and one of their affiliate lawyers. Both were arrested while fighting urban evictions. The lawyer, as it happens, was thrown in jail the same night Mandela passed away. Through a characteristic transmutation of past and present through these symbolic lineages, Abahlali proposes they are answering Mandela's call to return to the streets:

> The struggle we are facing today we were facing it even when Mandela was still alive. The evictions, beatings, arrests, torture, assassinations, corruption and violation of our rights were taking place when Mandela was still alive. . . .
>
> Nelson Mandela fought for justice, democracy and freedom for all. He did not say that the poor were excluded. . . . We will continue to take Mandela's struggle forward. . . .
>
> The ruling party is fighting for membership and the sustainability of the party rather than addressing the peoples' concerns. . . . Today people do not volunteer for the party because they want to join the struggle for justice, equality and democracy. Today people join the party to invest in the party so that tomorrow it will be their turn to eat our future. . . .
>
> Today as Mandela has passed on the ANC is an organisation that has harmed us and that will continue to harm us. But Mandela lived for us and not for the ANC. He clearly said that if the ANC does to us what the apartheid government did to us then we must not fear to do to the ANC what we did to the apartheid government. Nobody can deny that in Cato Crest the ANC is doing to us what the apartheid government did to us.
>
> [Mandela] always made it clear that there is still a long walk to freedom. . . . It is the responsibility of our generation to continue this journey. . . .
>
> This is how we will show our respect for Mandela's struggle. . . . This new phase of the struggle is just beginning.[8]

As the press release suggests, by tracing these lineages of sacrifice, which inspire collective feeling and sanctify leaders, Abahlali endeavors to multiply publics that sympathize with the movement. By invoking the aura of liberation icons, they lend themselves and these publics moral authority. Abahlali names themselves, and those living in townships and shack settlements more broadly, as legitimate heirs to Mandela's legacy. It should be noted that this invocation of Mandela often stands in tension with some communal histories of Cato Manor, where the ANC long has occupied an ambivalent position. In 1993, when Mandela visited the area, for instance, African residents refused to meet with him (Edwards 1994).

Abahlali's general secretary—who has been acquitted on all charges of "public violence"—wrote a "Letter from Prison" circulated online and among members, echoing these themes while alluding to the sacred qualities of mass action. Her letter suggests that communion with the sacred is taken in through the body:

> My seven days in prison gave me time to think. . . . I had to sit back and ask myself: "Why did I join this movement?" I had a chance to back off, but once something is inside you, once you live it, once it is injected inside you no one else can stop it. Ubuhlali [the spirit of Abahlalism] runs in my veins. I am unable to distance myself from it any more. I don't need ubuhlali, but my life needs it. It is what I live and breathe. . . . Evictions, beatings, arrests and murder are not suffered alone if you are in this movement. This makes us strong. And as repression gets worse it drives more people into the movement. It makes us stronger and stronger.[9]

As the letter suggests, there is a tension between sacrificing and *being* sacrificed by external forces. The politicization of the arrest, injury, and death of activists is a means of shifting agency from these external forces to the internal body, at once individual, collective, and spiritual.[10] In the same "Letter," she emphasizes that sacrifice sustains movements, but also implies forms of consumption that deplete them. Resonating with idioms of migrant labor, one member said in reference to the Marikana massacre and Nzuza's death: "The rich are sacrificing the lives of the poor to feed themselves."

As this suggests, again, through symbolic condensation, sacrifice is understood as intimately transmuting between the mine, ostensibly a space of masculine wage labor, and the shack settlement, ostensibly a space of feminine domestic labor. In the *Guardian*, Zikode said South African cities are like ATMs, sites of extraction and circulation, where everyone is taking a cut: the Lonmin CEO, the Durban mayor, and the local "hit man."[11] Like Abahlali's networks, these are global transactions. The general secretary sums up Abahlali's emergent idiom of sacrifice by declaring in her "Letter": "No judg-

ment, imprisonment or bullet will silence me while we . . . are being oppressed by those whose daily bread is the poverty and blood of the poor,"[12]
suggesting the centrality of consumption, the body, and its violation as categories of an emergent political theology (see also Bernstein 2013).

The Limits of Sacrifice as Rites of Passage

Although, thus far, I have focused upon highly visible instantiations of Abahlali's living politics, sacrifices that are politically consecrated but *not* publicized are as revealing as what becomes the subject of mass gatherings or
headline news. An arrest may be a rite of passage into leadership, but many
just want to put their lives back together again. Those who refuse an elected
mantle are treated with reverence and respect within the movement, whether
or not they remain active. These narratives highlight how unreported cases of
police violence contribute to Abahlali's idiom.

As previous chapters have examined, occupying land or illicitly connecting service supplies are routine practices that risk injury, arrest, and even
death in South Africa. These sacrifices are enacted as a means of securing
urban life where ordinary means of economic and political mobility are not
available. Because these are commonplace yet criminalized practices, they
rarely make headline news and are not entirely legible as politics in the eyes
of the law. Abahlali members, however, view these practices, and the sacrifices they entail, as the raison d'être of their living politics.[13] Abahlali held
a commemorative march, for instance, on the occasion of the thirty-third
anniversary of the 1976 Soweto uprising, when security forces gunned down
schoolchildren protesting against teaching Afrikaans.

Among those killed was Hector Pieterson, whose lifeless body carried by
his schoolmate in the posture of the Pieta became a galvanizing image for
global anti-apartheid movements. The Abahlali Youth League statement,
drawing upon this history, spoke to the everyday sacrifices carried by "born
frees" like Nzuza. In the statement, they stressed education, employment,
and other forms of social mobility, as well as toilets, electricity, and access to
urban infrastructure in newly desegregated cities:

> The poor have to survive as we can. . . . We live in shacks. We live in shit and
> fire. We are evicted. We have no safe and easy transport. The police treat us
> as criminals. They beat us if we try to organise. If you are young and poor
> you are treated as a threat to society and not as the future our society. Hec-
> tor Peterson [*sic*] . . . and other comrades who died for our Freedom and
> Democracy did not die for this. We do not respect their sacrifice by accepting
> that this is Freedom. Freedom and Democracy is not just about voting. It is

not about being in nice fancy places [like nightclubs and movie theaters]. It is about being able to think, and do things for yourself. . . . It means being able to take responsibility for your own life and your own future. It means building a society in which everyone counts. It means sharing land, wealth and power. We are the youth of today. We want to continue where Hector Peterson [sic] and others have left from. This is how we should respect their sacrifice.[14]

As the statement suggests, everyday sacrifices are felt throughout one's life, and through a life cycle distended or cut short. These sacrifices shape youthful political action, as they did for previous generations. Yet these sacrifices also respond to emergent historical processes. The Youth League statement, for instance, points to recently desegregated movie theaters as key sites of "born free" identity making. Abahlali Youth League members criticize "born frees" who seek individual economic mobility as an end in itself, or to escape poverty through consumption. Youth League members urge "born frees," instead, to eschew "fancy" things, and collectively right past and present structural wrongs by taking to the streets as community activists.

Often this politicization came with broad reflections upon wealth inequality in post-apartheid society. For instance in such rhetorical questions as "Why, now that democracy has come, is Lonmin mine still owned by the British?" Or "Why do white 'bosses' and 'madams' remain in the same well-paid jobs and secure suburban homes?" "Why are police, notorious for apartheid-era violence, still plying their trade in the same police stations?" "Why is the new Black middle class, our comrades and neighbors, not redistributing while they enjoy the benefits of corporate or political office?" These questions, like an idiom of sacrifice itself, serve to distinguish and identify a political community, and thereby collective identification among members as a racialized poor, premised upon ongoing lived, material conditions in shack settlements and townships.

As discussed in chapter 3, Abahlali meetings during my research between 2008 and 2010 would sometimes run for multiple days, overnight without break, so that every participant can have his or her say for however long he or she is willing to speak. Even so, in any organization, speech acts and events, such as press releases and mass meetings, encode certain kinds of internal structural differences and asymmetrical relations. Sometimes members themselves would read these as gendered, racialized, ethnicized, geographic, or age-based. When women in a new branch undergoing eviction complained of their laundry getting dirty as a major concern, for example, it did not feature prominently in the press release. Or when a Youth League member took issue with an elder woman shaming him for dating too liberally within the movement, he did not fight back or "cough out" his embarrassment at a meeting. These differences, and how they are mobilized between members also often are more complex than categories of gender and age.[15] The women whose laundry woes did not make it into a press release belonged to a small and recently adopted, and hence less influential, branch in the movement. The shamed Youth League member had been gaining prominence in the movement, not for his dating choices, but for his respected leadership and influential oration, inspiring jealousies.

That is not to say Abahlali's living politics is only concerned with the injurious qualities of shack life. As they did when coughing out, members frequently spoke of joyous moments, too, which inform, even if they are not reducible to, movement politics. Some of these joyous moments stemmed from taking pride in one's community, the social bonds formed among kith and kin, the strides made in organizing a soccer match or beauty pageant, mediating a conflict, or setting up a neighborhood watch. What I have argued is that Abahlali's living politics responds to liberalization by borrowing from the liberation struggle through ritual practices, symbolic kinship, and producing globally networked publics. These ritual practices, at the same time, draw upon the power invested in new technologies. I do not suggest that Abahlali's idiom of sacrifice paints a totalizing picture of South Africa's first post-apartheid generation. However, it does lend insight into how sacrifice— and politics more broadly—might be seen as neither wholly entangled in the market or outside of it. It also points to how "born frees," who politicians of all stripes have been wooing as an emerging electoral constituency, are taking up the mantle of sacrifice as their own. At the same time, it is important to register Nzuza's death. In the same week Nzuza was shot, a South African government report estimated a 218 percent increase in police brutality in 2013, including 4,047 cases of assault, and 275 deaths in custody.[16] The highest number of political killings since 1994 is in the province of KwaZulu-Natal, where Cato Manor is located (Bruce 2014). Many more assassinations have followed. Yet it is worth putting in broader context that the vulnerability of black youth to surveillance, arrest, and violence by police has become a flashpoint of protests in cities across the globe.[17] What Abahlali's idiom lastly might suggest is that violent policing is not a likely strategy for demobilizing protest. In South Africa, the dramatic hearings of the Truth and Reconciliation Commission, the hopeful adoption of a new Constitution, and a massive overhauling of the security cluster have signaled an end to some arbitrary functions of state sovereignty. But it is not an end that had been popularly imagined.

Living Politics Revisited

The preceding chapters of this book have examined the everyday practices and interactions that constitute collective self-identification as "the poor," premised upon shared material life across historically race-based communities. Focusing on the elements of fire, water, air, and land reveals how the urban poor transform material into technological innovations, which build communities and collective politics. Living politics reimagines, leverages, and even redirects power within the compromised confines of liberal democracy. The politicization and criminalization of material life also serves as a site of cultivating new practices, for instance, through the courts and digital media technologies. Along with building shelters, occupying land, and illicitly

Residents voting in a branch launch in Durban, 2008. (Photo by author)

connecting to the electric grid, these are forms of community organizing that constitute Abahlali's living politics. This politics, while aiming to make urban life viable and secure by accessing infrastructure, also seeks to make visible and audible those whose very appearance is deemed illicit (Gordon 2012).

Mapping the production of political and criminal agents points to a need for understanding the infrastructural imagination at multiple scales. Although embedded in local practices, interactions, and identities, element of living politics circulate as globally intelligible icons and idioms of popular discontent in broader geographies of anger (Appadurai 2006). Fire, water, air, and land are being taken up by a new generation of activists beyond South Africa who find themselves formally included, but effectively shut out of mainstream politics and waged work in the context of liberalism. As mass unemployment relegates more and more people to the shadows of urban life, fire on the streets appears, for instance, where ungovernable populations threaten power, and where communities are bereft of infrastructure.

Activists are sharing their politics cross regionally and transnationally—as previous generations did, but through novel channels and circuits. Through networks in part made possible by Internet-enabled cell phones, Abahlali members have real-time linkages to activists taking to the streets in countries such as Egypt, Haiti, and the United States. Residents of an Abahlali-affiliated community can upload photographs of a burning road blockade to their website, which may be viewed nearly instantaneously by affiliates in Russia, the United Kingdom, or Turkey. Abahlali shares news of shack conflagrations in India, Brazil, and Kenya, where many poor residents rely on open flame and where some delegates of the movement have traveled for invited lectures, workshops, and conferences. These exchanges suggest how living politics, like the dynamics of power it mirrors, is locally enacted yet globally entangled.

What I want to capture by analyzing living politics, is the contradiction and ambivalence in the ways that people experience the post-apartheid world, and how people use the materials of their lives to respond to its conditions. Some residents I talked to are saving money to send a child to an elite school, something previously not allowed. Others are protesting water disconnections and yet see themselves as benefiting from previously unavailable social grants. Many feel alienated from mainstream political parties, and yet they do not deny their ability to vote as a real and recent gain. As this suggests, future nostalgia, longing for a foreseeable time that "replaces untoward pasts" (Piot 2010, 20), has been replaced by a critical reappraisal of the material forms that have made South Africa a globalized liberal democracy.

Notes

Introduction

1. Nearly every resident I spoke with told me this story of the birth of the Kennedy Road settlement. However, historical records suggest that the Kennedy Road settlement was founded earlier—in the late 1970s—on land classified as "Indian" under apartheid. The mythical founding date echoes the centrality of the mid-1980s and opposition to white control over the land to imaginaries of post-apartheid urban struggle.

2. By "late liberation struggle," I am referring the mid-1980s until the official fall of apartheid in 1994.

3. The Gini-coefficient is a widely used metric of economic inequality that represents statistical distributions of income. In some, especially rural areas, the unemployment rate is estimated as high as 65 percent.

4. Estimated at 5.2 million, or 10 percent of the population. Some sources suggest 16 percent of the population, or 8.3 million, roughly the entire city of New York.

5. Membership is highly variable and fluid.

6. Se-Ann Rall, "Council Vows to Get Rid of Shack-Dwellers," *The Mercury*, October 30, 2006.

7. Asinamali later was used by anti-apartheid workers and township residents in the 1960s, as well as today in Johannesburg by the Social Movements Indaba (SMI).

8. The residents who ended up in Arnett Drive were those who fell through the cracks of a forced relocation to KwaMashu.

9. See Chance 2004.

10. As a mass movement and political party that inhabits most major apparatuses of the democratic state, the ANC has insisted upon centralization (see also Brown 2016). Under apartheid, as a matter of political and physical survival, the exiled leadership called for cohesion and discipline among factions in the movement: exiles, political prisoners, "inziles," and the rank and file working within South Africa. Throughout its negotiations with the National Party, the ANC explicitly rejected federalism as a structure of the new democratic government, not least because of the threat posed during the transition by regionally based parties like the Zulu-nationalist Inkatha Freedom Party (IFP), and organizations such as the white racist militia, the AWB. The government then has a three-tiered structure: national, provincial, and regional bodies, with the ANC regional offices acting as intermediaries. Though other tiers may act locally,

with the ability to pass provincial legislation, the national government (the party of the ANC) retains a hold on most law-making functions of the state and dictates policy, ranging from the construction of RDP homes to macroeconomic matters. Following the end of apartheid, the ANC also has occasionally purged its ranks of noncomplying members of the party, most notably over economic policies that affect "the poor." Activist networks, such as Abahlali have often mirrored the structures of the ANC. The Poor People's Alliance, for instance, has national executive, provincial, and regional bodies, with local branch committees acting as intermediaries to communities.

11. Michael Wines, "Shantytown Dwellers in South Africa Protest Sluggish Pace of Change," *New York Times*, December 26, 2005, http://www.nytimes.com/2005/12/25/world/africa/shantytown-dwellers-in-south-africa-protest-sluggish-pace-of-change.html.

12. "Five Protests a Day in SA—ISS," *News24*, February 7, 2014, http://www.news24.com/SouthAfrica/News/Five-protests-a-day-in-SA-ISS-20140207. Counting protests is a matter of contestation between residents and state agents. Some scholars, citing police reports, reckon as many as ten thousand protests per year nationwide (Lee 2009).

13. Notably, the Anti-Privatization Forum from Gauteng, the Concerned Citizens Forum from KwaZulu-Natal, and the Anti-Eviction Campaign from the Western Cape.

14. Stefaans Brümmer, "A New War for the Allegiance of the Poor," *Mail & Guardian*, September 6, 2002.

15. Ibid.

16. The iterations of this antagonism, circulated prior to the march in news media and the academy, are now as familiar in activist circles as among members of the South African Parliament. In brief, the ANC committed itself to economic liberalization, influenced by the fall of communism and state socialism in Eastern Europe, but chiefly under pressure from corporations, and international institutions like the World Bank. As early as 1990, the ANC undertook negotiations with the World Bank, hammering out plans for the repayment of apartheid-era loans. In 1995, the ANC officially abandoned its early plans for development with the RDP (Reconstruction and Development Plan) and replaced it with a centrist development plan known as GEAR (Growth, Employment, and Redistribution). Effectively the ANC election platform, the RDP, was widely hailed as "pro-poor" and consistent with the redistributive principles of the 1955 Freedom Charter, which articulated core principles of the ANC and anti-apartheid movements.

GEAR, critics claimed, was "antipoor," representing the worst of "Washington Consensus" neoliberalism. As one veteran anti-apartheid activist put it, GEAR is founded on a trickle-down logic, wherein "if you can't pay, you can't have it." During the summit march, protesters on the streets and the news referred to this policy shift, in part with songs and slogans tied to both the anti-apartheid struggle and the antiglobalization movement, aimed at GEAR, the United States, the ANC, and the World Summit on Sustainable Development (dubbed by activists the "W$$D"). Activists also proposed that new state policies and regulations against the poor have continuities with the past: "When we fought for our rights under apartheid they imprisoned us. Now, when we fight for our rights, they still imprison us. . . . What has changed?" (South African Press Association, "March Stopped Outside Wits," August 25, 2002.)

17. In part, these explanations arose from a problem of scale. Although macro efforts to track protests on the streets can be revealing, it failed to capture why residents, from their own perspectives, were protesting in the first place.

18. "NIA Launches Probe into Riots," *Sunday Times*, May 29, 2005.

19. Agence France Presse, "Mbeki Warns of 'Threat' from Township Rioting in South Africa," May 25, 2005.

20. Ibid.

21. The term "third force," moreover, recalls the apartheid regime's use of *swart gevaar* (black threat in Afrikaans) and *rooi gevaar* (red, or communist, threat). Often used interchangeably, under apartheid, these terms were meant to capture the imminent threat posed to the race-based state. Formerly tied to "blackness" and "communism," today these threats are tied to the criminalized activist networks of "the poor."

In Durban, protesters in 2005 began to appropriate and redeploy the term "third force." As Abahlali president S'bu Zikode observed, street protests in Durban and other towns and cities may not be formally organized with each other, but they are related, insofar as those identifying as the poor articulate similar concerns about life in shack settlements. Zikode wrote an article that has been translated and published internationally in multiple languages titled "We Are the Third Force" (November 2005, http://abahlali.org/node/17). In his article, Zikode proposes that, in fact, there are four "forces" that have given rise to living politics: (1) the struggle against apartheid; (2) the promise of democratic citizenship; (3) material life in shack settlements; and (4) a future redemptive politics of the poor:

> Those in power are blind. . . . My appeal is that leaders who are concerned about peoples' lives must come and stay at least one week in the *jondolos* (shacks). They must feel the mud. They must share 6 toilets with 6,000 people. They must dispose of their own refuse while living next to the dump. They must come with us while we look for work. They must chase away the rats and keep the children from knocking the candles. They must care for the sick when there are long queues for the tap. . . . We are driven by the Third Force, the suffering of the poor. Our betrayers are the Second Force. The First Force was our struggle against apartheid. The Third Force will stop when the Fourth Force comes.

22. "The KwaZulu-Natal Elimination and Prevention of Re-emergence of Slums Act, 2007," *Extraordinary Provincial Gazette of KwaZulu-Natal*, August 2, 2007, available at http://abahlali .org/files/KZN%20Slums%20Act.pdf.

23. Rall, "Council Vows to Get Rid of Shack-Dwellers."

24. As I discuss further in chapter 5, despite having been presented as a minor figure in international news coverage, President Jacob Zuma's role was hotly debated in South Africa, as has been the "Zuma factor" in the pogroms. Zuma had ousted Thabo Mbeki earlier that year as ANC president. Reports have circulated of attackers singing Zuma's controversial trademark song, "Bring Me My Machine Gun." Some of the shacks that were demolished were tagged with pro-Zuma graffiti, and Zuma's rallies have often taken on a decidedly ethnic character, with his supporters wearing "100% Zulu Boy" T-shirts.

25. Touching on classic theoretical debates, political anthropologists have analyzed how democracy is constituted by civic participation in public life (Arendt 1994); the distribution of sovereign power (Schmitt [1932] 1996; Foucault 2006), and state-civil society relations (Hegel [1820] 1949; Marx [1932] 1978; Gramsci 1971). Recent scholarship, notably reflecting on the criminalization of politics, has been dedicated to examining the nature of prerogative power in postcolonial liberal democracies. Partha Chatterjee, looking at slums in Bombay, has argued that anticolonial liberation struggles were waged and mass culture forged upon the notion that democracy would diminish, if not cancel the violent and arbitrary functions of the state (Chatterjee 2004). Though

democratic transitions have constituted new relations between states and citizens, prerogative power has not so much been destroyed as redeployed with new targets and mechanisms of force and consent. Many theorists in the mid-2000s attempted to describe liberal democratic prerogative through two interlocking theoretical assertions: governmentality and biopolitics (Agamben 1998; Brown 1995; Chatterjee 2004; Mbembe 2006; Sharma and Gupta 2006). Significant to the early stages of my research, and rarely noted, is that Foucault dedicates his 1976 lecture on governmentality to a reading of *The Prince*, which is the culmination of his thinking on Machiavelli that appears in all his work as it shifts from disciplinary power to its intersection with regulatory mechanisms and the role of the state.

According to Foucault, *The Prince* never ceased to function as an object of implicit and explicit rejection, relative to which "the whole literature on government established its standpoint" (Foucault 2006, 132). In the sixteenth century as well as in his rediscovery in the eighteenth century, it is said by Machiavelli detractors and supporters alike that the prince, that *Ur* figure of traditional sovereignty, stood in a relation of singularity and externality, and thus also transcendence, to his principality (Foucault 2006, 132). This has a threefold meaning. *First*, that the prince's link to his principality is purely synthetic without a fundamental, essential, natural, or juridical tether between the prince, the territory, and its people. This synthetic-ness, that is to say arbitrariness, Foucault in *Discipline and Punish* regards only as fully realized after the figurative and literal beheading of the king in the eighteenth century. *Second*, that the prince's link to his principality is fragile and continually under threat—of revolution or other usurpations—from outside enemies and from the people within, who have no a priori reason to accept his rule. *Third*, the objective of the exercise of power is to strengthen and protect that fragile and synthetic link between the prince, the territory, and the people by identifying dangers and developing techniques for manipulating relations of force.

Against traditional princely sovereignty, the anti-Machiavellian literature calls for an "art of government" premised on self-governing and morality, the family, and above all the economy (Foucault 2006, 135). Where the princely raison d'être is to draw a line between his power and any other, the "art of government" literature tries to establish a continuity of power that flows both "upwards and downwards" (Foucault 2006, 134). Upward, that is, to the sovereign and downward to the family. Here, historically speaking, we find an introduction of the modern notion of economy, which in Machiavelli's day meant the proper management of households. Later in the eighteenth century, the term would enter the realm of governmental practice, a new field of intervention with new (biopolitical) targets. Unlike the Machiavellian prince who exercises sovereign power on a territory and its people, the literature on the "art of government" concerns itself with what Foucault calls "the right disposition of things" (Foucault 2006, 135). Backed by a "science of statistics" and sociological typologies, government then becomes concerned with "men in their relations, their links, their imbrication with those other things which are wealth, resources means of subsistence, their territory with its specific qualities, climate, irrigation, fertility; men in their relation to that other kind of things, customs, habits, ways of acting and thinking; lastly men in their relation to that other kind of things, accidents and misfortunes such as famine, epidemics, death" (Foucault 2006, 136).

The purpose of the "art of government" is not merely to manage these things, but to do so in a way that is directed toward a pursuit of perfection and an "intensification for the processes which it directs," where tactics—including law itself—is deployed to arrange things so that the ends of government may be achieved (Foucault 2006, 137). It means, in short, an increasing rationalization of the state and centrality of political economy, which depends on the wealth and welfare of a "new subject": the population. In a later lecture, Foucault explains that between the regulatory and disciplinary mechanisms of governmental power, which, respectively, targets the body and the population, is "life," the biological processes of man-as-species.

Foucault read Machiavelli as a cipher for the emergence of new disciplinary and regulatory mechanisms, which he concludes must be the enemy of princely prerogative. Agamben, by contrast, reads in Machiavelli an "inner solidarity" (Agamben 2005, 46). Citing the *Discourses on Livy*, Agamben refers to the suspension of the law in the Roman republic (*Iustitium*). Against the *tumultus* of the plebs, Machiavelli advises "breaking the order to save it," which Nissan describes as a "vacuum" and which Carl Schmitt characterizes as a "quasi-dictatorship" (Agamben 2005, 46). Agamben sides with Nissan, and proposes that the state of exception is an indeterminate zone, wherein the law is not abrogated (abolished or repealed) but suspended, a legal suspension of the law premised upon stripping certain subjects of their legal and political status.

One of the few examples of biopower offered by Michel Foucault is a nineteenth-century slum: the working-class housing estate. For Foucault, the layout of a housing estate, which at least in theory localizes poor families (one to a house) and individuals (one to a room), and their spatial location within the town, is aimed at controlling bodies, making individuals and their behavior more visible and policing more possible. In addition to these disciplinary measures aimed at bodies, there are regulatory mechanisms, which apply to the population. These "encourage patterns of saving related to housing, to the rendering of accommodations and, in some cases, their purchase. Health-insurance systems, old-age pensions, rules on hygiene that guarantee optimal longevity of the population; the pressures that the very organization of the town brings to bear on sexuality and therefore procreation; child care, education, et cetera" (Foucault 2003, 251). As discussed in chapter 4, the working-class housing estate was designed, perhaps above all, to remove the urban poor from crowded back-alley slums, long regarded as criminal and ungovernable. Filling the housing estate with bodies and populations typically required the destruction of an existing slum and the forced removal of its inhabitants, which could be said to have as much to do with princely prerogative as its gentler counterpart in "the art of government." In time, as I completed my research, what I found relevant in these debates about biopower is not so much the overarching paradigm of the prison, the hospital, or the housing estate put forward by Foucault, but rather the suggestion that democratic state prerogative is characterized by welfare-granting regulations *and* relations of force that often abrogate the law.

26. See also United Nations Human Settlements Programme 2003; Seabrook 1996; Amis and Lloyd 1990; Obudho and Mhlanga 1988; Tranber Hansen and Vaa 2004; and Patton 1998.

27. In South African public discourse, the term "ungovernable" implies operating without centralization to break the law, and forcibly targeting material manifestations of the political and economic order. Ungovernability, therefore, stands in tension with theories of democratic representation that emphasize becoming counted by state agents through legitimating legal rights, or operating within the bounds of the law. The ungovernable are a close relative of autonomists who practice in "the art of not being governed" (Scott 2009), but seek political inclusion and economic redistribution by becoming visible and audible to state agents. I suggest that ungovernability is characteristic to new activist networks, crowds, and insurgencies beyond South Africa, which have correlates and coordinates with mobilizations that preceded them. Yet these groupings also act upon new terrains. A woman burning a tire on the streets in Kennedy Road, for instance, may appear before a court as a respondent, calling upon rights in national policy and legislation. She may build a shack for her family on occupied state land, yet present her community as dutiful constituents to a local councillor. She may illicitly connect energy

supplies, while praying to God to give her a job to feed the prepaid meter. Like all identities, practices, and interactions, they are multiple, and often contradictory, once they are performed as living politics.

28. The "poor" in South Africa is a racialized identity, one constructed in precarious and complex historical ways. But I emphasize that "the poor" is a category under construction, especially by state agents and their corporate partners in post-1994 development projects, which residents of townships and shack settlements are newly politicizing as a collective self-identification. I make this observation not to dichotomize race and class, but rather to suggest how both are implicated in the making of citizenship after apartheid. Race, here, broadly refers to a naturalized system of differentiation tied to the body and kinship. By poverty, I underscore not only an inability to find work or attain certain standards of economic mobility, but also an extreme scarcity of basic infrastructure and other necessities of life, such as housing. Race and poverty, therefore are understood as socially constructed but lived categories that vary across temporal and spatial scales, as well as institutional formations. My work underscores how race and poverty adhere in everyday materials.

Chapter One

1. "Five Protests a Day in SA—ISS," *News24*, February 7, 2014, http://www.news24.com/ SouthAfrica/News/Five-protests-a-day-in-SA-ISS-20140207. Shack fires, like street protests, are difficult to measure, especially as some are not statistically recorded, even if police arrive on the scene. As previously noted, some scholars, citing police reports, reckon as many as 10,000 protests per year nationwide (Lee 2009).

2. Slindile Maluleka, "Electricity Theft Kills Eight Pupils," *IOL*, March 29, 2010, http://www .iol.co.za/news/south-africa/electricity-theft-kills-8-pupils-477860; "Violent Protesters Blamed for Police Use of Force," *eNCA.com*, October 2, 2013, http://www.enca.com/south-africa/violent -protesters-blamed-police-use-force.

3. "Winnie Mandela: South Africa's Divisive Diva," *Guardian*, April 17, 2011, http://www .guardian.co.uk/theobserver/2011/apr/17/observer-profile-winnie-mandela.

4. "Nelson Mandela's Statement from the Dock at the Opening of the Defence Case in the Rivonia Trial," April 20, 1964, available at http://www.anc.org.za/content/nelson-mandelas -statement-dock-rivonia-trial.

5. African National Congress, "Statement to the Truth and Reconciliation Commission," Department of Justice and Constitutional Development website, August 1996, http://www .justice.gov.za/trc/hrvtrans/submit/anctruth.htm.

6. Notably, the Vlakplaas police unit (ibid.).

7. On necklacing, see Moses Mackay, "Necklacing Up in Khayelitsha," *Sowetan*, March 30, 2012, http://www.sowetanlive.co.za/news/2012/03/30/necklacing-up-in-khayelitsha.

8. The Inkatha National Cultural Liberation Movement was founded in 1975, later to become the Inkatha Freedom Party (IFP) in 1990.

9. The state, here, is not a unified totality, but a varied set of hegemonic institutions, discourses, agents, and tactics that must be understood in its absence as much as in its presence (Fanon 1965; Foucault 1991; Gramsci 1971; Rancière 1998).

10. As the movement noted in a press statement: "Abahlali does not condone violence by its members. We define violence as harm to persons. We do not consider burning a tire in

the street, or forming a road blockade to be violence." See "Fact Sheet: Abahlali Laying False Rumors to Rest," Abahlali baseMjondolo website, November 25, 2010, http://abahlali.org/node/ 7599/.

11. On this exchange between the Treatment Action Campaign and Abahlali, see "Abahlali baseMjondolo of the Western Cape Replies to the Treatment Action Campaign," Abahlali base-Mjondolo website, October 13, 2010, http://abahlali.org/node/7364/.

12. Fire on the streets also serves to make visible fire in the home, caused by a lack of electricity. Many activists view burning road blockades and shack conflagrations as interrelated insofar as both arise from constrained political and economic mobility.

13. "Shack Fire Takes a Life in eMmaus," Abahlali baseMjondolo press release, May 1, 2011, http://abahlali.org/node/8022/.

14. "KwaMashu, South Africa's Murder Capital," *Waza Online*, March 1, 2010, https:// wazaonline.com/en/archive/kwamashu-south-africas-murder-capital.

15. "Memorial Service for 16 Year Old Sakhephi Emmanuel Zenda," Abahlali baseMjondolo press release, July 29, 2009, http://abahlali.org/node/5571/.

16. It might also be added between *zoe* and *bios*, which Giorgio Agamben (1998) proposes as a fundamental distinction in modern politics between bare life, or the biological man-as-species, and the citizenry, or those who belong to a common political community. Here, by contrast, the urban poor use life itself to contest demarcations of modern politics.

Chapter Two

1. Natasha Prince, *The Cape Argus*, June 13, 2009, 6.

2. Analysis of political belonging in anthropology has a rich tradition in anthropology. Some of the earliest studies were of so-called nonstate systems (see Malinowski [1922] 1961; Radcliffe-Brown 1940; Fortes and Evans-Pritchard 1940). A resurgence of anthropological interest in political belonging, often critical of previous generations, happened in the 1990s amid debates over national citizenship and globalization (see Anderson [1991] 2006; Brubaker 1998; Chatterjee 1991; Appadurai 1990; Ong 1999; Petryna 2003; Sassen 1996; Tilly 1996). Anthropologists returned to the topic again in the 2000s in studies of how power and sovereignty affects state−citizen relations (see Holston 2008; Trouillot 2003; Li 2007; Benhabib 2002; Rajan 2003; Bhabha 2004; Das et al. 2001; Biehl 2013). Studies of diaspora, as well as the role of race, class, and gender have been central to many of these debates, especially in recent literature (see Stoler 2013; Thomas 2009; Bonilla 2015; Ralph 2015). Drawing from these studies, I focus on how urban citizenship is materialized by water, which itself carries debts of the past particularly as a substance of exchange. I suggest further that urban citizenship emerges from political belonging within a township or shack settlement.

3. In a similar move of retelling colonial history through water, Abahlali members at times recounted the 1838 Battle of Blood River. Pushed out of the Cape Colony by the British, Afrikaner Voortrekkers (pioneers in Afrikaans) invaded the Zulu Kingdom (Dlamini 2001; Guy 2006). The Voortrekkers used the river to protect their flanks against King Dingane's powerful military. By narrating the battle, which ended in the bloody seizure of Zulu territory, Abahlali members link colonial-era belonging to present-day water struggles among the urban poor. In their telling, it was control over water—not merely guns, or bibles—that hastened South Africa's colonization. The Battle of Blood River, in other words, turned not on firepower or the fear of God, but upon waterpower and the fear of thirst.

4. This infrastructure, at times, served to build a labor pool around cities or negotiate with powerful existing precolonial political authorities such as the Zulu Kingdom (Guy 2006).

5. John Locke ([1690] 1980) uses the example of drawing a pitcher of water from a fountain as the moment when a common supply becomes not merely consumed, but possessed.

6. As James Miller writes, "If solid ground has been conventionally associated with reason, water has for centuries been the symbolic element of unreason: 'Madness is the liquid and streaming exterior of rocky reason,' and water an 'infinite, uncertain space,' the oceanic element of 'dark disorder'" (1980, 100). For residents in Abahlali settlements, however, water is what is gathered to establish a home, and evidences the fertility of South Africa, at the same time that it is the vehicle for the arrival of white colonists such as Jan Van Riebeeck in the Cape.

7. The Vaal uprising erupted out of an already tense situation in Transvaal townships and in response to rent increases in Evaton, Sebokeng, Sharpeville, Bophelong, and Biopatong. Violence broke out between protesters and police, which ended in numerous deaths and injuries.

8. "Electricity Cut Off at Mandela Home," *International News*, May 22, 1987, AM cycle.

9. Ibid.

10. Associated Press, "Explosions Cut Electricity in Pretoria," *International News*, November 13, 1981, PM cycle.

11. See also Morris 2011.

12. In 1982, with the passing of the Black Local Authorities Act, the apartheid regime established a system of racially segregated local councils, which propped up black councillors to oversee and mediate urban township governance. Until that legislation was passed, local councils were white-only. Black local councillors, some who were targeted for assassination, were perceived as apartheid stooges, spies, and collaborators.

13. David Crary, "Soweto City Council Drops Campaign to Crush Rent Boycott," *International News*, December 9, 1988, PM cycle.

14. "Electricity Cut Off at Mandela Home."

15. Ibid.

16. Tom Cohen, "Government to Cut Lights, Water to Some Townships," *International News*, August 30, 1990, PM cycle.

17. "S. Africa to Cut Services in Defiant Areas," *Los Angeles Times*, August 30, 1990, http://articles.latimes.com/1990-08-30/news/mn-618_1_essential-services.

18. "South Africa's Local Councils in Crisis: Conservative Officials Cut Off Water Supplies to Nearby Townships, Fueling National Debate," *Christian Science Monitor*, October 30, 1990. Liberation activists' efforts to demobilize the rent and services boycotts could be seen as compatible with the interests of apartheid during this period. However, as Desmond Tutu said at the time, the terms of future payment plans could only be agreed upon if activists and community leaders were given greater freedom of movement through the townships, and "not harassed or detained as they consulted with residents" (ibid.). Selling water as a "nonracial" commodity, in other words, could be seen as facilitating key activist leaders' access to the movements' base and on a consolidation around that leadership. In effect, the white councils had to legitimate the exercise of localized democratic participation.

19. David Crary, "Soweto City Council Drops Campaign to Crush Rent Boycott," *International News*, December 9, 1988, PM cycle.

20. South African Press Association, "ANC Expresses 'Serious Concern' after Councils Cut Off Services," October 19, 1990.

21. See www.worldbank.org and Chance 2004.

22. The General Mining Corporation owned Ermelo at the time. The General Mining

Corporation later would become Gencor, Ltd., and eventually the energy company Engen. The corporation was described by the *New York Times* "a base for apartheid profits"; December 18, 1991, http://www.nytimes.com/1991/12/18/business/a-base-for-post-apartheid-profits.html.

23. "South Africa's Local Councils in Crisis."

24. Ibid.

25. Ibid.

26. Ibid.

27. Ibid.

28. Ibid.

29. Ibid.

30. "Nelson Mandela's Speech to Launch the Masakhane Campaign," February 25, 1995, available at http://www.anc.org.za/content/nelson-mandelas-speech-launch-masakhane-cam paign.

31. Ibid.

32. African Eye News Service (South Africa), "20,000 Residents in the Dark After Not Paying Bills," May 20, 1997.

33. Ibid.

34. Ibid.

35. Ibid.

36. For more on debt and infrastructure, see Ruiters 2002. Also see Rustomjee 2006.

37. Residents paying a flat rate of R70 per month (approximately $7) suddenly were charged between R400 and R500 (approximately $40 or $50), an amount completely unaffordable for many, even those with formal sector jobs.

38. "Water Privatization Test Case 'A Total Debacle,'" *Mail & Guardian*, November 16, 2001.

39. Ibid.

40. Ibid.

Chapter Three

1. Social scientific approaches to effervescence, and the fizzing "social glue" that it emits, have relied upon the dyadic relationship between the individual and collective (Durkheim [1912] 1995; Habermas 1984; Arendt 1998). I emphasize the role of nonhuman, climatic agents in shaping this relationship by analyzing how practices in poor African, Indian, and Coloured communities transform particulates in the air.

2. This structure was in use from 2005 until about 2014 when, partly in response to the emergence of the Economic Freedom Fighters (EFF), Abahlali elected to cease imitating the ANC national structures and invent their own, but without the military overtones that the EFF has espoused.

3. Arguing against Elaine Scarry's insoluble separation between language and body, Judith Butler suggests the forceful ways in which words might actually constitute the physical body and its corresponding social identities, as much as threaten their existence (Butler 1997, 13). According to J. L. Austin, language has not only direct effects on the body through illocutionary utterances, but also foreshadows its effects through perlocutionary utterances. The address of an Other brings the addressee in material existence—that is to say, at once linguistically, socially and physically—not simply by being recognized, "but in a prior sense, of being recognizable" (Butler 1997, 5). Language constitutes the body but also invades and takes residence in it. As Butler suggests, "One need only consider the way in which the history of having been called an

injurious name is embodied, how the words enter the limbs, craft the gesture, live and thrive in and as the flesh of the addressee" (Butler 1997, 159). Using performative utterances in narrativizing memory may suggest the ways that words might heal the wounds created by a violence done to the body, identity, and community. In Abahlali, and especially through the practice of coughing out, words are seen as reconstituting the speaker, as language "composes, without determining the cultural sense of the body, and . . . the body disorient[s] that cultural sense" (Butler 1997, 159). Members' voices and conceptions of violence then again are reaffirmed as a having a central place in gathering memory through a collective practice of coughing out.

4. The Dlamini King Brothers no longer live in Kennedy Road. They were among the residents chased out of the settlement during the 2009 attacks examined in chapter 5.

5. Michel Foucault, in his studies of modern sexuality, characterizes incitement as pleasurably proliferating in discourse that which is nevertheless banned (Foucault 1978). While singing in this way might be viewed as a reinscription of mine bosses' power, performers view it as an assertion of masculinity.

6. Abahlali members identify not only as Anglican and African Zionist but also as Methodist and Catholic.

7. Although Christianity is the dominant religious background of members within the movement, some settlements are made up of largely Hindu or Muslim constituents. In these contexts, such as Zinzi's community, coughing out may take on another valence altogether, depending on the constellation of religious persuasions within any given settlement. Christian traditions in South Africa are incorporated into secular political life and reflect political theological underpinnings of activist networks from the ANC to Abahlali.

8. "Abahlali baseMjondolo Attacked in eShowe by Councillor Warlords," Abahlali baseMjondolo press release, August 18, 2009, http://abahlali.org/node/5646/.

9. Pseudonyms are used for Sisipho and Bulelani. The account of their experiences, including quotations, draws on Chance 2010.

10. Recent literature on pollution in postindustrial and impoverished contexts in the United States, likewise, captures the spirit of this critique (Taylor 2015; Walley 2013; Fortun 2014).

Chapter Four

1. State agents in different regions called the camps by different names. Officially, they were called "temporary relocation areas" in Cape Town, "transit camps" in Durban, and "decant areas" in Johannesburg. In spite of this semiotic variation—or obfuscation—they are materially alike.

2. Transit camps to house the urban poor are an increasingly international phenomenon: camps have been established in Brazil, Angola, and Kenya. See Huchzermeyer 2004.

3. At the time of my research, little was publicly known of the camps by dint of their location on invisible peripheries of the city and the dearth of scholarly and journalistic inquiry about their conditions.

4. To examine how residents like Monique and her neighbors use the land to establish territory, I draw from theories of urban space, studies of informal dwelling, and research on postcolonial power (Appadurai 2006; Pieterse 2008; Brenner et al. 2011; Bertelsen, Tvedten, and Roque 2013; Harms 2013; Huchzermeyer 2011; Fennel 2015; Holston 2008; Gupta 2012; Rao 2012; Ross 2010; Roy 2011; Pithouse 2006; von Schnitzler 2013; Cousins et al. 2013). Across these literatures, scholars—particularly those working on the African continent—have emphasized two interlocking theoretical assertions to characterize contemporary forms of territorial sovereignty:

namely, governmentality and biopolitics (Breckinridge 2014; Chari 2006; Ferguson 2006; Chatterjee 2004; Mbembe 2003; Hansen and Stepputat 2005; Piot 2010). As previously noted, one of the few, and rarely noted, examples offered by Michel Foucault is the nineteenth-century housing project. Transit camps, which share a few of its features, illustrate how these large-scale institutional processes work intimately together at the level of urban land and housing. However, Foucault does not attend to how the urban poor transform housing projects.

5. Rosalie De Bruijn, "AbM Launches Right to the City Campaign in Cape Town," Abahlali baseMjondolo website, May 30, 2010, http://abahlali.org/node/6750.

6. Quoted in Huchzermeyer 2006, 47.

7. "Breaking New Ground: A Comprehensive Plan for the Development of Sustainable Human Settlements," August 2004, available at http://abahlali.org/files/Breaking%20new%20ground%20New_Housing_Plan_Cabinet_approved_version.pdf.

8. Insofar as water and land fall under contractual relationships with the post-apartheid state, these elements materialize citizenship. However, unlike water, which is posited as a "special kind of property," access to land is regarded as a right to be progressively realized—not a basic life necessity.

9. See also Kerry Chance, Marie Huchzermeyer, and Mark Hunter, "Listen to the Shack-dwellers," *Mail & Guardian*, June 24, 2009, https://mg.co.za/article/2009-06-24-listen-to-the-shackdwellers.

10. Lennox Mabaso, "Mabaso: Slums Bill Not a Zimbabwe-Style 'Operation Murambatsvina,'" *The Witness*, July 18, 2007, available at http://abahlali.org/node/1720/. Lennox Mabaso was then the spokesperson for the MEC for Housing, Local Government, and Traditional Affairs. His article included quotations from the MEC.

11. "Operation Murambatsvina Comes to KZN," Abahlali baseMjondolo press release, June 21, 2007, http://www.abahlali.org/node/1629.

12. "Breaking New Ground," p. 7.

13. "Jo'burg Cleans Out Inner City Slums," *IOL*, November 4, 2002, http://www.iol.co.za/news/south-africa/jo-burg-cleans-out-inner-city-slums-1.31118#.UeHAekTNob0.

14. "Safety and Crime in South Africa," *SouthAfrica-Travel.net*, http://www.southafrica-travel.net/miscellaneous/southafrica_safety.html, accessed July 12, 2013.

15. S'bu Zikode, "We Are the Third Force," Abahlali baseMjondolo website, November 2005, http://abahlali.org/node/17.

16. The original plans for the N2 Gateway were modified over time, not least in response to the rotation and sacking of elected officials and project partners. The purpose here, in other words, is not to measure the extent that policy is different from its enactments on the ground, for it will be by definition. Rather, the plans lend insight into the pragmatics of a "world-class city" articulated at various levels of the state. For residents of Symphony Way, the plans—in part, made public by community participation exercises—are cited as necessary to understanding why they, in the first place, occupied unfinished houses and built a shack settlement at the N2 Gateway site.

Of the twenty-five thousand homes under construction, the majority were to accrue value for investors. Rental and bonded units were too costly for shack dwellers like Monique and her neighbors. In part, their exclusion was by design: the Breaking New Ground policy document identifies a middle-income population, households from R3,500 to R7,000 per month (approximately $332 to $665 USD), slipping through the cracks between private and governmental housing markets. The inaugural residents of the "low-cost" rentals went on rent boycott for several years, after Thubelisha failed to repair major defects, including huge cracks in the walls, leaking roofs, and faulty keys. The keys issued to residents could open not only their own flats, but also all the other flats in the building, requiring residents to devise their own systems for security. The bonded units were to be built on land occupied by the long-standing Joe Slovo shack settlement, home to some twenty thousand families. (See also Legassick 2008.)

17. The size of transit camps compares unfavorably to Reconstruction and Development Plan (RDP) houses, the most common concrete block structures built after 1994, which are about 30 square meters with two rooms. They are also smaller than the notorious "matchbox" houses built in townships under apartheid, which were typically 52 square meters with four rooms and a living area.

18. "Operation Murambatsvina Comes to KZN."

19. Pearlie Joubert, "A Lethal Find," *Mail & Guardian*, December 1, 2007, http://www.mg.co .za/articlePage.aspx?articleid=326470&area=/insight/insight__national/.

20. Dianne Hawker, Niemah Davids, and Leila Samodien, "We're Not Budging—Delft Residents," *IOL*, February 7, 2008, http://www.iol.co.za/news/south-africa/were-not-budging ---delft-residents-388404.

21. Ibid.

22. Department of Housing, "N2 Gateway Must Be Protected from Anarchy," February 19, 2008, http://www.info.gov.za/speeches/2008/08022009451002.htm, accessed July 29, 2015.

23. Housing Minister Sisulu, quoted in Verashni Pillay, "Delft Residents Stranded," *News24*, February 19, 2008.

24. Ibid.

25. Ibid.

26. Asa Sokopo, Murray Williams, and Andisiwe Makinana, "Delft Refuse, Resist Eviction," *The Star*, February 19, 2008.

27. "Blockades" would become the signature of the AEC as it expanded branches to Chicago, Detroit, and Los Angeles during the American foreclosure crisis.

28. On other occasions, however, Cassim noted that his mother had had his front teeth removed when he was a child.

29. Residents' proposed plans include in situ upgrades and interim basic services where they live, which reaffirms some of the principles set out in BNG policy.

Chapter Five

1. As noted in previous chapters, *im*Pondo is an ethnicity associated with Mpondoland in the Eastern Cape province on the coast south of KwaZulu-Natal. See, for instance, Nigel Gibson and Raj Patel, "Democracy's Everyday Death: South Africa's Quiet Coup," *Pambazuka News*, October 8, 2009, http://www.pambazuka.org/en/category/features/59322. Also Jeff Guy, "Justice Delayed and Denied for 12 Kennedy Road Accused," *The Mercury*, May 13, 2010, available at http://www.abahlali.org/node/6699; and Losier 2010.

2. This is the estimated number of members currently registered in Abahlali's database. That is, card-carrying members from officially launched branch areas. Databases of previous years have been lost, such that it cannot be determined, on that basis, to what extent and how they may have changed or been constituted across time. Beyond this, membership, be it to a sports club, church, dance group, union, or social movement entails meaningful practices, organizational principles and criteria, both de facto and codified to varying degrees, elaborate to greater or lesser extents, particular to that social grouping and that change across time.

3. Abahlali members consider the movement operating "underground" until a street protest on Human Rights Day 2010. The street protest was initially banned by the eThekwini Municipality.

4. During one day at court, a group of young men flanking a woman wearing a dress emblazoned with the ANC logo—after loudly identifying herself as an ANC local councillor—approached a reverend standing with Abahlali members shouting, "We can kill you" and other threats, which were captured on video.

5. Thando Mgaga, *The Witness*, October 16, 2009.

6. "The *Mail & Guardian* conducted a survey of the 88 people who signed the attendance register at the 'stakeholders' meeting. Nineteen were provincial government representatives, 12 from the municipality and eight from the police. After subtracting media and representatives of other community policing forums and clusters, the register reflected 14 ANC members, seven South African National Civic Organisation (SANCO) members and seven people claiming to be 'residents' of Kennedy Road. . . . Telephone calls confirmed most of those claiming to be ordinary Kennedy Road residents or inhabitants with ANC affiliations were in fact from other areas, such as the Puntan's Hill, Sydenham Heights and the Foreman Road settlement." Niren Tolsi, "Kennedy Olive Branch a Sham," *Mail & Guardian*, October 11, 2009, http://www.mg.co .za/article/2009-10-11-kennedy-olive-branch-a-sham.

7. On September 28, 2009, students at the University of KwaZulu-Natal organized a small campus meeting to plan for the collection of food, blankets, and clothing for those displaced in the Kennedy attacks. Within hours of this meeting, an organizer received a personal e-mail from the spokesperson for the provincial minister of Safety and Security. Students at the meeting regarded this e-mail as a measure of state intimidation. The e-mail included the quotation in the text, with an attached, and later circulated, press statement.

8. Thanks to Dara Kell and Chris Nizza, filmmakers of *Dear Mandela*, for sharing raw footage of the state press conference and "stakeholders" meeting, and also for their transcribed notes from September 26.

9. Colleagues provided thirty additional transcribed or recorded testimonies. Thanks are due to Kalinca Copello and Francesco Gastaldon for transcribed or recorded copies of testimonies by those who witnessed the attacks, and for clarification and thoughts on these testimonies.

10. Gibson and Patel, "Democracy's Everyday Death."

11. See Nelson Mandela's speech on Heritage Day, 1996: http://www.info.gov.za/speeches/ 1996/960925_0x12696.htm, accessed March 30, 2010.

12. The identity of Xhosa speakers breaks down further into ethnic subgroupings that are geographically defined and connected with histories of chieftaincy, largely in the Eastern Cape. The *ama*Pondo are the predominant Xhosa ethnic subgrouping in Kennedy Road. The identity of Zulu speakers has no equivalent subgroupings; however, distinctions often are made between urban and rural Zulus, wherein the former are viewed as ethnically dissipated.

13. As noted, the charismatic rise of President Jacob Zuma, iconically, is associated with a modular ethnic reanimation. Some viewed Mbeki's ouster as a militarization of party politics—at least, metaphorically. Zuma was the former head of the ANC's military wing, Umkhonto we Sizwe (the MK) reflected in his election theme song, the liberation anthem, "Bring me my machine gun" (*Umshini wami*).

Unlike Mandela and other ANC leaders, who hailed from apartheid-era royalty or activist elites, Zuma was known as a "pro-poor populist" with modest roots. Also unlike other ANC leaders in prison or exile, he had scraped out his existence as an "inzile"—living as a soldier underground and on the run. Residents, some who viewed Abahlali as anti-ANC, told me that

Zuma—by virtue of once sharing the same impoverished soil—would mean economic salvation for shack dwellers in Durban, for he was to pay tribute to his ancestral home.

14. In Cape Town in 2009, in another regional and racial context, two Abahlali affiliates—one Coloured, the other Xhosa—were targeted with petrol bombs.

15. Online and in local newspapers, Abahlali issued strong statements against ethnonationalism, and organized public marches. In one of their most widely circulated statements, Abahlali said, "The anger of the poor can go in many directions." Because Abahlali's own mobilizations were premised on popular effervescent mobilizations, they knew that the kith and kin networks of poor communities in Durban were living and breathing entities. They were intimately connected to each other, and, as such—through rumor, cell phone text message, or/ and technologies—could animate effervescent ungovernability on the streets, whether toward pro-poor populism or toward fiery ethnonationalism.

16. The first Abahlali press release about the armed attacks, published on September 27, 2009, reported a lack of clarity on the number of deaths, suggesting that anywhere between two and five people were killed and that two of the dead might have been the attackers.

17. State agents, in particular local security forces and the local ANC councillor, had their own stakes in this battle.

18. Many in the settlement attributed *ukubambisana* to the presence of a provincial crime intelligence officer, who had been based regularly in the Kennedy settlement since 2008. As noted, he told me he cut his teeth in intelligence during the 1980s in southern KwaZulu-Natal. The fact of his presence alone inspired talk among some residents about whether he was investigating not gang activities, but Abahlali's activities. In 2005, in the wake of so-called service delivery protests and the movement's emergence in Kennedy Road, the National Intelligence Agency announced their intention to identify instigators across the country. Most residents, however, welcomed the provincial crime intelligence officer as a sympathetic intermediary to the local police. The officer was often at Kennedy—in homes, in shebeens, at the Community Hall, in the Abahlali Office—sharing food, talking with residents and responding to incidents in his capacity as the police. For years before his arrival, the local police refused to respond to calls from residents or to go inside the settlement. If a woman was beaten by her boyfriend—as the woman I stood with on the road was—she would be told to go to the Hall or walk to the police station to report the crime. Police would not come to her home.

19. A meeting and mediation was held at the local police station with Abahlali leaders and the provincial crime intelligence officer present. The Forum was released, and the incident declared resolved by the two parties, who walked home together peacefully.

20. Like the Zuma-aligned police commissioner who devised it, the "shoot-to-kill" policy originated from the murder capital of KwaZulu-Natal.

21. Richard Davies, "Criminals in the Dwang, Warns Deputy Minister," *Mail & Guardian*, July 1, 2009, https://mg.co.za/article/2009-07-01-criminals-in-the-dwang-warns-deputy-minister.

22. David Smith, "South Africa Considers 'Shoot to Kill' Policing Ahead of World Cup," *Guardian*, September 16, 2009, https://www.theguardian.com/world/2009/sep/16/south-africa-police-world-cup.

23. Abahlali-affiliated settlements demobilize and remobilize with regularity, although some have sustained their connections to the movement for the past decade. By demobilization, I mean that the branch no longer holds regular meetings, pays dues, or attends Abahlali events. Some demobilized branches, however, will continue to have standing elected committee members, and participate irregularly, or on an individual basis. Abahlali regularly dis-

cusses demobilized communities and at times complains that settlements only join the movement when they are undergoing an immediate crisis, such as the threat of an eviction. The most routinely cited reasons for demobilization are consistent with what I have observed since 2006. These reasons include forced eviction, often accompanied by gutting defeats in drawn out court battles, and explicit repression in the form of sanctioned police violence by police or security forces. Xenophobic pogroms, which target movement members, have also resulted in demobilization. Frequently, when demobilization occurs, members take up participation in other community-based activities, notably Pentecostal churches or political parties.

24. In addition to the upgrading project in Kennedy, Abahlali was negotiating with the ANC-led municipality via an NGO called Public Participation Trust, one of the many post-apartheid organizations to which the government outsourced its technocratic governance. The NGOs were the infrastructural "middlemen" between state agents and residents. These negotiations resulted in the municipality earmarking fourteen Abahlali-affiliated settlements for new infrastructures, including electricity in Kennedy Road and five other settlements. Kennedy would be included in a permanent upgrading project, which meant that houses would be built on site, and ideally residents could stay where they had lived for many years. Amid street protests in 2005, Kennedy residents had resisted being forcibly relocated to distant sites, where access to jobs, transportation, shops, and other urban amenities would prove a challenge. At the same time, Abahlali was in negotiations with provincial state agents across political parties to address basic infrastructure—notably toilets—as well as corruption in the allocation of placements in new housing projects.

25. Two women once affiliated with Abahlali, but no longer, stood nearby watching the scene. They waited for two of the Forum members to finish with the police and the crime intelligence officer, as one woman wanted to report that her boyfriend, a taxi driver, who had beaten her in the past, now was threatening to hunt her down and kill her. The local police already had a call earlier at an intersection near Kennedy and close to near the local Councillor's office, where a crowd of about fifty had gathered on the street, with no ambulance present, around the body of a bloodied young man, face down on the pavement.

26. The time is estimated by witnesses, even as they are consistent across separate accounts: for example, KRDC members said between 11:15 p.m. and midnight, the first man reported at about 11:30 p.m.; the family reported sometime before midnight; and the women reported 11:20 p.m. These include statements from witnesses unaffiliated with any committee—whether the KRDC, Abahlali, or the Forum—as well as Abahlali members, leaders, or their families.

27. A friend phoned the next day to say that the armed men did return, at an unknown hour, early in the morning. When they did not find her, they turned to looting, taking clothes, furniture and other belongings. Later that day, her home was demolished. Her friend said that local police officers were present, but did not stop the men. A man, neighboring one of those killed, saw members of the armed group outside his shack, moving silhouettes carrying sticks. He, and those staying with him, remained inside, hiding. They heard the "screams" outside. They called the police. All fled the settlement at daybreak. After the state press conference and "stakeholders" meeting in the Hall, on September 28, he returned to pick up some belongings. Two men came to his shack, warning, "There are still fights here. People are looking for you. They say you were working with the Forum." At about 6:30 p.m., a few hours later, two police officers knocked on his door. They asked what happened. He told them he did not work with the Forum—which he did not—and did not know. His home was burned down later that night; he lost everything, while he was staying with a friend outside Kennedy Road.

28. Note that a "hundred men" is an estimate, cited by separate witnesses. However, some

said "three hundred men" in total; still others, said "too many" to count. Variance also could be due to the different locations of the settlement that witnesses were positioned. One man also reports that one of the throngs of armed men carried "a bucket" toward the Simunye shop, which he said is associated with *muthi*, a protection in a call to "war."

29. The following night, at 8:30 p.m. on September 27, the Zikodes' shack was demolished, the walls torn down, their belongings stolen or slashed through with bush knives.

At approximately 12:00 midnight, neighbors of the Zikodes—a man, his wife, and their six-year-old child living across the road—awoke to shouts, and saw that armed men were banging on the walls of the food shop. The "mob" came toward his home, throwing bottles. They shouted to him, "We'll finish with the others, then come back to get you." The family hid. Early the next morning at an uncertain hour, walking back to his home, he saw a man from his "village" in the Eastern Cape running—a "mob" was behind him. Fearful, he ran to the nearby Foreman Road settlement, where he called his wife. They left for the Eastern Cape and have not returned to Kennedy. Both have since lost their jobs.

30. The gangs in Kennedy, at that time, were primarily 27s and 28s, the former associated with law-preserving violence and the latter associated with lawmaking violence (Benjamin 1978). See Steinberg 2004.

31. Even though some among them, gathering at the main taxi rank next to the Hall, shouted anti-imPondo slogans, two witnesses said the armed men were not themselves ethnically homogeneous. For instance, one said, "They were Zulus, Bhacas, Xhosas, all kinds of people."

32. Some said singing "The Struggle Allows It," others said songs that were "calls to war," or "warlike songs," or "aggressive songs."

33. One witness said the dog van unit and two officers were from Durban Central.

34. Police from Durban Central, Sydenham, and Inanda stations, witnesses said, were seen later in the night, and early in the morning, as well as in the days that followed.

35. The police were not available to interview at the time of research. However, daily, intensive research entailed the observation of many day-to-day interactions with Sydenham police officers within the settlement and at their police station. These interactions included routine surveillance of residents and of me (shadowing by car, stopping for questioning, etc.). Immediately following the attacks at Kennedy Road, the Sydenham police conducted a violent and bloody raid of a nearby Abahlali-affiliated settlement, Pemary Ridge ("Pemary Ridge under Police Attack Now; Shooting Continues," Abahlali baseMjondolo press release, November 13, 2009, http://www.abahlali.org/node/6032). Beyond these sociological facts, this event history aims to compare the "official" public record with witnesses, residents specifically, across a broad range of affiliations, not the personal perspectives of police officers.

36. Two of the Forum members accompanied the Italian journalist to a meter-taxi around 11:45 p.m. Around 1:00 a.m., the film crew was told by the KRDC to move their private car from the road inside the Hall, where it would be safer. The provincial crime intelligence officer with another Metro van dog unit is said to have returned around 1:00 a.m. This time, he and the Metro police went inside the settlement, following the sound of chanting behind and below the Hall. They returned to the Hall, telling KRDC members that they believed the trouble was over, and departed. When the police vehicles pulled into the road the settlement momentarily "went quiet." Various witnesses saw armed men hide inside shacks, in darkened pathways, and in the bush.

37. Soon thereafter, according to the Youth League president recounting their interaction, the provincial crime intelligence officer pulled up to the fence, near some of the armed men. He

lowered his car window and spoke to the Forum members. The Youth League president asked the officer if it was safe to open the gate to allow camp participants to leave, and whether the armed men planned to hurt them. The officer said, "No, they know who they are looking for." He closed his car window, about to drive away, before an armed man nearby shouted, "Give us S'bu!" The officer opened his window again, and said, "I suggest you all go home and resolve this matter in the morning. You have already heard that Zikode is not here."

38. At this time, the KRDC, still at the Abahlali Office, said the road looked clear for the film crew and some members from other settlements to depart.

39. Another woman and her husband, living in two separate shacks, were both operating *spaza* shops. Away for the weekend, they returned to find their homes and shops destroyed, looted. The husband said the only item he found left in the debris was a document for a car. The next day, they used the car to depart for the Eastern Cape.

Conclusion

1. Nkululeko Nene, "Claim 'Third Force' Behind Settlement Unrest," *Daily News*, October 17, 2013.

2. For a complete list of signatories, see "M&G: Open Letter to James Nxumalo, Senzo Mchunu & Jacob Zuma," Abahlali baseMjondolo website, October 2, 2013, http://abahlali.org/node/12296/.

3. On crime and policing, see also Gillespie 2008 and Hornberger 2013.

4. It should be noted that similar rites apply in many guerilla and gang contexts (Feldman 1991; Aretxaga 2000; Steinberg 2004).

5. "Today We Protest in Cato Crest in Honour of Nelson Mandela," Abahlali baseMjondolo press release, December 9, 2013, http://abahlali.org/node/13328/.

6. Signs produced in Cato Crest also are in *isi*Xhosa.

7. "Today We Protest in Cato Crest in Honour of Nelson Mandela."

8. Ibid.

9. Bandile Mdlalose, "I Will Not Be Silenced," *IOL*, October 10, 2013, http://www.iol.co.za/dailynews/opinion/i-will-not-be-silenced-1589748#.UtjXWtK1ZA8.

10. The general secretary has since left Abahlali to launch another movement after disputes with the current Abahlali leadership, suggesting the fluctuation of these affective sentiments across time.

11. S'bu Zikode, "Despite the state's violence, our fight to escape the mud and fire of South Africa's slums will continue," *Guardian*, November 11, 2013, http://www.theguardian.com/profile/sbu-zikode.

12. Mdlalose, "I Will Not Be Silenced."

13. In contrast to theories of violence that distinguish between the socioeconomic and the political, Abahlali members view these as one and the same. Abahlali's idiom of "sacrifice," therefore, also falls into tension with the South African Truth and Reconciliation Commission's framing of violence, which as Fiona Ross (2003) has demonstrated, emphasized individual bodily injury over collective injury, men's wounds over women's wounds, and the political over the socioeconomic.

14. "AbM Youth League: Building Tomorrow's Leaders Today," Abahlali baseMjondolo press release, June 14, 2013, http://abahlali.org/node/9790/.

15. Some authors who have written about Abahlali have failed to recognize the complexities of gender within the movement, and within relevant theoretical literatures more broadly. Rather than gender being understood as a fixed essence (man/woman), biologically determined (penis/vagina), or uniformly constituting power across times and places (powerless women/powerful men), I approach gender as a relational identity. Often these relational identities take on a fractally recursive character (Gal 2002). Therefore, a young female member of Abahlali may be more powerful than an older man, depending upon their respective positions within the movement. A meeting in which this young woman is speaking and an old man is listening may be misrecognized as an upending of ordinary power relations, when, in fact, it is the status quo. Where a younger man and older woman disagree in a meeting and hold equal positions in the movement, the older women's opinion would be deferred to by virtue of her seniority by age. Therefore, a younger man challenging an older woman in a meeting may be indicative of an upending of ordinary power relations, rather than what might appear to the casual observer, as reproducing the status quo. My point is not to ignore gender asymmetries but to better understand their complexities.

16. See Chance 2013; and Sarah Evans, "IPID Report: Sharp Increase in Assault by Police Cases," *Mail & Guardian*, October 2, 2013, http://mg.co.za/article/2013-10-02-ipid-report-sharp-increase-in-assault-by-police-cases.

17. On July 14, 2017, the Durban Magistrate's Court found the police officer who shot Nzuza "guilty of murder beyond a reasonable doubt." Sentencing is pending, and the magistrate's decision is likely to be appealed. Nzuza's family, who have been attending the hearings, will have to wait years for the outcome of the trial.

References

Agamben, Giorgio. 1998. *Homo Sacer: Sovereign Power and Bare Life.* Translated by Daniel Heller-Roazen. Stanford, CA: Stanford University Press.

———. 2005. *State of Exception.* Chicago: University of Chicago Press.

Agence France Presse. 2005. "Mbeki Warns of 'Threat' from Township Rioting in South Africa." May 25.

Alexander, Peter, Thapelo Lekgowa, Botsang Mmope, Luke Sinwell, and Bongani Xezwi. 2012. *Marikana: A View from the Mountain and a Case to Answer.* Johannesburg: Jacana Media.

Amis, Philip, and Peter Lloyd, eds. 1990. *Housing Africa's Urban Poor.* Manchester, UK: Manchester University Press.

Anand, Nikhil. 2011. "Pressure: The PoliTechnics of Water Supply in Mumbai." *Cultural Anthropology* 26 (4): 542–64. http://dx.doi.org/10.1111/j.1548-1360.2011.01111.x.

Anderson, Benedict. (1991) 2006. *Imagined Communities.* London: Verso Books.

Appadurai, Arjun. 1988. *The Social Life of Things.* Cambridge: Cambridge University Press.

———. 1990. "Disjuncture and Difference in the Global Cultural Economy." *Public Culture* Spring 2 (2): 1–24.

———. 2006. *Fear of Small Numbers: An Essay on the Geography of Anger.* Durham, NC: Duke University Press.

Appel, Hannah. 2012. "Walls and White Elephants: Oil Extraction, Responsibility, and Infrastructural Violence in Equatorial Guinea." *Ethnography* 13 (4): 439–65. http://dx.doi.org/10.1177/1466138111435741.

Apter, Andrew. 1992. *Black Critics and Kings.* Chicago: University of Chicago Press.

Arendt, Hannah. 1994. *Essays in Understanding, 1930–1954: Formation, Exile, and Totalitarianism.* Edited by Jerome Kohn. New York: Schocken Books.

———. 1998. *The Human Condition.* Chicago: University of Chicago Press.

Aretxaga, B. 2000. "A Fictional Reality: Paramilitary Death Squad and the Construction of State Terror in Spain." In *Death Squad*, edited by Jeffery A. Sluka, 46–69. Philadelphia: University of Pennsylvania Press.

Ashforth, Adam. 2005. *Witchcraft, Violence and Democracy in South Africa.* Chicago: University of Chicago Press.

Austin, J. L. 1965. *How to Do Things with Words.* Cambridge, MA: Harvard University Press.

Badiou, Alain. 2012. *The Rebirth of History: Times of Riots and Uprisings*. Translated by Gregory Elliott. New York: Verso.

Balakrishnan, Gopal, ed. 1996. *Mapping the Nation*. London: Verso.

Balibar, Etienne. 2006. "Uprisings in the French Banlieues: Race? Nation? Or Class?," Public lecture, May 10, University of Chicago, Franke Institute for the Humanities and the Chicago Center for Contemporary Theory.

Balibar, Etienne, and Immanuel Wallerstein, eds. 1991. *Race, Nation, Class: Ambiguous Identities*. London: Verso.

Ballard, Richard, Adam Habib, and Imraan Valodia, eds. 2006. *Voices of Protest: Social Movements in Post-Apartheid South Africa*. Scottsville, South Africa: University of KwaZulu-Natal Press.

Bank, Leslie. 2001. "'Duncan's Inferno': Fire Disaster, Social Dislocation, and Settlement Patterns in a South African Township," In *Transforming Settlement in Southern Africa*, edited by Chris de Wet and Roddy Fox, 147–62. Edinburgh: Edinburgh University Press.

Banks, Marcus. 1996. *Ethnicity: Anthropological Constructions*. London: Routledge.

Bayat, Asef. 2000. "From 'Dangerous Classes' to 'Quiet Rebels': Politics of the Urban Subaltern in the Global South." *International Sociology* 15 (3): 533–57. http://dx.doi.org/10.1177/026858000015003005.

Beinart, W. 2001. *Twentieth Century South Africa*. Oxford: Oxford University Press.

Beinart, W., and C. Bundy. 1997. *Hidden Struggles in Rural South Africa: Politics and Popular Movements in the Transkei and Eastern Cape, 1890–1930*. Berkeley: University of California Press.

Benhabib, Seyla, ed. 1996. *Democracy and Difference: Contesting the Boundaries of the Political*. Princeton, NJ: Princeton University Press.

———. 2002. *The Claims of Culture: Equality and Diversity in the Global Era*. Princeton, NJ: Princeton University Press.

Benjamin, Walter. 1978. "Critique of Violence." In *Reflections: Essays, Aphorisms, Autobiographical Writings*, edited by Peter Demetz; translated by Edmund Jephcott, 277–300. New York: Schocken Books.

Bernstein, A. 2013. "An Inadvertent Sacrifice: Body Politics and Sovereign Power in the Pussy Riot Affair." *Critical Inquiry* 40 (1): 220–41.

Bertelsen, Bjørn Enge, Inge Tvedten, and Sandra Roque. 2013. "Engaging, Transcending and Subverting Dichotomies: Discursive Dynamics of Maputo's Urban Space." *Urban Studies* 51 (13): 2752–69. http://dx.doi.org/10.1177/0042098013512872.

Bhabha, Homi. 2004. *The Location of Culture*. New York: Routledge.

Biehl, João. 2013. *Vita: Life in a Zone of Social Abandonment*. Oakland: University of California Press.

Biko, Steve. (1969) 2002. *I Write What I Like*. Chicago: University of Chicago Press.

Billig, Michael. 1995. *Banal Nationalism*. London: Sage.

Birkinshaw, Matt. 2008. "A Big Devil in the *Jondolos*: The Politics of Shack Fires." Abahlali baseMjondolo, August. http://abahlali.org/files/Big_Devil_Politics_of_Shack_Fire.pdf.

Bond, Patrick. 2004a. "South Africa's Resurgent Urban Social Movements." University of KwaZulu-Natal, Centre for Civil Society Research Report No. 22, 1–34.

———. 2004b. *Talk Left, Walk Right: South Africa's Frustrated Global Reforms*. Durban: University of KwaZulu-Natal Press.

———. 2011. *Politics of Climate Justice*. Pietermaritzburg: University of KwaZulu-Natal Press.

Bonilla, Yarimar. 2015. *Non-sovereign Futures: French Caribbean Politics in the Wake of Disenchantment.* Chicago: University of Chicago Press.

Bourdieu, P. 1977. *Outline of a Theory of Practice.* Cambridge: Cambridge University Press.

Boyer, Dominic. 2014. "Energopower: An Introduction." *Anthropological Quarterly* 87 (2): 309–33. http://dx.doi.org/10.1353/anq.2014.0020.

Brass, P. 1991. *Ethnicity and Nationalism: Theory and Comparison.* London: Sage.

Breckenridge, Keith. 1998. "Men, Race, and Masculinity on the South African Goldmines." *Journal of Southern African Studies* 24 (4): 669–93.

———. 2014. *Biometric State: The Global Politics of Identification and Surveillance in South Africa, 1850 to the Present.* Cambridge: Cambridge University Press.

Brenner, Neil, et al. 2011. *Cities for People, Not Profit.* New York: Routledge.

Brown, Julian. 2016. *The Road to Soweto: Resistance and the Uprising of 16 June 1976.* Johannesburg: Jacana Press.

Brown, Wendy. 1995. *States of Injury: Power and Freedom in Late Modernity.* Princeton, NJ: Princeton University Press.

Brubaker, R. 1998. *Citizenship and Nationhood in France and Germany.* Cambridge: Harvard University Press.

Bruce, David. 2014. "Political Killings in South Africa: The Ultimate Intimidation." Institute for Security Studies, November 3. http://www.issafrica.org/publications/policy-brief/political-killings-in-south-africa-the-ultimate-intimidation.

Bunn, David. 1994. "Our Wattled Cot: Mercantile and Domestic Space in Thomas Pringle's African Landscapes." In *Landscape and Power,* edited by W. J. T. Mitchell, 127–73. Chicago: University of Chicago Press.

Burawoy, Michael, and Katherine Verdery, eds. 1999. *Uncertain Transition: Ethnographies of Change in the Postsocialist World.* London: Rowan and Littlefield.

Butler, Judith. 1997. *Excitable Speech.* London: Routledge.

———. 2002. *Antigone's Claim.* New York: Columbia University Press.

Caldeira, Teresa. 2000. *City of Walls.* Berkeley: University of California Press.

Carter, Erica, James Donald, and Judith Squires. 1993. *Space and Place: Theories of Identity and Location.* London: Lawrence and Wishart.

Castells, Manuel. 1983. *The City and the Grassroots: A Cross-Cultural Theory of Urban Social Movements.* Berkeley: University of California Press.

Chalfin, Brenda. 2013. "Public Things, Excremental Politics, and the Infrastructure of Bare Life in Ghana's City of Tema." *American Ethnologist* 41 (1): 92–109.

Chance, Kerry Ryan. 2004. "Cut Off: Water and Electricity Politics in the 'New' South Africa." Master's thesis, University of Chicago.

———. 2010. "The Work of Violence: A Timeline of Armed Attacks at Kennedy Road." School of Development Studies Research Report No. 83, University of KwaZulu Natal. http://www.sds.ukzn.ac.za/default.php?3,6,684,4,0, accessed June 5, 2010.

———. 2013. "SAPS Violence Shakes the Foundation of Democracy." *Daily Maverick,* October 7. http://www.dailymaverick.co.za/opinionista/2013-10-07-saps-violence-shakes-the-foundation-of-democracy/#.U_ZzsRYnhg0.

———. 2015a. "Sacrifice after Mandela: Liberation and Liberalization among South Africa's First Post-Apartheid Generation." *Anthropological Quarterly* 88:857–79.

———. 2015b. "'Where There Is Fire, There Is Politics': Ungovernability and Material Life in Urban South Africa." *Cultural Anthropology* 30 (3): 394–423.

Chari, Sharad. 2004. "Political Work: The Holy Spirit and the Labours of Activism in the Shadows of Durban's Refineries." In *The Development Decade?: Economic and Social Change in South Africa, 1994–2004*, edited by Vishnu Padayachee, 427–43. Cape Town: Human Science Research Council.

———. 2006. "Imperial Debris and Political Striving in Durban." Paper presented at the American Association of Geography Conference, March 9.

———. 2010. "State Racism and Biopolitical Struggle: The Evasive Commons in Twentieth-Century Durban, South Africa." *Radical History Review* 108:73–90. http://dx.doi.org/10.1215/01636545-2010-004.

Chatterjee, Partha. 1991 "Whose Imagined Community?" *Millennium* 20 (3): 521–25.

———. 1994. *The Nation and Its Fragments: Colonial and Postcolonial Histories*. Princeton, NJ: Princeton University Press.

———. 2004. *The Politics of the Governed: Reflections on Popular Politics in Most of the World*. New York: Columbia University Press.

Chu, Julie Y. 2014. "When Infrastructures Attack: The Workings of Disrepair in China." *American Ethnologist* 41 (2): 351–67. http://dx.doi.org/10.1111/amet.12080.

Cohen, Anthony. 1994. *Self-Consciousness: An Alternative Anthropology of Identity*. London: Routledge.

———, ed. 2000. *Signifying Identities: Anthropological Perspectives on Boundaries and Contested Values*. London: Routledge.

Coles, Kim. 2004. "Election Day: The Construction of Democracy through Technique." *Cultural Anthropology* 19 (4): 551–79.

Colony of Natal. 1901. *Acts of the Parliament of the Colony of Natal, Passed in the Fifth Session of the Second Colonial Parliament, 1901*. Natal: "Times" Printing and Publishing. Available at https://books.google.com/books?id=SnlDAQAAMAAJ&printsec=frontcover&source=gbs_ge_summary_r&cad=0#v=onepage&q&f=false.

Comaroff, Jean. 1985. *Body of Power, Spirit of Resistance*. Chicago: University of Chicago Press.

Comaroff, Jean, and John L. Comaroff. 1991. *Of Revelation and Revolution*, vol. 1, *Christianity, Colonialism, and Consciousness in South Africa*. Chicago: University of Chicago Press.

———. 2001. "Naturing the Nation: Aliens, Apocalypse, and the Postcolonial State." *Journal of Southern African Studies* 27 (3): 627–51. http://dx.doi.org/10.1080/13504630120065301.

———, eds. 2006. *Law and Disorder in the Postcolony*. Chicago: University of Chicago Press.

Cooper-Knock, Sarah. 2009. "Symbol of Hope Silenced." *Daily News* (South Africa), November 13. Available at http://abahlali.org/node/6029/.

Coplan, D. B. 1987. "Eloquent Knowledge." *American Ethnologist* 14:413–33.

Cousins, Ben, Jackie Dugard, and Tshepo Madlingozi. 2013. *Socio-Economic Rights in South Africa*. Cambridge: Cambridge University Press.

Daniel, E. Valentine. 1996. *Charred Lullabies: Chapters in an Anthropology of Violence*. Princeton, NJ: Princeton University Press.

Danner, Mark. 2004. *Torture and Truth: America, Abu Ghraib and the War on Terror*. New York: New York Review of Books.

Das, Veena, Arthur Kleinman, Margaret M. Lock, Mamphela Ramphele, and Pamela Reynolds. 2001. *Remaking a World: Violence, Social Suffering, and Recovery*. Berkeley: University of California Press.

Davis, Mike. 2006. *Planet of Slums*. New York: Verso.

Day, G., and A. Thompson. 2004. *Theorizing Nationalism*. Basingstoke: Palgrave Macmillan.

Deleuze, Gilles, and Felix Guattari. 1987. *A Thousand Plateaus*. Minneapolis: University of Minnesota Press.

Desai, Ashwin. 2002. *We Are the Poors: Community Struggles in Post-Apartheid South Africa*. New York: Monthly Review Press.

Dezeuze, Anna. 2006. "Thriving on Adversity: The Art of Precariousness." *Mute*, September. http://www.metamute.org/en/Thriving-On-Adversity.

Dieckhoff, Alain, and Natividad Gutierrez, eds. 2001. *Modern Roots: Studies of National Identity*. Aldershot: Ashgate.

Disterhoft, Jason. 2011. "11 Numbers You Need to Know about the Global Housing Crisis." *Human Rights Now Blog* (Amnesty International), October 6. http://blog.amnestyusa.org/africa/human-right-to-housing-11-numbers-you-need-to-know/.

Dlamini, Nsizwa. 2001. "The Battle of Ncome Project: State Memorialism, Discomforting Spaces." *Southern African Humanities* 13 (1): 125–38.

Donnan, Hastings, and Thomas M. Wilson. 1999. *Borders: Frontiers of Identity, Nation and State*. Oxford: Berg.

Douglas, Mary. 1966. *Purity and Danger*. New York: Routledge.

Durkheim, Emile. (1912) 1995. *Elementary Forms of Religious Life*. New York: Free Press.

Edwards, I. 1994. "Cato Manor: Cruel Past, Pivotal Future." *Review of African Political Economy* 61 (21): 415–27.

eThekwini Municipality. 2007. "Air Quality Management Plan for eThekwini Municipality." April. http://www.saaqis.org.za/documents/ETHEKWINI%20METROPOLITAN%20MUNICIPALITY%20AQMP.pdf.

Elyachar, Julia. 2003. "Mappings of Power: The State, NGOs, and International Organizations in the Informal Economy of Cairo." *Comparative Studies in Society and History* 45 (3): 571–605.

Eriksen, T. 1993. *Ethnicity and Nationalism: Anthropological Perspectives*. London: Pluto Press.

Evans-Pritchard, E. E. (1937) 1976. *Witchcraft, Oracles, and Magic among the Azande*. Oxford: Oxford University Press.

Fanon, Frantz. 1965. *The Wretched of the Earth*. Translated by Constance Farrington. New York: Grove Press.

Farquhar, Judith, and Margaret Lock, eds. 2006. *Beyond the Body Proper: Reading the Anthropology of Material Life*. Durham, NC: Duke University Press.

Feldman, A. 1991. *Formations of Violence: The Narrative of the Body and Political Terror in Northern Ireland*. Chicago: University of Chicago Press.

Fennell, Catherine. 2011. "'Project Heat' and Sensory Politics in Redeveloping Chicago Public Housing." *Ethnography* 12 (1): 40–64. http://dx.doi.org/10.1177/1466138110387221.

———. 2015. *Last Project Standing: Civics and Sympathy in Post-Welfare Chicago*. Minneapolis, MN: University of Minnesota Press.

Ferguson, James. 2006. *Global Shadows: Africa in the Neoliberal World Order*. Durham, NC: Duke University Press.

———. 2013. "A Rightful Share: Distributive Politics beyond Gift and Market." Paper presented at the Harvard Africa Workshop Conference, Cambridge, MA, April 26.

Ferme, Mariane. 1998. "The Violence of Numbers: Consensus, Competition, and the Negotiation of Disputes in Sierra Leone." *Cahiers d'Études Africaines* 38 (150–152): 555–80. http://www.jstor.org/stable/4392881.

———. 2001. *The Underneath of Things: Violence, History and the Everyday in Sierra Leone*. Berkeley: University of California Press.

Fortes, M., and E. E. Evans-Pritchard. 1940. *African Political Systems.* Oxford: University Press.

Fortier, Anne-Marie, ed. 2000. *Migrant Belongings: Memory, Space, Identity.* Oxford: Berg.

Fortun, Kimberley. 2001. *Advocacy after Bhopal: Environmentalism, Disaster, New Global Orders.* Chicago: University of Chicago Press.

———. 2014. "From Latour to Late Industrialism." *HAU* 4 (1): 1–55.

Foucault, Michel. 1978. *History of Sexuality, Vol. 1.* New York: Random House.

———. 1991. *The Foucault Effect.* Edited by Graham Burchell. Chicago: University of Chicago Press.

———. 2003. *Society Must Be Defended: Lectures at the Collège de France, 1975–1976, Vol. 1.* Edited by Mauro Bertani, Alessandro Fontant, and Francois Ewald. New York, NY: Picador.

———. 2006. "Governmentality." In *The Anthropology of the State: A Reader,* edited by Akhil Gupta and Aradhana Sharma, 131–43. Malden, MA: Blackwell.

Fraser, Nancy. 1990. "Rethinking the Public Sphere." *Social Text* 25:56–80.

Freund, B. 2007. *The African City.* Cambridge: Cambridge University Press.

Gal, Susan. 2002. "A Semiotics of the Public/Private Distinction." *Differences: A Journal of Feminist Cultural Studies* 13 (1): 77–95.

Gal, Susan, and Gail Kligman, eds. 2000. *Reproducing Gender: Politics, Publics and Everyday Life after Socialism.* Princeton, NJ: Princeton University Press.

Ganguly, Keya. 2001. *States of Exception: Everyday Life and Post-Colonial Identity.* Minneapolis: University of Minnesota Press.

Geary, P. 2002. *The Myth of Nations: The Medieval Origins of Europe.* Princeton, NJ: Princeton University Press.

Gedalof, Irene. 1999. *Against Purity: Rethinking Identity with Indian and Western Feminisms.* Gender, Racism, Ethnicity. London: Routledge.

Gellner, Ernest. 1983. *Nations and Nationalism.* Oxford: Basil Blackwell.

Geschiere, Peter. 2013. *Witchcraft, Intimacy, and Trust: Africa in Comparison.* Chicago: University of Chicago Press.

Geschiere, Peter, and Birgit Meyer, eds. 1999. *Globalization and Identity.* Oxford: Blackwell.

Ghertner, D. Asher. 2011. "Rule by Aesthetics: World-Class City Making in Delhi." In *Worlding Cities: Asian Experiments and the Art of Being Global,* edited by Ananya Roy and Aihwa Ong, 279–306. Malden, MA: Wiley-Blackwell.

Gibson, Nigel C. 2011. *Fanonian Practices in South Africa: From Steve Biko to Abahlali baseMjondolo.* New York: Palgrave Macmillan.

Gillespie, Kelly. 2008. "Moralizing Security: 'Corrections' and the Post-Apartheid Prison." *Race/Ethnicity: Multidisciplinary Global Contexts* 2 (1): 69–87. http://www.jstor.org/stable/25595000.

Gordon, Lewis. 2012. "Of Illicit Appearance." *Truth Out,* May 12. http://www.truth-out.org/news/item/9008-of-illicit-appearance-the-la-riots-rebellion-as-a-portent-of-things-to-come.

Graeber, D. 2011. *Debt: The First 5000 Years.* New York: Melville House.

Gramsci, Antonio. 1971. *Selections from the Prison Notebooks.* Edited and translated by Quentin Hoare and Geoffrey Nowell Smith. New York: International Publishers.

Greenberg, Stephen. 2004. "Post-Apartheid Development, Landlessness and the Reproduction of Exclusion in South Africa." University of KwaZulu-Natal, Centre for Civil Society Research Report No. 17, 1–42.

Guibernau, M., and J. Hutchinson, eds. 2004. *Understanding Nationalism.* Cambridge: Polity Press.

Guibernau, M., and J. Rex, eds. 2010. *The Ethnicity Reader: Nationalism, Multiculturalism and Migration.* 2nd ed. Cambridge: Polity Press.

Gupta, Akhil. 2012. *Red Tape: Bureaucracy, Structural Violence, and Poverty in India.* Durham, NC: Duke University Press.

Gupta, Akhil, and James Ferguson, eds. 1997. *Culture, Power, Place: Explorations in Critical Anthropology.* Durham, NC: Duke University Press.

Guy, Jeff. 2006. *Remembering the Rebellion: The Zulu Uprising of 1906.* Durban: University of KwaZulu Press.

Habermas, Jürgen. 1984. *The Theory of Communicative Action, Vol. 1: Reason and the Rationalization of Society.* Translated by Thomas McCarthy. Boston: Beacon Press.

Hall, John, ed. 1998. *The State of the Nation: Ernest Gellner and the Theory of Nationalism.* Cambridge: Cambridge University Press.

Hansen, Thomas Blom. 2008. "The Political Theology of Violence in Contemporary India." *South Asia Multidisciplinary Academic Journal* [online]. http://samaj.revues.org/1872.

Hansen, Thomas Blom, and Finn Stepputat. 2005. *Sovereign Bodies.* Princeton, NJ: Princeton University Press.

Hardt, Michael. 2010. "Two Faces of Apocalypse: A Letter from Copenhagen." *Polygraph* 22:265–74.

Hardt, Michael, and Antonio Negri. 2004. *The Multitude.* New York: Penguin Press.

Harms, Eric. 2013. "Eviction Time in the New Saigon: Temporalities of Displacement in the Rubble of Development." *Cultural Anthropology* 28 (2): 344–68.

Hart, Gillian. 2014. *Rethinking the South African Crisis: Nationalism, Populism, Hegemony.* Athens: University of Georgia Press.

Hart, Keith. 1973. "Informal Income Opportunities and Urban Employment in Ghana." *Journal of Modern African Studies* 11 (1): 61–89.

Harvey, David. 2005. *A Brief History of Neoliberalism.* New York: Oxford University Press.

———. 2012. *Rebel Cities.* London: Verso.

Harvey, Penny, and Hannah Knox. 2012. "The Enchantments of Infrastructure." *Mobilities* 74: 521–36. http://dx.doi.org/10.1080/17450101.2012.718935.

Hechter, Michael. 2000. *Containing Nationalism.* Oxford: Oxford University Press.

Hegel, Georg Wilhelm Friedrich. (1820) 1949. *Hegel's Philosophy of Right.* Translated by T. M. Knox. Oxford: Clarendon Press.

Heller, Patrick. 2001. "Moving the State: The Politics of Democratic Decentralization in Kerala, South Africa, and Porto Alegre." *Politics & Society* 29 (1): 131–63. http://dx.doi.org/10.1177/0032329201029001006.

———. 2012. "Democracy, Participatory Politics and Development: Some Comparative Lessons from Brazil, India and South Africa." *Polity* 44 (4): 643–65.

Herzfeld, Michael. 2009. *Evicted from Eternity.* Chicago: University of Chicago Press.

Hickel, Jason. 2014. "'Xenophobia' in South Africa: Order, Chaos, and the Moral Economy of Witchcraft." *Cultural Anthropology* 29 (1): 103–27. http://dx.doi.org/10.14506/ca29.1.07.

Holland, Dorothy, William Lachicotte, Debra Skinner, and Carole Cain. 2001. *Identity and Agency in Cultural Worlds.* Cambridge: Harvard University Press.

Holston, James. 2008. *Insurgent Citizenship: Disjunctions of Democracy and Modernity in Brazil.* Princeton, NJ: Princeton University Press.

Hornberger, J. 2013. "From General to Commissioner to General: On the Popular State of Policing in South Africa." *Law & Society* 38 (3): 598–614.

Hubert, H., and M. Mauss. (1899) 1981. *Sacrifice.* Chicago: University of Chicago Press.

Huchzermeyer, Marie. 2004. *Unlawful Occupation.* Johannesburg: Africa World Press.

———. 2006. "The New Instrument for Upgrading Informal Settlements in South Africa: Contributions and Constraints." In *Informal Settlements: A Perpetual Challenge?,* edited by Marie Huchzermeyer and Aly Karam, 41–61. Cape Town: Juta/University of Cape Town Press.

———. 2011. *Cities with "Slums": From Slum Eradication to a Right to the City in Africa.* Cape Town: Juta/University of Cape Town Press.

Hutchinson, John, and Anthony Smith. eds. 1994. *Nationalism.* Oxford: Oxford University Press.

James, Paul. 1996. *Nation Formation: Towards a Theory of Abstract Community.* London: Sage.

Jensen, Steffan. 2008. *Gangs, Politics and Dignity in Cape Town.* Chicago: University of Chicago Press.

Khuzwayo, S'Celo. 2011. "Investigate Shack Fire, Says Mlaba." eThekwini Municipality. http://www.durban.gov.za/City_Government/Pages/Investigate_Shack-Fire_Says_Mlaba.aspx, accessed July 21, 2017.

Kockelman, Paul. 2016. "Grading, Gradients, Degradation, Grace: Part 1, Intensity and Causality." *HAU* 6 (2): 389–423.

Kosek, Jake. 2006. *Understories: The Political Life of Forests in Northern New Mexico.* Durham, NC: Duke University Press.

Laclau, Ernesto, and Chantal Mouffe. (1985) 2001. *Hegemony and Socialist Strategy: Towards a Radical Democratic Politics.* New York: Verso.

Langford, Malcolm, Ben Cousins, Jackie Dugard, and Tshepo Madlingozi, eds. 2013. *Socio-Economic Rights in South Africa: Symbols or Substance?* Cambridge: Cambridge University Press.

Larkin, Brian. 2008. *Signal and Noise: Infrastructure and Urban Culture in Nigeria.* Durham, NC: Duke University Press.

Latour, Bruno. 2013. *An Inquiry into Modes of Existence.* Cambridge: Harvard University Press.

Lee, Christopher. 2009. "Sovereignty, Neoliberalism, and the Postdiasporic Politics of Globalization: A Conversation about South Africa with Patrick Bond, Ashwin Desai, and Molefi Mafereka ka Ndlovu." *Radical History Review* 2009 (103): 143–61.

Lefort, Claude. 1989. *Democracy and Political Theory.* Minneapolis: University of Minnesota Press.

Legassick, Martin. 2008. "Western Cape Housing Crisis: Writings on Joe Slovo and Delft." Western Cape Anti-Eviction Campaign website, February. https://westerncapeantieviction.files.wordpress.com/2008/03/joeslovo_delft-leggasick.pdf.

Li, Tania Murray. 2007. *The Will to Improve: Governmentality, Development, and the Practice of Politics.* Durham, NC: Duke University Press.

Locke, John. (1690) 1980. *The Second Treatise on Government.* Indianapolis, IN: Hackette.

Lodge, Tom. 2001. *Consolidating Democracy.* Johannesburg: University of Witwatersrand Press.

Losier, Toussaint. 2010. "A Quiet Coup: South Africa's Largest Social Movement under Attack." *libcom.org,* June 2. http://libcom.org/news/quiet-coup-south-africa%E2%80%99s-largest-social-movement-under-attack-world-cup-looms-02062010.

Lumsden, Fiona, and Alex Loftus. 2003. "Inanda's Struggle for Water through Pipes and Tunnels: Exploring State–Civil Society Relations in a Post-Apartheid Informal Settlement." University of KwaZulu-Natal, Centre for Civil Society Research Report No. 6, 1–35.

Maarsdorp, G. G., and Humphreys, A. S. B., eds. 1975. *From Shantytown to Township: An Economic Study of African Poverty and Rehousing in a South African City.* Cape Town, South Africa: Juta.

Machiavelli, Niccolò. (1532) 1958. *The Prince.* Translated by W. K. Marriott. New York: E. P. Dutton.

Madikizela-Mandela, Winnie. 2013. *491 Days: Prisoner Number 1323/69.* Athens: Ohio University Press.

Mageo, Jeannette, ed. 2001. *Cultural Memory: Reconfiguring History and Identity in the Postcolonial Pacific.* Honolulu: University of Hawai'i Press.

Makhulu, Anne-Maria. 2010. "The Question of Freedom: Post-Emancipation South Africa in a Neoliberal Age." In *Ethnographies of Neoliberalism*, edited by Carol Greenhouse, 131–45. Philadelphia: University of Pennsylvania Press.

Malinowski, Bronislaw. (1922) 1961. *Argonauts of the Western Pacific.* New York: Dutton.

Mamdani, Mahmood. 1996. *Citizen and Subject.* Princeton, NJ: Princeton University Press.

Mandela, Nelson. 1994. *A Long Walk to Freedom.* New York: Back Bay Books / Little, Brown.

Marais, Hein. 2011. *South Africa Pushed to the Limit: The Political Economy of Change.* London: Zed Books.

Marshall, Ruth. 2009. *Political Spiritualities.* Chicago: University of Chicago Press.

Marx, Karl. (1932) 1978. "The German Ideology: Part I." In *The Marx-Engels Reader*, 2nd ed., edited by Robert C. Tucker, 146–200. New York: W. W. Norton.

Mauss, Marcel. 1954. *The Gift: Forms and Functions of Exchange in Archaic Societies.* London: Cohen and West.

Mavhunga, Clapperton Chakanetsa. 2013. "Cidades Esfumaçadas: Energy and the Rural-Urban Connection in Mozambique." *Public Culture* 25 (2): 261–71. http://dx.doi.org/10.1215/08992363-2020593.

———. 2014. *Transient Workspaces.* Cambridge: MIT Press.

Maylam, P. 1983. "The 'Black Belt': African Squatters in Durban 1935–1950." *Canadian Journal of African Studies* 17 (3): 413–28.

Mbali, Mandisa. 2005. "The Treatment Action Campaign and the History of Rights Based Patient-Driven HIV/AIDS Activism in South Africa." University of KwaZulu-Natal, Centre for Civil Society Research Report No. 29, 1–23.

Mbembe, Achille. 2003. "Necropolitics." Translated by Libby Meintjes. *Public Culture* 15 (1): 11–40. http://dx.doi.org/10.1215/08992363-15-1-11.

———. 2006. "On Politics as a Form of Expenditure." In *Law and Disorder in the Postcolony*, edited by Jean Comaroff and John Comaroff. Chicago: University of Chicago Press.

Mbembe, Achille, and Sarah Nuttall. 2008. "Writing the World from an African Metropolis." *Public Culture* 16 (3): 347–72.

McDonald, David A., and John Pape, eds. 2002. *Cost Recovery and the Crisis of Service Delivery in South Africa.* London: Zed Books.

Mchunu, Ken. 2008. "Electricity Thieves to Face Heat." eThekwini Online, November 5. http://www1.durban.gov.za/durban/services/services_news/electricity-thieves-to-face-heat.

McKinley, Dale. 2004. "A Disillusioned Democracy: South African Elections Ten Years On." University of KwaZulu-Natal, Centre for Civil Society.

Mdlalose, Gugu. 2009. "Unsafe Electricity Installations." eThekwini Online, November 13. http://www1.durban.gov.za/durban/government/media/press/privatepressitem.2009-11-13.5860188301.

Meyer, B. 2013. "Material Mediations and Religious Practices of World-Making," In *Religion across Media*, edited by K. Lundby, 1–19. New York: Peter Lang.

Miller, James. 1980. *The Passion of Michel Foucault.* Cambridge: Harvard University Press.

Mitchell, Timothy. 2009. "Carbon Democracy." *Economy and Society* 38 (3): 399–432. http://dx .doi.org/10.1080/03085140903020598.

Moodie, Dunbar. 1994. *Going for Gold.* Berkeley: University of California Press.

Morley, David, and Kevin Robins. 1995. *Spaces of Identity: Global Media, Electronic Landscapes and Cultural Boundaries.* London: Routledge.

Morris, Rosalind C. 2006. "The Mute and the Unspeakable: Political Subjectivity, Violent Crime, and 'the Sexual Thing' in a South African Mining Community." In *Law and Disorder in the Postcolony*, edited by Jean Comaroff and John L. Comaroff, 57–101. Chicago: University of Chicago Press.

————. 2011. "A Pound of Sugar, a Basket of Eggs, and the Spillage of Milk: Worldly Itineraries of Domestic Commodities (or, Recipe for a Personal History of the World, circa 1986/7, with Reference to Henri Lefebvre and Gertrude Stein, via Karl Marx and Mao Zedong)." Paper presented at "The Lives of Things" conference, Chicago, IL, April 29–30.

Morrison, Minion K. C., and Peter C. W. Gutkind, eds. 1982. *Housing the Urban Poor in Africa.* Syracuse: Maxwell School of Citizenship and Public Affairs.

Mudimbe, V. Y. 1994. *The Idea of Africa.* Bloomington: Indiana University Press.

Munn, N. 1992. *The Fame of Gawa.* Durham, NC: Duke University Press.

Murray, Martin J. 2009. "Fire and Ice: Unnatural Disasters and the Disposable Urban Poor in Post-Apartheid Johannesburg." *International Journal of Urban and Regional Research* 33 (1): 165–92.

Nash, June. 2005. *Social Movements: An Anthropological Reader.* Malden, MA: Blackwell.

Neuwirth, Robert. 1994. *Shadow Cities: A Billion Squatters, a New Urban World.* New York: Routledge.

Ngcongco, Nondu. 2011. "Electricity 'Thieves' Arrested." eThekwini Online, January 21. http:// www1.durban.gov.za/durban/government/city-government-news/electricity -2018thieves2019-arrested.

Nordstrom, Carolyn, ed. 2004. *Shadows of War: Violence, Power, and International Profiteering in the Twenty-First Century.* Berkeley: University of California Press.

Obarrio, Juan. 2004. "Beyond Equivalence: the Gift of Justice." *Anthropological Theory* 10 (1–2): 163–70.

Obudho, Robert A., and Constance C. Mhlanga, eds. 1988. *Slum and Squatter Settlements in Sub-Saharan Africa.* New York: Praeger.

Ong, Aihwa. 1999. *Flexible Citizenship: The Cultural Logics of Transnationality.* Durham, NC: Duke University Press.

Paley, Julia. 2001. *Marketing Democracy.* Berkeley: University of California Press.

Parry, Jonathan, and Maurice Bloch, eds. 1989. *Money and the Morality of Exchange.* Cambridge: Cambridge University Press.

Patel, Raj. 2008. "A Short Course in Politics at the University of Abahlali baseMjondolo." *Journal of Asian and African Studies* 43 (1): 95–112. http://dx.doi.org/10.1177/0021909607085587.

Paton, Alan. 1945. *Cry, The Beloved Country.* New York: Charles Scribner's Sons.

Patton, Carl V., ed. 1988. *Spontaneous Shelter.* Philadelphia: Temple University Press.

Peacock, James, Patricia Thornton, and Patrick Inman, eds. 2007. *Identity Matters: Ethnic and Sectarian Conflict.* Oxford: Berghahn.

Peebles, G. 2012. "Filth and Lucre: The Dirty Money Complex as Taxation Regime." *Anthropological Quarterly* 85 (4): 1229–56.

Petryna, Adriana. 2003. *Life Exposed: Biological Citizens after Chernobyl.* Princeton, NJ: Princeton University Press.

Phillips, Anne. 1991. *Engendering Democracy.* University Park: Pennsylvania State University Press.

Pieterse, Edgar. 2008. *City Futures: Confronting the Crisis of Urban Development.* London: Zed Books.

Piot, Charles. 2010. *Nostalgia for the Future: West Africa after the Cold War.* Chicago: University of Chicago Press.

Pithouse, Richard. 2006. "Our Struggle Is Thought, on the Ground, Running." University of KwaZulu-Natal, Centre for Civil Society Research Report No. 41, 1–43.

Poole, Ross. 1999. *Nation and Identity.* Ideas series. London and New York: Routledge.

Pooley, Simon. 2012. "Recovering the Lost History of Fire in South Africa's Fynbos." *Environmental History* 17 (1): 55–83. http://dx.doi.org/10.1093/envhis/emr117.

Povinelli, Elizabeth. 2016. *Geontologies: A Requiem for Late Liberalism.* Durham, NC: Duke University Press.

Pype, Katrien. 2012. *The Making of the Pentecostal Melodrama.* Oxford: Berghahn Books.

Radcliffe-Brown, A. R. 1940. Preface to *African Political Systems.* London: Oxford University Press.

Rademeyer, Julian. 2013. "Claim That 94% in SA Have Access to Safe Drinking Water . . . Doesn't Hold Water." *Africa Check,* April 29. http://africacheck.org/reports/claim-that-94-of-south-aclaim-that-94-in-sa-have-access-to-safe-drinking-water-doesnt-hold-water/#sthash.kgZgkp0j.dpuf.

Rajan, Sunder Rajeswari. 2003. *The Scandal of the State: Women, Law, and Citizenship in Postcolonial India.* Durham, NC: Duke University Press.

Ralph, Michael. 2015. *Forensics of Capital.* Chicago: University of Chicago Press.

Rancière, Jacques. 1998. *Disagreement: Politics and Philosophy.* Translated by Julie Rose. Minneapolis: University of Minnesota Press.

Rao, Vyjayanthi. 2006. Risk and the City: Bombay, Mumbai, and Other Theoretical Departures. *India Review* 5 (2): 220–32.

———. 2012. "Slum as Theory: Mega-Cities and Urban Models." In *The SAGE Handbook of Architectural Theory,* edited by C. Greig Crysler, Stephen Cairns, and Hilde Heynen, 671–86. London: SAGE Publications.

Rapport, Nigel, and Andrew Dawson, eds. 1998. *Migrants of Identity: Perceptions of Home and Improvement in a World of Movement.* Ethnicity and Identity Series. Oxford, New York: Berg.

Redfield, Peter. 2012. "Bioexpectations: Life Technologies as Humanitarian Goods." *Public Culture* 24 (1): 157–84. http://dx.doi.org/10.1215/08992363-1443592.

Richter, Gerhard. 2003. "Enduring Freedom: War, Corporate Television, and the Delusion of the Delusion." *Qui Parle* 14 (1): 73–97.

Ross, Fiona. 2003. *Bearing Witness.* London: Pluto Press.

———. 2010. *Raw Hope, New Life: Decency, Housing, and Everyday Life in a Post-Apartheid Community.* Cape Town: University of Cape Town Press.

Roy, Ananya. 2011. "Slumdog Cities: Rethinking Subaltern Urbanism." *International Journal of Urban and Regional Research* 35 (2): 223–38. http://dx.doi.org/10.1111/j.1468-2427.2011.01051.x.

Ruiters, Gregory. 2002. "Debt and Disconnection: The Case of Fort Beaufort, Queenstown and Stutterheim." In *Cost Recovery and the Crisis of Service Delivery in South Africa*, edited by David A. McDonald and John Pape. London: Zed Books.

Rustomjee, Cyrus. 2006. "From Economic Debt to Moral Debt: The Campaigns of Jubilee South Africa." In *Voices of Protest: Social Movements in Post-Apartheid South Africa*, edited by Richard Ballard, Adam Habib, and Imraan Valodia. Scottsville, South Africa: University of KwaZulu-Natal Press.

Sassen, Saskia. 1996. *Losing Control? Sovereignty in an Age of Globalization.* New York: Columbia University Press.

Schmitt, Carl. (1932) 1996. *The Concept of the Political.* Chicago: University of Chicago Press.

Schneider, Cathy Lisa. 1995. *Shantytown Protest in Pinochet's Chile.* Philadelphia: Temple University Press.

Schopflin, George. 2000. *Nations, Identity, Power: The New Politics of Europe.* London: C. Hurst.

Scott, James. 2009. *The Art of Not Being Governed: An Anarchist History of Upland Southeast Asia.* New Haven, CT: Yale University Press.

Seabrook, Jeremy. 1996. *In the Cities of the South.* London: Verso.

Seekings, Jeremy, and Nicoli Natrass. 2005. *Class, Race, and Inequality in South Africa.* New Haven, CT: Yale University Press.

Selmeczi, Anna. 2011. "'From Shack to the Constitutional Court': The Litigious Disruption of Governing Global Cities." *Utrecht Law Review* 7 (2): 60–76. http://persistent-identifier.nl/URN:NBN:NL:UI:10-1-101282.

Sharma, Aradhana, and Akhil Gupta, eds. 2006. *The Anthropology of the State.* Oxford: Blackwell.

Siegel, James T. 1998. *A New Criminal Type in Jakarta: Counter-Revolution Today.* Durham, NC: Duke University Press.

Simone, AbdouMaliq. 2004a. *For the City Yet to Come.* Durham, NC: Duke University Press.

———. 2004b. "People as Infrastructure: Intersecting Fragments in Johannesburg." *Public Culture* 16 (3): 407–29.

———. 2014. *Jakarta, Drawing the City Near.* Minneapolis, MN: University of Minnesota Press.

Smart, Alan. 1992. *Making Room: Squatter Clearance in Hong Kong.* Hong Kong: Hong Kong University Press.

Smith, James. 2008. *Bewitching Development.* Chicago: University of Chicago Press.

Sparks, Allister. 1995. *Tomorrow Is Another Country: The Inside Story of South Africa's Road to Change.* Chicago: University of Chicago Press.

Stadler, A. W. 1973. "Birds in the Cornfield: Squatter Movements in Johannesburg, 1944–1947." *Journal of Southern African Studies* 6 (1): 93–123.

Statistics South Africa. 2013. "South Africa—General Household Survey 2011." Central Microdata Catalogue, January 9. http://microdata.worldbank.org/index.php/catalog/1297.

Steinberg, Jonny, ed. 2001. *Crime Wave: The South African Underworld and Its Foes.* Johannesburg: Witwatersrand University Press.

———. 2004. *The Number: One Man's Search for Identity in the Cape Underworld and Prison Gangs.* Johannesburg: Jonathan Ball.

———. 2009. *Thin Blue: The Unwritten Rules of South African Policing.* Johannesburg: Jonathan Ball.

Stoler, Anne, ed. 2013. *Imperial Debris: On Ruins and Ruination.* Durham, NC: Duke University Press.

Strathern, M. 1990. *The Gender of the Gift: Problems with Women and Problems with Society in Melanesia.* Berkeley: University of California Press.

Tambiah, Stanley J. 1997. *Leveling Crowds*. Berkeley: University of California Press.

Taylor, Marcus. 2015. *The Political Ecology of Climate Change Adaption: Livelihoods, Agrarian Change, and the Conflicts of Development*. New York: Routledge.

Thomas, Deborah A. 2009. "The Violence of Diaspora: Governmentality, Class Cultures, and Circulations." *Radical History Review* 103 (2009): 83–104.

Tilly, Charles. 1996. *Citizenship, Identity, and Social History*. Cambridge: Cambridge University Press.

Tranber Hansen, Karen, and Mariken Vaa. 2004. *Reconsidering Informality*. Uppsala: Nordiska Afrikainstitutet.

Trouillot, Michel-Rolph. 2003. "North Atlantic Universals: Analytical Fictions, 1492–1945." *South Atlantic Quarterly* 101 (4): 839–58.

Turner, Victor. 1967. *The Forest of Symbols*. Ithaca, NY: Cornell University Press.

United Nations Human Settlements Programme. 2003. *The Challenge of Slums: Global Report on Human Settlements, 2003*. London: Earthscan Publications.

Van Onselen, Charles. 2001. *New Babylon, New Nineveh*. Johannesburg: Jonathan Ball.

Verdery, Katherine. 1991. *National Identity under Socialism: Identity and Cultural Politics in Ceausescu's Romania*. Berkeley: University of California Press.

———. 1996. *What Was Socialism and What Comes Next?* Princeton, NJ: Princeton University Press.

von Schnitzler, Antina. 2013. "Traveling Technologies: Infrastructure, Ethical Regimes, and the Materiality of Politics in South Africa." *Cultural Anthropology* 28 (4): 670–93. http://dx.doi .org/10.1111/cuan.12032.

Walley, Christine. 2013. *Exit Zero: Family and Class in Postindustrial Chicago*. Chicago: University of Chicago Press.

Wedel, Janine R. 2001. "Mafia without Malfeasance, Clans without Crime: The Criminality of Post-Communist Europe." In *Crime's Power: Anthropologists and the Ethnography of Crime*, edited by Philip C. Parnell and Stephanie C. Kane, 221–24. New York: Palgrave Macmillan.

Weiner, A. 1992. *Inalienable Possessions: The Paradox of Keeping-while-Giving*. Berkeley: University of California Press.

White, Hylton. 2004. "Ritual Haunts: The Timing of Estrangement in a Post-Apartheid Countryside." In *Producing African Futures: Ritual and Politics in a Neoliberal Age*, edited by Brad Weiss, 141–66. Leiden, Netherlands: Brill.

Wicker, Frans-Rudolf. 1997. *Rethinking Nationalism and Ethnicity: The Struggle for Meaning and Order in Europe*. London: Berg.

Winther, Tanja. 2008. *The Impact of Electricity: Development, Desires and Dilemmas*. New York: Berghahn.

Zikode, S'bu. 2009. "Democracy Is on the Brink of Catastrophe." Talk given at Rhodes University, Grahamstown, South Africa, October 30, 2009. Available at http://www.abahlali.org/ node/5962.

Žižek, S. 2004. "From Antigone to Joan of Arc." *HELIOS* 31 (1–2): 51–62.

Index

Abahlali, 5, 7–10, 13–14, 16–17, 19–22, 25–28, 30–31, 33, 36, 39–40, 43–47, 49, 51, 54, 61, 63–64, 71–72, 74, 76, 80, 83, 85–86, 88, 90, 93, 95, 99, 104–5, 111–18, 120–22, 124, 129–30, 133, 147–48n10, 152–53n10, 153n3, 155n2, 159n3, 159n4, 159–60n13, 160n16, 160n18, 160n19, 161n24, 161n25; "born frees," 142–43; Branch Area meetings, 66; Branch Launch meetings, 69; "coming out of silence," 69, 77; coughing out, 78, 143; and demobilization, 160–61n23; dispatches of, 23; Emergency Meetings, 67; ethnonationalism, statements against, 160n15; faith of, 156n6, 156n7; and gender, 164n15; "Letter from Prison," 140; liberation struggle, borrowing from, 143; living politics of, 141, 143–45; mass meetings, 65–70; members, number of, 6, 158n2; movement buildings, 67; Movement Meetings, 66; as national movement, 6; policy, challenging of, 12; pollution, approach to, 81–82; protests of, 11–12; the rapture, 75; sacrifice, idiom of, 134–35, 137–38, 140–43, 163n13; shack fires, 34; as target, in pogrom, 107–10; Youth League Camp, 66, 123, 125–27, 141–43, 162–63n37

Act of Parliament (1901), 48–49

Africa, 10–11

African, Indian, and Coloured communities, 18, 32, 48, 55, 58, 64, 65, 72, 91, 111, 119, 155n1

African National Congress (ANC), viii, 3, 6, 8–12, 19–20, 25, 29–32, 44, 52–53, 55, 57, 65, 68, 74, 87, 91, 96, 107–11, 114–16, 119–21, 122, 125, 127–29, 135, 138–40, 155n2, 156n7, 159n4, 159n6, 161n24; centralization of, 147–48n10, 159–60n13; economic liberalization, commitment to, 148n16; as liberation movement, 138; as mass movement, 27; Umkhonto

we Sizwe (MK), military wing of, 28, 51, 159–60n13

African studies, 15

African Zionism, belief in rapture, 74–75

Agamben, Giorgio, 149–51n25, 153n16

AIDS/HIV, viii, 41, 69, 82, 98, 117, 122

air, 22, 63–64, 74, 77, 80, 82, 85, 144–45; social glue, 155n1; and sociality, 70. *See also* pollution

*ama*Bhaca, 112

Amafela, 7

Amnesty International, 109

ancestors, 73, 75; ancestral rites, 81; spirits of, 71–72

Anglicanism, 75; colonization, complicit with, 74

Angola, 156n2

Anti-Eviction Campaign (AEC), 21, 66, 87–88, 90, 93, 95, 99, 101–4, 114–15

antiglobalization, 10

apartheid, 6–7, 9–10, 31, 46, 48–50, 94, 112, 120, 154n12; anti-apartheid activities, 66; Black Jacks, 73; dismantling of, and citizenship rights, 91; fall of, vii–viii, 4, 8, 30, 43, 54, 60, 73, 91, 95, 136, 147n2; fire, and street politics, 32; fire, link to, 27; honeymoon period, 8; pass laws, 28; and pollution, 81; racial belonging under, 111; secret police force, 12; and water, 52–57, 59. *See also* post-apartheid

Asinamali, 7–8

Austin, J. L., 155–56n3

AWB, 147–48n10

"Bantustans," 7, 65, 76, 111–12

Barclays, 96

"Battle in Seattle," 10

Battle of Blood River, 153n3

Bellcourt, 30–31

Berea, 64

Biko, Steve, 2, 74

biopower, 15–16, 149–51n25

Biwater, 57–59

Black Consciousness movement, 2, 74

Black Local Authorities Act, 154n12

Black Panthers, 119

Bombay, 149–51n25

Boston, 4

Boycott Movement, 51

boycotts: consumer boycotts, 46, 51, 54, 57–58; political belonging, 51; rent boycotts, 6–8, 51, 154n18; and water, 46, 51–52, 54, 57–58

Boy Scouts, 31

Brazil, 67, 120, 145, 156n2

Breaking New Ground (BNG), 21, 87, 91–92, 157–58n16; new housing vision, 95; urban informality, 93

Brutus, Dennis, 1

Bulelani, 78–80

Busisiwe (teacher), 5, 31–32, 37–38, 48, 63, 66, 69, 76–77, 82, 107, 120

Butler, Judith, 134, 138, 155–56n3

Cape Flats, 101–2, 104

Cape Town, vii, 4, 11, 19–21, 33, 40, 43–44, 47, 51, 59, 86, 88, 91–96, 99, 102–3, 109, 113–15, 156n1; Coloured District Six in, 8

Cassim, Ashraf, 101–2

Cato Crest shack settlement, 133–39

Cato Manor, 7, 138–40, 143; forced removal, 136

Chatterjee, Partha, 149–51n25

Chicago, 4, 6

Chicago Anti-Eviction Campaign, 138

cholera, 58

Chomsky, Noam, 109

citizenship, 48, 58; post-apartheid conception of, 55; as race-based, 43

Clare Estate, 1

climate science, 81–82

colonialism, 3

colonization, and Anglicanism, 74

Commercial Industrial Workers Union, 7

community policing, 3, 117, 119–21, 124, 159n6. See also policing

Congolese Solidarity Campaign, 116

Congress Alliance, 65–66

Congress of South African Trade Unions (CO-SATU), 57–58

Congress of the People (COPE), 110, 114–16, 120, 127

Copello, Kalinca, 159n9

Corrod, Graham, 58

coughing out, 64–65, 69, 74, 78, 143, 155–56n3, 156n7; izangoma (traditional healers), 72; musical roots of, 70–71; past and present risk, bur-

den of, 77; Pentecostal practices, overlapping with, 75; witchcraft, warding off, 72

Cry, the Beloved Country (Paton), 7

Dear Mandela (film), 159n8

decolonization, 18, 74

Defiance Campaign, 27–28

de Klerk, F. W., 56–57

Delft transit camp, 18, 86, 88, 90, 93–94, 96–101, 103–4

democracy, viii, 18, 55, 77, 137, 139, 141, 142, 149–50n25; civic participation, 149–51n25; liberal democracy, 15, 17, 144–45

Democratic Alliance (DA), 87, 115

Dhlomo, Zithulele, 3, 5–6, 39; death of, 1–2; memorial of, 2

Dingane, King, 153n3

Discipline and Punish (Foucault), 149–51n25

Discourses on Livy (Machiavelli), 149–51n25

District Six, 8, 43, 94; eviction of, 94

Dlamini King Brothers, 69–71, 112–13, 117, 156n4

Dube, Lucky, 54, 57

Durban, 1, 3–4, 6–7, 10–12, 19–21, 25–26, 29–31, 35, 37, 39–41, 60, 64, 66, 70, 72, 75–78, 80–82, 86, 88, 97, 99, 107, 113, 115–16, 122, 133, 140, 149n21, 156n1, 159–60n13; Cato Manor in, 8; race-based tensions in, 111

Durban Housing Department, 109

Dutch East India Company, 47

Eastern Cape, 18, 21, 159n12

Economic Freedom Fighters (EFF), 9, 155n2

Egypt, 145

electricity bandits, 27, 36

Ermelo coal mine, 53–54

Eskom, 36, 43, 56

ethnicity, 14, 19, 107, 128; as modular, 112–14; and xenophobic pogroms, 114

ethnonationalism, 111, 160n15; ethnonational pogroms, 115; as intensifying, 113; territorial sovereignty, 116

Europe, 148n16

evictions, 4, 6–8, 10, 12–13, 20–22, 30, 85, 87, 94, 100–104, 113, 126, 136, 139; citizen rights, 95; safeguarding against, 92; urban poor, 88

Fairey, Shepard, 113

Faku (street hawker), 5, 25, 38, 54, 63, 65–66, 72–73, 75–76, 82, 107, 113, 115, 120–21, 133

fire, 23, 31, 43, 144–45; as affordable, 32–33; collective anger, galvanizing of, 33; collective rebuilding, 34; as democratized, 28; destructive capacities of, 34; difference, lines of, 30, 39–40; electricity, lack of, 35; as existential condition, 34; injuries associated with, 37; living politics, 33; and riots, 17–18; rituals, use in, 33; shack

fires, 21–22, 25–28, 30, 34–35; spiritual consciousness, 33; urban insurgency, importance to, 28; urban poor, 111; as weapon, 28
First National Bank, 96
Foucault, Michel, 149–51n25, 156n5, 156–57n4
Freedom Charter, 65, 148n16
Freedom Day, 11
funerals, as sites of mobilization, 32

Gandhi, Mohandas, 27
gift giving, commodity exchange, 134
globalization, 153n2
Global North, 40
Global South, viii, 40
global warming, 81–82
Goldstone Commission, 12
governmentality, and biopolitics, 149–51n25
Graceland (Simon), 69
Grootboom, Irene, 92
Group Areas Act, 7–8, 47, 94
Growth, Employment, and Redistribution (GEAR), 148n16
Gwala, Nkululeko, 135

Haiti, 67, 145
"Happy Valley" transit camp, 98
Heritage Day, 111–13, 115–17, 123. See also "Shaka Day"
housing, vii–viii, 1, 4, 8, 19, 30, 51, 55, 67–68, 83, 87, 100–101, 149–51n25, 152n28, 157–58n16; as formalized, 21, 88–91, 96; housing policy reform, 91–92, 95, 102–3; housing projects, 5, 12–13, 21, 95–97, 122–23, 156–57n4, 161n24; informal housing, 6, 12, 17, 36, 88–90, 93, 99; and land, 86, 88–93, 95, 102, 133–35; new housing vision, 92, 95; as state-owned, 50; urban space, 91–92
Hubert, Henri, 134
Human Rights Day, 11, 159n3
Human Rights Watch, 109

imfene dance group, 113, 116–17, 120; witchcraft, association with, 109
impimpi, 32
India, 67, 145
informality, 68, 85, 129, 134, 138; formalizing of, 96; informal barbeque stalls, 63; informal convenience stores, 20, 51, 114; informal economy, 4, 90, 91, 97, 107, 110, 112–13, 117, 129; informal settlements, 6, 12, 36, 88–90, 92–93, 99; informal space, 104; informal territorial sovereignty, 91, 93, 122, 123; informal trade, 110, 116, 121; land, contested claims to, 91; and space, 90; spatial practices, 88, 90–91, 96, 101–3; urban informality, 88, 93
informal territorial sovereignty, 91, 122–23;

"world-class cities," efforts to build, 93. See also territorial sovereignty
infrastructure, 2–4, 6–9, 11, 16, 26–27, 30, 35, 39–40, 44–46, 51, 53–54, 59–60, 87, 95, 97, 99, 101, 107, 109, 112, 141, 145, 152n28, 154n4, 161n24; colonial governance, imprint of, 47; political belonging, 122–23; space and informality, 90; territorial power, 121; territorial sovereignty, claiming of, 122–23; urban space, 103
Inkatha Freedom Party (IFP), 29, 31–32, 115, 147–48n10, 152n8. See also Inkatha National Cultural Liberation Movement
Inkatha National Cultural Liberation Movement, 152n8. See also Inkatha Freedom Party (IFP)
isicathamiya, 69, 76, 113; empowered masculinity, assertion of, 71; migrant miners, 70–71
izangoma (traditional healers), 72

Joe Slovo shack settlement, 100, 104, 157–58n16; eviction in, 103
Johannesburg, 4, 7–10, 19–21, 86, 88, 99, 113, 115, 135, 139, 156n1

Kell, Dara, 159n8
Kennedy Road Community Hall, 63–64, 72, 107–9, 111, 115, 117, 122–30, 161n27, 162n36
Kennedy Road settlement, 1–5, 14, 18, 20–22, 31, 35, 40, 60, 69, 76, 80, 85, 87, 131, 147n1, 161n24; as ANC stronghold, 19; Community Hall, 63–64, 72, 111, 115, 117, 122–30, 161n27, 162n36; community policing, 117–18, 120–21, 124; criminalization of, 116; ethnicity in, as modular, 112–13; ethnonationalism in, 115; fire, use of, 30; "the Forum," 117–20, 123–26, 160n19, 161n25, 161n27, 162n36, 162–63n37; gangs in, 162n30; informal entrepreneurs in, 117; informal liquor trade, policing of, 116, 121; pogrom in, 107–10, 116, 119, 121–30, 159n7, 162n35; protests in, 11; Shack Fire Summit, 37, 39; territorial sovereignty, 116; ukubambisana (hand-in-hand cooperation), 117–19, 160n18
Kenya, 145, 156n2
Kliptown, 65
Kriel, Hernus, 52, 58
KwaMashu, 39
KwaZulu-Natal, 12–13, 19–21, 27, 30, 32, 96, 112, 114–15, 125, 143, 160n18
Kyoto Protocol, 81–82

Ladysmith Black Mambazo, 69, 73
land, 22, 82–83, 123, 141, 144–45; and belonging, 104; contested claims to, 91; distribution of, along racial lines, 85; land ownership, as race-based, 92; land reform, 92; land restitution, 92; land tenure, 93; land tenure, and inclusive citizenship, 95; land tenure reform,

land (*continued*)
    92; living politics, 85; post-apartheid housing,
    86; power over, 88; rural space, indexing of,
    92; spatial practices, 101–2; territorial sover-
    eignty, 85; transaction, currency of, 92; urban
    space, 91
Land Act, 86
Land Invasions Unit of the South African Police
    Service, 6
Landless People's Movement (LPM), 21
Lefebvre, Henri, 90
liberal contract theory, 48–49
liberalism, 145
liberation movements, 26–27, 30, 40, 52, 59, 66,
    111, 134, 137–38, 143, 149–51n25
Lindani, 111–13, 118
Lindela repatriation center, 14
living politics, viii, 6, 9, 14, 16, 20, 22, 31, 34, 40,
    59, 67, 80, 102, 104, 107, 111, 118, 121, 133, 141,
    143–45, 149n21, 151–52n27; and air, 21; collec-
    tive self-identification of, 4; and fire, 21, 33;
    fragility of, 110; and land, 21; land, as central
    to, 85; nonracial citizenship, 112; as organic
    intellectual concept, 15; as public dramas, 17;
    sacrifice, as central to, 134; and urban poor, 17,
    103; and water, 21, 45
lobola (marriage rite), 71
Locke, John, 154n5
London, 48, 51, 58
Long Walk to Freedom, A (Mandela), 137
Lonmin mine, 135, 140, 142

Mabaso, Lennox, 157n10
Machiavelli, Niccolò, 149–51n25
Mahlangu, Solomon, 57
Mahlathini, 69
Mandela, Nelson, 1, 3, 8, 10, 14–15, 27–28, 47,
    50, 52, 57–58, 65, 74–75, 111, 133, 137, 140,
    159–60n13; as "father," 138–39; legacy of, 140;
    Masakhane Campaign, 54–56; moral authority
    of, 139; street politics, as icon of, 138
Mandela, Winnie, 28, 49–50, 53; water boycotts,
    participation in, 51–52
Marconi Beam, 54–55
materiality, and semiosis, 16
Mauss, Marcel, 134
mbanganga, 69
Mbeki, Thabo, 10–11, 13, 58, 114, 149n24,
    159–60n13
M'du, 43–45, 47, 59, 133
Mendini Hills, 6–8, 18, 20, 63, 73, 76
Metro Customer Services Centre, 36
Miller, James, 154n6
missionization, 74
Mnikelo, 34, 39
mob justice, and necklacing, 120

Monique, 86–87, 91, 93–94, 97, 99–102, 104,
    157–58n16
Mpanza, James, 7–8, 85, 94, 101
Mpondoland, 18
Mudimbe, V. Y., 134

National Intelligence Agency (NIA), 11, 160n18
National Party (NP), 8, 94, 147–48n10
national services riots, 9
Native Urban Areas Act, 7
Ndlovu, Thuli, 135
necklacing, 29–30, 113, 120
neoliberalism, 15, 54
new social movements, 9
Nissan, 149–51n25
Nizza, Chris, 159n8
Nombeka, 107, 130–31
Nortown, 31–32, 48
N2 Gateway Project, 86–88, 92, 96–97, 99–103,
    157–58n16
Nzuza, Nqobile, 133–35, 138, 140–41, 143, 164n17

Obama, Barack, 113
Operation Khanyisa, 35
Operation Wanya Tsotsi, 119

Pan Africanist Congress (PAC), 58
pantsula dancers, 113
Paton, Alan, 7
Peel, Robert, 119
Pemary Ridge Settlement, 41, 162n35
Pentecostalism, 81; Pentecostal churches, youthful
    appropriation of, 75
Phillip, Rubin, 2
Phola township, 56; boycotts in, 57
Pieterson, Hector, 141–42
pogroms, 14, 108–9, 116, 149n24; and criminaliza-
    tion, 116; as ethnonationalist, 107, 115; living
    politics, 110; as xenophobic, 4, 13, 78, 79, 104,
    114, 115, 160–61n23
policing: Broken Windows Policy, 119; national
    anxiety over, 118–19; Operation Wanya Tsotsi,
    119; shoot-to-kill policy, 119–20; and vigilan-
    tism, 118–19. *See also* community policing
political anthropology, 15; nonstate systems, 153n2
political mobilization, 4, 22, 27, 34, 58, 82, 111
politics, criminalization of, 149–51n25
pollution, 21–22, 48, 60, 63–64, 67, 74, 80–82
Poor People's Alliance (PPA), 10, 21, 95, 147–48n10
Population Registration Act, 8
post-apartheid, 3–4, 9–12, 16, 20, 27–28, 33–36,
    44, 47, 55, 58–60, 69, 74, 77, 81, 86, 88, 89,
    94–95, 98–99, 101, 103, 137, 142, 145, 157n8,
    161n24; evictions, safeguarding against, 92;
    housing, providing of, 92; pass laws, lifting of,
    91; post-apartheid reforms, 93; rural land, and

urban housing, 93; urban migration, 91. *See also* apartheid
Pretoria, 53
Prevention and Elimination of Reemergence of Slums Act, 12–13, 21
Prevention of Illegal Eviction from and Unlawful Occupation of Land Act (PIE Act), 12–13
Prevention of Illegal Squatting Act, 8, 94
Prince, The (Machiavelli), 149–51n25
protest: civil disobedience, viii; as "third force," 12, 149n21
Public Participation Trust, 161n24
public space, 4, 40, 64, 71

QR settlement, 43, 45, 47, 57, 59; and water, 44
Qumbela, Thembiknkosi, 135

race: and class, 18, 34, 112; and poverty, 5, 9, 152n28
racism, and xenophobia, 14
rainbow nation, viii, 9
Reconstruction and Development Plan (RDP), 55, 148n16, 158n17
Red City transit camp, 76–77, 98–99
Red Cross, 14, 25
rent and services boycotts, 51, 154n18
Riotous Assemblies Act, 65
Robben Island, 47, 50
Rock, Chris, 14
Ross, Fiona, 163n13
Rural Network (RN), 21
rural space, and land, 92
Russia, 145

Sandon, 10
sangoma, 72–74
São Paulo, 6
Scarry, Elaine, 155–56n3
Schmitt, Carl, 149–51n25
Separate Amenities Act, 49, 53
Shack Fire Summit, 37, 39, 67
shack settlements, 1, 5, 20, 40, 43, 46–47, 49, 58, 67, 94, 102, 104, 107, 111, 120, 131, 133, 136, 138, 140, 149n21; air in, 63; air pollution, 22; belonging, as fragile, 104; chronic respiratory illnesses, 82; community policing, 119; "coughing out," 64, 69; criminalization of, 2; elbow tests, 14; electricity banditry, 35–36; electricity theft, 35–36; and eviction, 8, 22, 85; fire, as weapon of protest, 25–28, 30; fire, criminalization of, 34–35; fire, use of, 22, 25, 34; as informal dwellings, 99; and land, 82; nonracial citizenship, 59–60; occupying land, 85; as politics of death, 104; pollution, management of, 81; protests in, 9, 11–12; racial and ethnic groups in, as diverse, 18–19; rent boycott, 7–8; and segregation, 8; shack fires, and illegal connections, 35;

shoot-to-kill policy, 120; slum clearance, 36; as "slums," recasting of, 4, 6; toilet project, 121–22; transit camps, forced eviction to, 22; upgrading project, 121; violence in, 104, 113–14; water in, 22, 54; xenophobic pogroms in, 13–14; youth churches, 75. *See also individual communities*
Shaka, King, 119
"Shaka Day," 111. *See also* Heritage Day
Sharpeville Massacre, 11, 28, 154n7
Sibiya, Edwin, 56–57
Siboniso (community activist), 5, 11, 25, 30–33, 38, 65–66, 76, 85, 87, 107, 111–12, 130, 133
Simon, Paul, 69
Sisipho, 78–80
Sisulu, Lindiwe, 96, 101
Skosana, Maki, 30
Slovo Park, 35–37, 75
slum populations: and crime, 95; eradication of, 91, 96, 103; evictions of, 4, 7, 88, 94, 101; police violence, 4; as term, 94–96; transit camps, 89; as ungovernable, 120
Slums Acts, 94, 96, 104
Social Movements Indaba (SMI), 10–11, 13
Social Movements United (SMU), 10
social spaces: ethnicization of, 30; racialization of, 30
Sofasonke movement, 7–8, 85, 101, 139
Sophiatown (Johannesburg), 8
South Africa, vii–viii, 3, 6, 10–11, 16–18, 22, 26–27, 36, 40, 56–58, 64, 74–75, 85, 88–91, 93, 95–96, 102, 104, 109–10, 113–14, 119, 130, 133–34, 137–38, 141, 145, 149n24, 153n3, 156n7; boycotts in, 51; citizenship, and racial status, 43; Constitutional Court, 12, 21, 91–92, 103; constitution of, 4, 45, 101, 143, 147–48n10; economic liberalization, 9; elbow tests, 14; elbow tests, and pencil tests, 14; and fire, 34; fire, use of by activists, 33; infrastructure in, 45–46; political liberalization, 9; and pollution, 82; poor in, as racialized identity, 152n28; refugee relief efforts, 14; slums, and racial rezoning, 94; as unequal, 4; ungovernability, as term, 151–52n27; water supplies, 45–49, 54
South African National Civic Organisation (SANCO), 159n6
South Durban, 64, 69
South Durban Community Environmental Alliance (SDCEA), 82
sovereignty, liminal terrain, 88
Soweto, 7, 51–52; uprising, 141
"Soweto Accord," 52
squatters, 7
street protests, 3–6, 8, 11, 14, 17, 26, 82, 102, 104, 118, 149n21, 152n1; civil disobedience, viii, 21; submitting a memorandum, 44–45

Suppression of Communism Act, 65
surveillance, 35–36, 66, 162n35; of black youth, 143
Symphony Way settlement (Cape Town), 87–88, 94, 97, 99–100, 102–4, 157–58n16

Tambo, Oliver, 28
territorial sovereignty, 22, 31, 116, 122–23; and biopolitics, 156–57n4; community policing, 120–21; and governmentality, 156–57n4
Thubelisha, 88, 96, 100–101, 104, 157–58n16
Tilly, Mohammed, 53
townships, viii, 4–7, 10, 12–14, 16, 22, 27, 33, 35, 40, 46–47, 49–53, 55, 57–59, 67, 87, 94–96, 102, 104, 111, 113, 119, 125, 136, 138, 140, 142, 152n28, 154n18, 157n17; shoot-to-kill policy, 120; as ungovernable, 8, 28. *See also individual townships*
transit camps, 13, 22, 87, 96, 104, 156n2, 156–57n4; excess population, 96; formal sector jobs, 97; as informal dwellings, 99; legal battles, over post-apartheid land, 88–89; as liminal zone, 88; poor, removal of, 89–90; protesting against, 99; size of, 158n17; slum eradication, 96; slum populations, 89; social networks, erosion of, 98; unwanted black populations, repatriation of, 94; urban poor, 90; water, access to, 97; work in, 97–98. *See also individual transit camps*
Truth and Reconciliation Commission (TRC), 12, 28–30, 50, 69, 143, 163n13
Tsunami transit camp, 100
Turkey, 67, 145
Tutu, Desmond, 154n18

Umkhonto we Sizwe (MK), 28, 51, 159–60n13. *See also* African National Congress (ANC)
umlilo (fire), 111, 116
umoya (air), 63, 68, 74–75, 85, 116; Holy Spirit, 111, 113
Unemployed Peoples' Movement (UPM), 21
ungovernability, 3, 17, 21, 27, 110, 111, 114, 116, 133, 145, 149–51n25; slum populations as, 120; as term, 28, 151–52n27; townships as, 8, 28
United Democratic Front (UDF), 8
United Kingdom, 145
United Nations, 114; COP 17 (17th Conference of the Parties), 81–82; United Nations Millennium Development Goals, 6, 96
United States, 67, 119, 145, 148n16
University of KwaZulu-Natal, 159n7
Unlawful Organization Act, 65
urban poor, 26, 102, 113, 144, 153n16; and air, 111; collective identity, 111; and fire, 111; spatial practices of, 90

urban space, 16, 39, 91, 102–3; housing, indexing of, 92
urban studies, 15

Vaal uprising, 50, 154n7
Victoria, Queen, 47
Voortrekkers, 153n3

water, 22, 40–41, 44, 64, 123, 144–45; carceral life, importance to, 49–50; citizen belonging, 56, 59; and citizenship, 58; as commodity, 55; consumer boycotts, use of, 46, 51, 54, 57–58; infrastructure of, 59–60; interrogations, use in, 50; liquid geographies of, 47; living politics, 45; national citizenship, binding to, 46; as nonracial commodity, 52–53, 59; political belonging, 43, 49; as political conductor, 46; privatization of, 57–59; as public good, 49; as race-based, 49; and segregation, 49; as special kind of property, 48–49
Water Services Act, 58
Way It Is, The (Dube), 54
Wesselton, 53–54
West Africa, 130
Western Cape, 21, 44, 104
witchcraft, 71; coughing out, 72
Women's League, 66
Wonder, Stevie, 69
World Bank, viii, 1, 8, 19, 53, 92, 148n16
World Cup (2010), 93, 96, 104, 110, 119; and evictions, 88
World Summit on Sustainable Development (WSSD), 9, 148n16; anti-marches, 10–11

xenophobia, 19, 78–79, 104, 116; and pogroms, 114–15; as racism, 14
Xhanti, Prince, 88, 96
Xhosa, 7, 110–17, 128, 159n12

youth churches, 76; Pentecostal traditions, 75
Youth Day, 6
Youth League, 66, 123, 127, 141–43

Zenda, Sakhephi, 38–39
Zikode, S'bu, 108–9, 115, 118, 125, 127, 137, 140, 149n21, 162n29, 162–63n37
Zille, Helen, 44–45, 47
Zinzi (traditional healer), 5–7, 63, 65–66, 73–74, 76, 82, 156n7
Žižek, Slavoj, 133, 138
Zulu, 7, 14, 31, 69, 71, 74, 111–15, 119, 124–25, 128, 153n3, 154n4, 159n12; as third force, 29
Zuma, Jacob, 109, 115, 149n24; modular ethnic reanimation, association with, 159–60n13; and Zumania, 114
Zyl, Van, 100